Wartime

Sexual

Violence

Wartime

Sexual

Violence

From Silence to Condemnation of a Weapon of War

Kerry F. Crawford

Georgetown University Press
Washington, DC

Library of Congress Cataloging-in-Publication Data

Names: Crawford, Kerry F., author.
Title: Wartime Sexual Violence : From Silence to Condemnation of a Weapon of War / Kerry F. Crawford.
Description: Washington DC : Georgetown University Press, 2017. | Includes bibliographical references and index.
Identifiers: LCCN 2016040464 (print) | LCCN 2016057830 (ebook) | ISBN 9781626164666 (pb : alk. paper) | ISBN 9781626164659 (hc : alk. paper) | ISBN 9781626164673 (eb)
Subjects: LCSH: Women and war. | Rape as a weapon of war. | Women—Violence against. | Sex crimes. | Violence—Economic aspects. | War—Economic aspects.
Classification: LCC JZ6405.W66 C73 2017 (print) | LCC JZ6405.W66 (ebook) | DDC 364.15/32—dc23
LC record available at https://lccn.loc.gov/2016040464

♾ This book is printed on acid-free paper meeting the requirements of the American National Standard for Permanence in Paper for Printed Library Materials.

18 17   9 8 7 6 5 4 3 2 First printing

Printed in the United States of America

Cover designed by Pam Pease.

Contents

Illustrations

Acknowledgments

This book would not have been possible without the good faith and encouragement of an entire community of colleagues, friends, and family. I have looked forward to writing these pages to express my thanks for quite some time.

The book—and I as a scholar—benefited immeasurably from the guidance of Jim Lebovic, Kimberly Morgan, Michael Barnett, and Aisling Swaine. They always seemed to know which rabbit holes were worth exploring and which were best left alone. Martha Finnemore, Susan Sell, and Elizabeth Saunders shared their time and sage advice many times over the course of several years. Kelly Bauer, Jake Haselswerdt, Michelle Jurkovich, Chloé Lewis, Melinda Adams, and Kristin Wylie read numerous half-baked drafts of chapters or sections, listened patiently to my partially formed ideas, and always offered constructive thoughts. To all these wonderful scholars and friends: Thank you.

I would like to thank the members and creators of three networks from which I have drawn support and inspiration. The Journeys in World Politics workshop and network of alumnae, led by Sara Mitchell and Kelly Kadera, gave me the courage to pursue this research. Barbara Miller and the entire Global Gender Program community helped me view the project through an interdisciplinary lens and provided a safe space to think and talk about the complexities of gender and international affairs. The Missing Peace Young Scholars Network—supported through a partnership of the US Institute of Peace; the Human Rights Center of the School of Law at the University of California, Berkeley; the Peace Research Institute Oslo; and Women in International Security—offered vibrant discussions and camaraderie through the various research and writing stages. Many thanks are due especially to Kathleen Kuehnast, Chantal de Jonge Oudraat, Kim Thuy Seelinger, and Inger Skjelsbæk for their encouragement.

I am grateful for the material support that allowed me to conduct research and set aside time to write. The American Political Science Association Centennial Center's Rita Mae Kelly Endowment Fellowship, the Woodrow Wilson National Fellowship Foundation, and the Columbian College and the Global Gender Program at George Washington

University provided support for the doctoral research that informed this book. The book in its current form owes much to the College of Arts and Letters at James Madison University for summer research support. The International Studies Association's James N. Rosenau Postdoctoral Fellowship provided me with the opportunity to devote my full attention to this project, and I am grateful for the support of the Association's headquarters and of the Department of Political Science at James Madison University for offering me the time and space to complete the book.

I also wish to thank Don Jacobs, the staff of Georgetown University Press, and the anonymous readers who shared their ideas for improving the book.

To the named and unnamed individuals who shared their time and experiences with me to inform my research: Thank you. I was fortunate to have the opportunity to meet incredible people who devote each day to ending the scourge of sexual and gender-based violence and considering each of the myriad implications of the current approaches to doing so.

Dr. Patricia Weitsman graciously read a full draft of the early version of this book and offered her profound and profoundly energizing insights. That she gave so much time to the project is a gift I will not forget. Her presence is sorely missed. Lieutenant Colonel Shannon Beebe eagerly assisted the pursuit of an answer to my research questions. His belief in the project's importance, from our very first conversation about it, has stayed with me even in his absence. It is my hope that they both would have been pleased with the final product and the questions it raises.

My family deserves and has my deepest appreciation. Ray and Pam Crawford instilled in their daughter a desire to learn, ask questions, stand up against injustice, and stubbornly challenge the status quo. Their love and support made me who I am. I am grateful to my family and friends—especially Tim and Cindy Belling; Jolie Giardino; Fred and Fran Fulford; Joyce Hurtubise; Connie, Bill, John, and Mary Robinson; and Walter Kutrik—for their encouragement. Tyler Belling remained my rock through all the ups and downs of the book's life cycle and life itself, always believing in me. My sweet Lucca offered me a constant reminder that the world, with all its wars and sadness, is still and will always be a beautiful place—we need only know where to look to find joy.

Introduction

> Whatever the explanation, every speaker who adds their voice to
> this debate is helping to end centuries of silence that have made
> rape an effective "secret weapon."
> —*Margot Wallström, special representative of the
> UN secretary-general on sexual violence in conflict*

The haunting stories of sexual violence in war are by now too familiar.
Several hundred thousand women and girls suffered sexual violence in
Berlin in 1945 at the close of World War II. Mass rapes and sexualized
violence against people of all ages and genders attended the street riots
and internments during the Holocaust. Rape was considered heinous
but inevitable and therefore insufficient to warrant formal prosecution
on its own grounds at the Nuremberg Trials (Henry 2011, 30–34). Between 20,000 and 80,000 women and girls were raped and tortured, and
an unknown number of men and boys were forced to witness or commit
sexual violence during the Japanese invasion of Nanjing in 1937. Several
hundred thousand women and girls were forced into sexual slavery by
the Japanese military during World War II. The Tokyo Trials addressed
the sexual violence committed in Nanjing as excessive military aggres-
sion but ignored the vast instrument of forced prostitution known as
the comfort women system (Henry 2011, 39; Askin 1997, 202). The
seeming ubiquity of sexual violence in war cemented its perception as
an inevitable aspect of armed conflict and cast sexual violence both as
taboo and as commonplace, stifling effective political and legal discussion and action. Wartime sexual violence failed to evoke international
condemnation, regardless of the knowledge of atrocities committed on
a massive scale.

In the mid-1990s, the silence gave way to determined calls for change.
The combination of increased transnational advocacy on behalf of human rights in general, transnational mobilization around the issue of
women's human rights in particular, and collective horror at the atrocities committed in Bosnia-Herzegovina, Croatia, and Rwanda led to increased popular awareness of wartime sexual violence and widespread

demands to hold perpetrators accountable. International tribunals declared sexual violence a war crime, a crime against humanity, and a
crime of genocide and held individuals accountable for committing sexual violence and for ordering or condoning subordinate combatants' offenses. But the fight for justice and recognition of survivors' experiences
did not end there.[1] After centuries of implicit and explicit tolerance
for sexual violence in armed conflict, international organizations (IOs),
states, and their respective political leaders have expressed a willingness
to take action and have adopted resolutions, policies, and initiatives that
seek to eradicate conflict-related sexual violence. Organizations and initiatives including (but certainly not limited to) the International Campaign to Stop Rape & Gender Violence in Conflict, United Nations
Action Against Sexual Violence in Conflict, the Missing Peace Initiative,
and the Preventing Sexual Violence Initiative (PSVI) exist specifically
to highlight and combat the scourge of sexual violence in war. Units
within international nongovernmental organizations (NGOs) and state
government agencies now work to implement policies and programs
in order to assist survivors of conflict-related sexual violence, improve
the capacity for investigation and prosecution of perpetrators in both
conflict and postconflict zones, and increase awareness of sexual and
gender-based violence. States, NGOs, and IOs now publicly condemn
and engage in costly efforts to prevent and respond to the use of sexual
violence in armed conflict.

What changed to bring about such a shift from deliberate silence to
transnational advocacy and political action? It is intuitively puzzling
that states would devote (and at times risk) resources, personnel, and
political capital to an issue that has dwelt for so long on the distant margins of the spectrum of international concerns. There is little evidence to
suggest that sexual violence related to armed conflict is more of a threat
now than it was in the past. It would also be inaccurate to suggest that
states and commanders of armed forces were unaware of the perpetration of sexual violence in past wars.[2] Instead, the phenomenon driving
the shift from silence to action was a basic change in how advocates and
decision makers think about and discuss conflict-related sexual violence.
The international community came to understand sexual violence as a
weapon of war, and this dominant image of sexual violence effectively
captured the attention of security-minded actors who were in a position
to advocate for, initiate, and fund policy changes and institutional mandates—which they did. Put simply: When the international community

began to view and discuss sexual violence as a weapon, states and IOs started to take the issue seriously.

It is rare to read an account of the protracted conflict in the Democratic Republic of the Congo (DRC) or of the actions of the self-proclaimed Islamic State in Iraq and Syria (ISIS)—to take two prominent examples—without encountering some variation of the phrase "rape as a weapon" (Crawford, Hoover Green, and Parkinson 2014). The fact that this weaponized image of sexual violence has gripped the popular and policy discourse on wartime sexual atrocities is now well documented in the academic literature.[3] Maria Eriksson Baaz and Maria Stern (2013, 3), for instance, have examined the emergence of the recognition of sexual violence as a weapon of war in the DRC and elsewhere, together with the dominant perception's "assumptions, ontologies, composition and limits." They contend that the "rape as a weapon of war" narrative has a tendency to ignore the complexity of sexual violence and the range of victims, survivors, perpetrators, and forms, which leads to flawed attempts to respond to sexualized violence. In applying securitization theory to the international recognition of sexual violence, Sabine Hirschauer (2014) argues that speaking about sexual violence in Bosnia and Rwanda as a security threat enabled the creation of the ad hoc criminal tribunals for the former Yugoslavia (International Criminal Tribunal for the Former Yugoslavia, ICTY) and Rwanda (International Criminal Tribunal for Rwanda, ICTR) and the precedent-setting prosecution of sexual violence in those conflicts. Recognition of sexual violence as an existential threat enabled the international community to take extraordinary measures that would not have been possible otherwise; thus Hirschauer argues that desecuritizing the issue would impede further efforts to respond to sexual violence. Both these approaches capture important dynamics at work in the international community's evolving efforts to condemn, prevent, and prosecute the use of sexual violence in war. The effects of the central understanding of sexual violence as a weapon of war—what I call the "weapon of war" frame throughout this book—on the behavior of states and IOs lead to an interesting question, which lies at the heart of this book: What is the legacy of the weapon-of-war frame? Phrased differently, how has the frame helped or hindered political efforts to recognize, respond to, and eradicate conflict-related sexual violence? Building on observations of the weapon-of-war frame's emergence, shortcomings, and persistence, I explore the frame's impact on the implementation of an anti–sexual violence agenda by strong states and, by extension, the United Nations Security Council.

My assumption at the start of the research for this book was that the conventional wisdom surrounding the definition, framing, and diffusion of new international issues and human rights norms would be sufficient to explain the emergence of international condemnation of and action in response to sexual violence. It quickly became clear that efforts to address wartime sexual violence have followed an interesting, often paradoxical, pattern. To argue that NGOs and principled civil society members engaged in transnational advocacy have been the only forces behind international political efforts to respond to wars involving sexual violence would obscure the more nuanced complete picture. Although these international actors—NGOs and norm entrepreneurs—are vital components of the story, theirs is not the whole story. The evolving political effort to stop wartime sexual violence reflects strategic trade-offs based on overlapping but distinct understandings of what constitutes this type of violence and how the international community ought to respond: Women's rights and human rights advocates have championed one frame, that of conflict-related sexual violence as a women's human rights issue rooted in gender norms; and advocates embedded in, affiliated with, or directly targeting state agencies have propagated another frame, that of sexual violence used as a weapon of war. The full and somewhat unexpected explanation of how and why the international community of states, IOs, NGOs, and principled individual advocates both within and outside states responds to wartime sexual violence in the way it does involves a strong element of power politics; the implementation of an international programmatic agenda addressing sexual violence is due in large part to the interplay between principled advocacy and the interests of strong states. The weapon-of-war frame has found favor among the world's normative and political gatekeepers, and thus it has shaped high-level rhetoric, policy responses, and humanitarian aid efforts.

To understand political action in response to wartime sexual violence, then, it is necessary to account for the roles played by strong states. These states wield tremendous influence over the framing of an issue; as the gatekeepers of international issues and new norms, they have the power to influence the international community's understanding of an issue by promoting or rejecting specific issue frames. The "weapon of war" frame for sexual violence narrows the scope of what the international community can and should address. Conceptually, the perception of sexual violence as a weapon simplifies a complex issue such that it becomes easily recognizable. When sexual violence is a weapon, it is no longer a regrettable by-product of war but a centerpiece of military strategy and an act that the international community can condemn and regulate, like any other weapon prohibited by international norms and humanitarian law. It is particularly important that action in response to sexual violence as a weapon usually does not directly threaten states' interests or credibility, even if this action is not cost-free. The "weapon-of-war" frame shields states' armed forces and other personnel from condemnation of their own acts of opportunistic sexual violence and exploitation during military or peacekeeping deployments and removes any sense of culpability that could arise from direct or indirect political-economic ties to armed conflict.[4] Nevertheless, international political action in response to wartime sexual violence is not driven purely by states' interests, as evidenced by two observations: First, the increasingly institutionalized commitment to condemning and eradicating sexual violence as a weapon of war holds states accountable in the face of inaction; and second, sexual violence, whether viewed as a weapon or more broadly conceived, is hardly what we would consider a traditional state security interest. Given these motivating observations, in the chapters that follow, I seek to place understandings of progressive humanitarian norms and state security interests in conversation. The "weapon of war" frame is a tool, one that advocates can (and do) use to appeal to states and security-focused IOs, and one that enables them to enter high-level political discourse and eventually (slowly) expand the understanding of the forms, victims/survivors, and perpetrators of sexual violence that states and organizations should recognize and prioritize.

Exploring the Impact of the Weapon-of-War Frame

This book, then, is an account of the impact of strategic framing and advocacy. The reality of wartime sexual violence has not changed; the world now simply pays attention.[5] But this attention is not equally given. Cases of wartime sexual violence in which the motives behind and scale of violence are more ambiguous—those cases that advocates cannot or will not deem examples of sexual violence as a weapon—fail to generate condemnation and commitments from states. Sexual violence that is used systematically and strategically against civilians, especially when those civilians are women and young girls, gets attention. Sexual violence used as a weapon of war resembles the more conventional weapons that states and IOs are accustomed to condemning and prohibiting.

At the close of the twentieth century, transnational advocates leveraged international political and moral outrage over the atrocities in the genocidal conflicts in the former Yugoslavia and Rwanda as a way to frame sexual violence as a women's rights issue within the broader push for expanded human rights and for accountability for war criminals in these conflicts specifically. The "weapon of war" frame emerged both during and after the discussions of systematic sexual violence being used as a tool of genocide. Although the broader understanding of sexual violence—including its many forms and implications—tied to women's rights and gender inequality motivates the work undertaken by individual advocates, NGOs, agencies within the UN, and some state agencies with a focus on gender or human rights, the "weapon of war" frame is more commonly reflected in the rhetoric, policies, and popular discourse surrounding sexual violence. Even when groups recognize the convoluted realities of conflict-related sexual violence, outwardly focused efforts tend to use the "weapon of war" frame strategically.

If states and IOs were to respond to the broader spectrum of sexual violence in war and postconflict situations, including opportunistic sexual violence and sexual exploitation, they would need to take on broader issues of gender inequality, human rights, and civil-military relations. The "weapon of war" frame demarcates a more manageable range of actions for states and IOs to attempt to regulate than the larger spectrum of abuses and injustices included in the women's human rights frame for sexual violence. Although NGOs and many advocates have championed and continue to call for a broader approach to the international response to sexual violence, action in the most influential spheres of the international community is almost entirely limited to the one clearly defined area of wartime sexual violence that resonates strongly with security-minded states and organizations as well as with international legal precedent. The response to wartime sexual violence as a weapon has opened the door to conversations about the broader spectrum of sexual violence; but at the time of writing, the international response is firmly rooted in the "weapon of war" frame.

A frame does not merely make an impact on the extent to which an issue is accepted or embraced by the international community; it also has real effects on how states craft their policies and organizations carry out their daily work (Carpenter 2005). The Ottawa Treaty on antipersonnel mines and the Chemical Weapons Convention demonstrate how shifts in the understanding of specific tactics in war can change states' behavior; both legally binding international agreements prohibit what were once considered acceptable weapons of war by exposing the immorality and human costs of their use (Price 1995; Rutherford 2000). Framing sexual violence as a weapon of war generated increased international attention to the occurrence of wartime sexual violence and led state and organizational leaders to understand the severity of this type of atrocity. The "weapon of war" frame is limited, but it is clear, conspicuous, and easily understood—all necessary attributes of successful frames (Kier and Mercer 1996, 87, 93–94). The frame has established that sexual violence is not an acceptable weapon of war and that it is appropriate for states and organizations to condemn sexual violence when it is used as a weapon of war. Most important, the "weapon of war" frame has led the international community to *act* in response to reports of sexual violence used as a weapon and has shaped national policies and IOs' agendas. I do not aim to identify the existence of a general internalized norm prohibiting sexual violence, but I do contend that the "weapon of war" frame has led to stronger and more consistent, even if still flawed and uneven, international responses to wartime sexual violence. The point at which representatives of states and IOs began to speak of sexual violence as a tactic or weapon marked a critical shift in the international community's willingness and ability to respond.

In examining the relationship between issue framing and the international response to a specific type of atrocity, I place premises from security studies and constructivist international relations in conversation while also integrating themes commonly found in realist and feminist approaches. Constructivist insights suggest that the international community condemns certain actions that are proscribed by norms and shared beliefs about what constitutes appropriate behavior and that these beliefs change over time. As Martha Finnemore (1996, 2) observes, "Interests are not just 'out there' waiting to be discovered; they are constructed through social interaction." So, too, are perceptions of right and wrong in warfare, as well as security priorities. The "weapon of war" frame for sexual violence, like any issue frame, required advocates to engage in strategic maneuvering and persuasion in order to secure mass appeal and support from essential allies, perhaps most notably those embedded in the upper echelons of states and the UN.

Securitization theory and the literature on transnational advocacy and issue framing provide the theoretical foundation for my study. Research on transnational advocacy networks and issue-framing strategies often focus on NGOs and norm entrepreneurs as advocates and state policymakers as the targets of advocacy efforts. Change is manifested in new international rights, prohibitions, and norms, which are presumed to have long-term constitutive and behavioral effects on those who accept and comply with them. Securitization theory similarly focuses on changing priorities, assuming that interests are shaped and not given or static, but state elites are the change-makers, and "change" is the prioritization of a specific issue through its communication as an existential security threat. Insights from securitization theory illuminate the process whereby advocates and policymakers may broaden the scope of what are considered security issues. The two approaches to framing and issue prioritization offer clarity regarding how particular frames for historically overlooked issues affect states' responses to those issues. Chapter 1 explores the central concepts and their theoretical roots in depth.

At its core, the argument presented here speaks to realist theories of international relations. Once a phenomenon is considered a weapon or threat, it is within the scope of potential threats to the state and its immediate interests. States may respond to sexual violence used as a weapon because they have some intrinsic interest in doing so or because the "weapon of war" frame has convincingly identified sexual violence as a threat to states' interests. Previous research has demonstrated that state leaders cite atrocities when they are on the warpath or when they must justify their belligerent actions to domestic and international publics. Although such arguments convincingly explain specific cases in which state leaders have graphically described adversaries' human rights violations or the systematic mistreatment of women to justify intervention (Hunt and Rygiel 2006; Ben-Porath 2007), they rarely explore the political dynamics that drive states and organizations to respond to atrocities in the *absence* of compelling existential threats to state interests, an impending intervention, or a strong international norm.

The frame's potency is explained in part by what the frame is *not* about. Framing sexual violence as a weapon of war projected the issue as a security issue and not a women's or gender issue. Sexual violence framed as a weapon is a phenomenon unto itself, committed by barbarous actors against vulnerable populations (Crawford, Hoover Green, and Parkinson 2014). States, in particular, are hesitant to condemn acts that their own citizens or military personnel may have committed. Sexual exploitation and opportunistic sexual violence historically accompany military deployments and peacekeeping operations, and continue to do so today; but these types of sexual violence have been marginalized in international political discussions of wartime sexual violence (Allred 2006). When cast as a broad spectrum of gender-based abuses, or when discussed as a result of gender norms in peacetime or within military cultures, conflict-related sexual violence does not gain the same traction with states and security-focused institutions; it appears too nuanced, messy, and intractable. Some states and the UN have attempted to deal with the issue of deployment-related sexual exploitation and opportunistic sexual violence committed by civilians or armed actors, but enforcement is limited and the broader and more consistent effort to condemn sexual violence as a weapon of war is suggestive of the fact that narrowly defined frames are more easily diffused through the international community.

Beyond the obvious possibility that a state will condemn sexual violence when it is used against its own citizens or allies by an adversary, a state's interests may involve justifying a belligerent action or unpopular foreign policy by citing an adversary's use of sexual violence against its own civilians in order to portray that adversary as barbaric.[6] A state's interests may also be murkier; the use of sexual violence by one or more parties to a proxy war in which a powerful state has an interest can be a destabilizing force or complicating influence. In this sense, condemnation of sexual violence is compatible with traditional security interests and indicates co-optation of anti–sexual violence efforts and advocacy. In this book, however, I make the case that condemnation of sexual violence is not indicative of pure co-optation of the issue to serve as cover for other interests. Although anecdotal evidence of state responses, such as the US response to politically motivated sexual violence in Iraq under Saddam Hussein's regime, suggests that condemnation of sexual violence functions as one of the many tools in a state's rhetorical or diplomatic toolbox (Ben-Porath 2007), self-interest alone cannot explain the sustained international focus on sexual violence as a weapon of war. The very observation that there is an increasingly institutionalized response to wartime sexual violence by multiple international actors runs counter to this logic. State interests have shaped, but not hijacked, implementation of the anti–sexual violence agenda.

As interests shift over time and through human interactions, the changing gender balance of state agencies and IOs is also relevant to my analysis of the "weapon of war" frame. The tireless work of women's rights NGOs and advocates and the leadership of both female and male policymakers with a genuine concern for sexual and gender-based violence has led to greater recognition of women's issues and consideration of the role of gender norms in war and postconflict reconstruction and peacebuilding. To assert a direct causal relationship between the mere presence of women in institutions and the way in which the international community recognizes wartime sexual violence would be to essentialize women and men and to ignore the nuanced contexts of each institution's culture and structure. Feminist scholars highlight the need for IOs to "reflect greater gender sensitivity and gender equality, lest they become part of the problem rather than the solution to global injustice" (True 2003, 378).[7] Gender equality and sensitivity are achieved through shifts in organizational and institutional cultures and structures as well as the concerted efforts of individuals committed to giving voice to marginalized perspectives (Cohen 2000; Pankhurst 2008; Kronsell and Svedburg 2012). It is indisputable that women's rights advocates—groups and individuals from the Global South, including conflict-affected regions, and the Global North alike—helped to secure the inclusion of sexual violence in the statutes of the International Criminal Court and the ad hoc tribunals, pushed the UN Security Council to adopt Security Council Resolution 1325 in October 2000, and made it possible for states and UN agencies to develop national action plans for the Women, Peace, and Security agenda and to champion a host of programs and initiatives to empower women all over the world.

Despite the role played by transnational women's human rights advocates, the relationship between more broadly focused women's human rights and gender equality efforts and the dominant discourse on sexual violence in war is a problematic one. Sexual violence is one of the many aspects of these efforts, but the view of sexual violence as a weapon of war does not offer an empowering view of women and is often at odds with the broader goals of the Women, Peace, and Security agenda introduced by Resolution 1325; the "weapon of war" frame focuses on women (and, far less commonly, men) as civilian victims of a wartime strategy. Framing sexual violence as a weapon secured the support of states and organizations at critical moments, and advocates' strategic choices were made within the same institutional contexts over periods of weeks or months, without changes in the influence of women in those institutions. The role of women, gender-sensitive men, and the gender balance of institutions are necessary components of any account of international action against sexual violence; but there is an important and persistent gap between the women's rights approach to addressing sexual violence and the actions resulting from the "weapon of war" frame that must not be obscured, as the following chapters discuss.

The lessons learned from the impact of the "weapon of war" frame do not apply solely to the issue of sexual violence; rather, they contribute to a more general understanding of how overlooked issues become global priorities and whether increased attention leads to real change. I seek to expand our understanding of how framing shapes international political action and fosters sustained commitments, while also contributing to the discussion of international action in response to wartime sexual violence.

Sexual Violence in War: Scope and Definitions

As is implied by the book's focus, wartime sexual violence constitutes a special type of atrocity. Sexual violence occurs as military strategy, as accepted practice, or as a by-product of the chaos and political, social, and economic instability before, during, and after armed conflict.[8] References to rape, abduction, forced marriage, enforced prostitution, forced maternity, forced abortion or sterilization, and sexual slavery are prevalent throughout historical accounts of warfare (Niarchos 1995, 659). Although sexual violence perpetrated by combatants arises from motivations at least partially specific to each war and combatant group's ideological leanings, as well as societal gender dynamics, common explanations also point to revenge, frustration, attempts to bolster troops' morale and foster unit cohesion, and genocide or ethnic cleansing as incentives or goals (Goldstein 2001, 362; Farr 2009; Cohen 2013). Sexual and gender-based violence, in wartime as in "peacetime," are most deeply and strong rooted in entrenched societal norms that reify masculinity and systematically discriminate against women and anyone who does not fit within the accepted image of the masculine man (Goldstein 2001; Leatherman 2011; Hudson et al. 2012; Davies and True 2015).

Sexual violence involves a range of gender-based uses of force or threats of force, including rape. The Rome Statute of the International Criminal Court provides a comprehensive, broad, and gender-neutral definition of sexual violence:

> "The perpetrator committed an act of a sexual nature against one or more persons or caused such person or persons to engage in an act of a sexual nature by force, or by threat of force or coercion, such as that caused by fear of violence, duress, detention, psychological oppression or abuse of power, against such person or persons or another person, or by taking advantage of a coercive environment or such person's or persons' incapacity to give genuine consent"

(1998, Article 7[1][g]-6). Extant accounts of wartime sexual violence most often highlight the disproportionate impact of wartime gender-based violence on women and girls for reasons ranging from data availability to the need to give voice to historically silenced experiences in war. Kelly Dawn Askin (1997, 12–13) observes that "the same atrocities which happen to the civilian male happen to the civilian female. . . . Yet, *additional* things happen to females which far less frequently happen to males. Apart from the brutalities committed against civilians of both sexes, females—women and children alike—are sexually assaulted with alarming regularity." To underscore the importance of addressing sexual violence is not to suggest that it is the only way in which women and girls suffer in war or that women and girls are the only people affected by such violence. Men and boys are targets, whether they themselves are sexually violated or whether they are forced to commit or witness sexual violence against a spouse, sibling, parent, child, or other family or community member. Lesbian, gay, bisexual, transgender, and queer (LGBTQ) individuals are also subjected to sexual violence, at times targeted in ways different from cisgender and heterosexual men and women as a means of "corrective violence" or "cleansing" (United Nations Security Council 2015a, 7). Scholars and practitioners are working to address the relative absence of data on sexual violence targeting men, boys, and LGBTQ individuals; but given the nearly complete focus on women and girls in international political rhetoric and initiatives—the focus of the book— the case studies presented herein refer most often to sexual violence against female civilians.[9] Where available data, documents, rhetorical statements, and interviews explicitly accounted for the effects of sexual violence on men, boys, and LGBTQ individuals, I have incorporated this information. In addition, chapter 5 discusses the problematic silencing of specific groups of victims and survivors by the "weapon of war" frame.

The documentation of women's experiences during the first half of the twentieth century, particularly during World War II, depicts widespread acts of unthinkable horror (Leatherman 2011, 2). During the Armenian genocide, the women who were considered physically and sexually desirable were auctioned off as sex slaves to military officials, whereas the remaining women and girls (including the very young and very old) were raped and beaten (Leatherman 2011, 51–52). It is estimated that 20,000 to 80,000 women and girls were systematically raped by Imperial Japanese Army personnel in the six weeks after the fall of the Chinese city of Nanjing in 1937. Male civilians, including celibate monks, were forced to commit rape and incest as part of a campaign of sexual brutality and torture. The Imperial Army also maintained a system of forced prostitution to improve morale and discipline throughout the expansionist military campaign; estimates of the number of women enslaved as "comfort women" range from 50,000 to 410,000 (Heineman 2008, 5). In Europe, Nazi concentration camps involved forced prostitution in brothels to boost productivity among male internees and as a service for members of the Schutzstaffel (Leatherman 2011, 52). At war's end, German women living in Berlin were raped and exploited by Soviet soldiers on their return home; estimates of the number of women affected range from 100,000 to 1 million (Heineman 2008, 5). These atrocities were met with a profound silence from the international community because the social taboo assigned to sexual violence inhibited public discussion of such atrocities, because all sides of the war reportedly had some involvement in or knowledge of sexualized attacks and exploitation, and because there was no consensus that sexual violence was anything other than inevitable in war.

Accounts from the second half of the twentieth century are no less grim; sexual violence remained a feature of armed conflict, despite changes in the scope and type of war as well as major changes in the structure of the international political environment. Members of the Pakistani army raped an estimated 200,000 Bengali women in an effort to crush the independence movement in 1971 in what was then East Pakistan (now Bangladesh) (Weitsman 2008, 563). Among US troops serving in the Vietnam War, the rape of Vietnamese civilians was "standard operating procedure," and brothels were established inside military compounds to maintain morale and discipline (Niarchos 1995, 667–68; Askin 1997, 236). Although sexual violence in both these cases was fairly common knowledge, international political recognition was almost completely stifled by the global political structure of the Cold War and the low priority assigned to abuses of human rights—especially women's human rights. Table I.1 presents a brief picture of the estimated scale of sexual violence in selected armed conflicts.

In some sense, sexual violence is "what war is all about" (Alison 2007, 80). Implicit acceptance of conflict-related sexual violence and exploitation as inevitable created an environment of international indifference toward the strategic use and opportunistic occurrence of sexual violence.

Throughout the book, I use the terms "wartime sexual violence" and "conflict-related sexual violence" interchangeably. Both terms include both systematic or strategic and opportunistic forms of sexual violence that occur in the build-up to, active fighting in, and aftermath of armed conflict. These terms reflect the presence of sexual violence in an armed conflict without regard to the purpose (or lack thereof) of such violence. Condemnation of sexual violence varies with respect to the perception of attacks as directly linked to wartime strategy or as a result of the lack of accountability or rule of law in conflict zones.

The terms "systematic sexual violence," "strategic sexual violence," "sexual violence as a weapon," and "sexual violence as a tactic" suggest that sexual atrocities are documented as, or widely presumed to be, the deliberate strategy of one or more parties to the armed conflict (combatants). In such cases, the use of sexual violence directly serves the interests of an armed group or the state; examples include mass rape as a tool of ethnic cleansing and widespread forced prostitution. The execution of strategic sexual violence may look different across conflicts; but regardless of its specific manifestation, it must serve some military or political purpose. Sexual violence can be a devastatingly effective weapon. It represents a violation of social and familial norms, carries long-lasting consequences, and conveys a message about identity—whether national, ethnic, racial, or gender (Goldstein 2001; Weitsman 2008; Buss 2009; MacKenzie 2010). To ensure consistency, I use these terms when policy documents, transcripts, and interviewees use them. The suggestion by policymakers that a case of sexual violence is a case of systematic sexual violence signals the *perception* that the sexual violence was strategic in nature, and the political or legal response is based on this view. Perception

Table I.1   The Estimated Scale of Sexual Violence in Selected Conflicts

Primary Location of Armed Conflict	Date Range of Estimate	Estimated Number of Sexual Violence Victims and Survivors (Combined)[a]
World War II, invasion of Nanjing	1937	20,000–80,000
World War II, comfort women system	1932–45	50,000–410,000
Post–World War II, Berlin	1945	100,000–1,000,000
Bangladesh	1971	200,000
Sierra Leone	1991–2002	50,000–64,000
Bosnia-Herzegovina	1991–93	20,000–60,000
Rwanda	1994	250,000–500,000
Democratic Republic of the Congo	2006–7	407,397–433,785

[a]The figures for Nanjing, the comfort women system, Berlin, and Bangladesh are cited in the text. The estimate for Sierra Leone reflects population-based research involving internally displaced persons; see Amowitz et al. (2002). The figure for Bosnia-Herzegovina reflects a range of estimates cited by the Women Under Siege Project; see Hirsch (2012). The figure for Rwanda reflects estimates cited in a Human Rights Watch report on the Rwandan genocide; see HRW (1996, 33–34). For the DRC, the figure reflects data-based calculations of women who had experienced sexual violence within the past twelve months (2006–7) in the DRC; see Peterman, Palermo, and Bredenkamp (2011).

matters, especially as advocates, policymakers, and other international leaders struggle to understand an issue. The book focuses heavily on systematic sexual violence as a reflection of the international political discussion of wartime sexual violence; international actors, especially states and IOs, are more likely to recognize systematic or strategic sexual violence than opportunistic sexual violence.

The term "opportunistic sexual violence" does not suggest that such violence is less egregious but instead accounts for the fact that it is not directly related to military strategy. Instances of opportunistic sexual violence stem from entrenched gender dynamics and a sexualized distribution of power during armed conflict. These may include, for example, acts of sexual violence committed by combatants without orders from or the consent of military commanders. Opportunistic sexual violence includes rape and the broad range of sexual and gender-based atrocities enumerated above; but it is important to note that it may *also* include cases of conflict zone prostitution and other forms of sexual exploitation, given that consent in such situations is highly suspect. Opportunistic sexual violence arises from combat units' inability to enforce norms or policies condemning sexual violence (Wood 2009); the intermingling of combatants and civilians in wars with blurred or nonexistent front lines;

and the economically, politically, legally, and socially unstable conflict environment.[10] The proliferation of "survival sex" and sexual exploitation and abuse by combatants, peacekeepers, and humanitarian workers is another form of opportunistic sexual violence (Whitworth 2004; Pankhurst 2010).[11] Civilians, including perpetrators of intimate partner violence, are also responsible for committing opportunistic sexual violence both during and after armed conflict. Although strategic or systematic sexual violence perpetrated as a conflict strategy is more likely to be the target for states' and IOs' recognition, opportunistic violence is pervasive in conflict zones, persists long after active fighting has ceased and peacekeeping operations are under way, and is entrenched in many military cultures.

There is variation in the prevalence and utility of sexual violence; it is neither universal nor inevitable, and it is therefore preventable and punishable. Elisabeth Wood (2009) examines variation in the perpetration of sexual violence in conflicts through a case study of the Liberation Tigers of Tamil Eelam in Sri Lanka, arguing that wartime rape is rare when military groups condemn sexual violence and are able to enforce the prohibition through discipline and a hierarchical structure. Dara Cohen (2013) discusses the impact of recruitment mechanisms on the occurrence of rape, arguing that rape is a common socialization technique used by armed groups that abduct or forcibly conscript combatants because this shared taboo act can foster cohesion within the group. Michele Leiby (2009) finds evidence from the civil wars in Guatemala and Peru that sexual violence was used as a weapon of war and that state authorities had knowledge of mass sexual violence but failed to respond to it. She contends that sexual violence can serve multiple purposes at different points in a single conflict. By establishing that sexual violence is not an inevitable occurrence in war but often (though not always) a deliberate strategy, this body of research suggests that the international community has sufficient agency—provided the political will exists—to condemn and mitigate the effects of wartime sexual violence.

Although my focus is on international political efforts to condemn and eradicate sexual violence, it is impossible to divorce states' and advocates' actions from their roots in the ad hoc tribunals and the International Criminal Court (ICC) statute.[12] Askin's (1997) work on the legal recognition of gender-based atrocities exposes both the historical neglect of wartime sexual violence and the formidable challenges that faced international legal efforts to prosecute perpetrators in the former Yugoslavia and Rwanda. Legal instruments are not isolated from political forces; indeed, their very existence is shaped by the distribution of power and influence among states and organizations. As Nicola Henry (2011, 130) contends, the proceedings of international court cases shape and preserve the "collective memory and the recognition of rape as a serious human rights violation." The crimes that courts recognize are the crimes that global society remembers and the experiences it validates. This is problematic because the establishment of international courts and postconflict justice mechanisms is by nature rooted in specific interpretations of wars, genocide, and the crimes committed therein; courts possess and perpetuate "selective memory" (Henry 2011, 117). Jelke Boesten's (2010, 2014) case study of the Truth and Reconciliation Commission in Peru demonstrates that a focus on rape as a weapon of war obscures the many other forms of sexual violence, including opportunistic rape and rape committed by acquaintances or intimate partners in both wartime and "peacetime." The limited focus on sexual violence used as a weapon impedes the transitional justice process and ultimately permits continued impunity for perpetrators of the overlooked forms of sexual violence. The legal frameworks in place to address sexual violence are imperfect, but international legal institutions have laid an important foundation for the criminalization of systematic wartime sexual violence. Tuba Inal (2013, 133–66) makes the case that the decisions and statutes of the ICTY, ICTR, and ICC constitute an international legal prohibition of sexual violence in war, a prohibition that would have been unthinkable before the existence of and advocacy surrounding these institutions. Consideration of—simply the act of recognizing and speaking about, let alone prosecuting—sexual violence at the ICTY, ICTR, and in the statute of the ICC went a long way toward understanding sexual violence as a security issue (Hirschauer 2014).

This book integrates and builds on the findings from the literature on sexual violence but approaches the issue from a different angle: I observe the recent increase in the international response to wartime sexual violence and analyze the impact of the "weapon of war" frame on states' and the UN's commitments related to the anti–sexual violence agenda. In so doing, I situate the issue of wartime sexual violence within the context of national and international political concerns about peace, security, and stability. My aim is to combine insights from International Relations and the literature on sexual violence in order to understand why the international community has begun to recognize and devote valuable resources to an issue that was once considered an inevitable consequence of warfare.

Methods and Cases

To examine the international response to wartime sexual violence over the course of the last two decades, I used process-tracing to craft the detailed historical narrative laid out in later chapters. Process-tracing allowed me to examine the causal mechanisms driving the international response in an environment characterized by critical conflicts, individual efforts, and the interaction of multiple international actors, which Alexander George and Andrew Bennett (2005, 206) call a "world marked by multiple interaction effects, where it is difficult to explain outcomes in terms of two or three independent variables." To construct the process-tracing narrative, I relied on transcripts of speeches and press conferences, press releases, policy documents, special reports and annual reports, and verbatim transcripts of hearings and meetings released by NGOs, IOs, tribunals, and government agencies.

To complement my documentary analysis, I conducted semistructured interviews with current and former government officials, NGO and IO staff members, activists, scholars, and international lawyers between September 2011 and April 2016. Each interview focused on specific aspects of the international response to wartime sexual violence relevant to the individual's work as well as the individual's reflection on general programmatic efforts to secure women's human rights and respond to sexual violence. All interviews were conducted with regard for the individual's privacy. Most interviewees spoke on a not-for-attribution basis and, in these cases, decided on a preferred reference (usually "staff" or "official" and the name of their organization or government bureau). In several cases, individuals who have spoken or written publicly about the issue of conflict-related sexual violence preferred to speak on the record, and in these cases I have included their names. In addition to the individual interviews, I conducted participant observation during several on-the-record meetings, symposia, debates, and hearings on the issue of sexual violence between September 2011 and November 2015.

The documentary evidence and insights from interviews and events helped me determine the impact of the "weapon of war" frame. I paid special attention to the following aspects of the discussion of sexual violence: (1) How individuals, organizations, and state agencies defined and discussed sexual violence; (2) the extent to which states, organizations, or individuals were responsible for a given action or response; (3) whether a given action or response focused on a specific conflict, group of conflicts, or the issue of wartime sexual violence in general; (4) whether a given action or response was part of a broader political action targeting a specific state or group of states; and (5) whether a given action or response constituted or was followed by a commitment of resources or other enforcement mechanism. By supplementing the insights from publicly available documents with interviews, I aimed to uncover the individual, political, and normative motivations behind specific actions or policy responses to sexual violence.

The response to wartime sexual violence at any given time may include diplomatic recognition or a discussion in a multilateral forum, policies or resolutions, speeches, international legal actions, material or personnel commitments, naming and shaming, or all or none of these efforts. I focus on the actions of three strong and normatively influential international actors: the United States, the United Kingdom, and the UN Security Council. The selection of these two states and the Security Council in no way implies that they are the only actors working to address conflict-related sexual violence or that other efforts are insignificant. Instead, the United States, the United Kingdom, and the UN Security Council are often the targets of transnational advocacy on behalf of progressive human rights agendas or provide the platforms through which advocacy efforts are diffused. Because my focus here is on the effect of a security frame for a human rights and gender-related issue, the cases center on the states and related institutions that are often singled out for both advocacy and efforts and criticism. Why do advocates target these powers? For better or for worse, they wield considerable wealth and military and political influence to pressure other states and organizations into adopting or at least superficially accepting new norms and taboos; getting these international entities to acknowledge sexual violence as a matter of security legitimizes advocates' claims about the severity of conflict-related sexual violence and generates resources. The Security Council's resolutions have binding force on UN member states, according to Article 25 of the UN Charter, and the legitimation of an issue by this body carries significant weight, especially within the UN and among member states seeking to improve their diplomatic reputations.[13] The Security Council is a key player in issues related to war and peace, and specifying a role for the council and its member states in addressing conflict-related sexual violence has been a central objective of advocacy efforts (Cook 2009, 130–31). For these reasons the United States, the United Kingdom, and the UN Security Council are intuitively interesting and informative subjects in a study of framing and security interests. The case studies in the following chapters include the evolution of US policies, rhetoric, and implementation of initiatives to address sexual violence in the DRC, the adoption of Security Council Resolution 1820 in June 2008, and the United Kingdom's launch of the PSVI in May 2012. In each of the three cases, the impact of shifting understandings of sexual violence is apparent; and by focusing on the responses of these influential entities whose priorities often lie in the security sector, I aim to incorporate power and strategy into what would otherwise appear to be a purely normative study.

Plan of the Book

The following chapters further explore the research question and central concepts and apply them to the three case studies. Chapter 1 establishes the book's central theory: The "weapon of war" frame for sexual violence became the dominant understanding among strong states and the UN Security Council because of its limited scope and easily identifiable compatibility with the priorities of powerful states; but, though the frame has limited the range of recognizable perpetrators, survivors, and forms of sexual violence, it has created meaningful policy and programmatic changes and both short-term and long-term commitments. The frame has enabled advocates to "sell" the anti–sexual violence agenda to states and the Security Council. The chapter provides an overview of the "weapon of war" frame's development and competition with previous frames for sexual violence to underscore the effectiveness of the now-dominant perception among stakeholders.

Chapter 2 presents an in-depth case study of the shifting US political response to sexual violence in the DRC. Using the State Department's human rights reports on Zaire (1990–96) and the DRC (1997–2014), congressional hearings on sexual violence, and other government documents related to sexual violence and the DRC during this period, I demonstrate that policymakers within the United States responded to anti–sexual violence advocacy but that official responses and dedication of aid were tied to the observation of sexual violence as a tactic or weapon. In this chapter I argue that, though politicians frequently condemn sexual atrocities as part of a broader effort to discredit an adversary in the build-up to war, efforts to condemn sexual violence do not resemble pure co-optation by the security sector, even though the security frame limits the cases and actions considered by policymakers. Instead, genuinely concerned embedded advocates have used the "weapon of war" frame to illustrate the centrality of sexual violence to US foreign policy issues and interests.

Chapter 3 explores the adoption of UN Security Council Resolution 1820 in June 2008. Resolution 1820, the second in the Security Council's Women, Peace, and Security agenda, explicitly recognizes sexual violence as a weapon of war. In this chapter I draw from interviews with advocates who were instrumental in the adoption of Resolution 1820 and UN personnel dedicated to the broader issues of gender-based violence and women's rights. Advocates utilized the narrow "weapon of war" frame in their efforts to convince council members that sexual violence was indeed something they could address; Resolution 1820 would not have passed without sufficient evidence of the peace and security implications of sexual violence. Subsequent resolutions have continued to utilize the "weapon of war" frame in an effort to strengthen the UN's commitment to preventing and mitigating wartime sexual violence.

Chapter 4 documents the formation and early efforts of the United Kingdom's PSVI, led by then–first secretary of state William Hague. The rhetoric surrounding PSVI—Hague's speeches and accompanying policy and promotional documents—takes an abolitionist stance on wartime sexual violence, evocative of one of Hague's reported role models, William Wilberforce. Despite its broader operational focus on the spectrum of conflict-related sexual violence, PSVI's rhetoric remains rooted in the "weapon of war" frame, which suggests advocates' awareness of the frame's importance. In June 2014 the UK government hosted the first-ever international summit devoted solely to addressing wartime sexual violence; delegations representing states and organizations gathered to condemn past and current sexual atrocities in war and to pledge to take action against perpetrators and on behalf of victims and survivors. PSVI is unprecedented in its magnitude and explicit focus on sexual violence, but uncertainty after the loss of the initiative's central advocate and criticism of the UK government's commitment to the effort suggest that resource-intensive responses to sexual violence are not automatically sustained at the international level.

Chapter 5 assesses the overall impact of the "weapon of war" frame on political efforts to respond to sexual violence, with particular emphasis on the forms of sexual violence and individuals who fall outside the frame. In this chapter I discuss the normative implications of the narrow "weapon of war" frame, including the perpetrators, victims, and survivors excluded from this understanding of sexual violence. I also explore what the frame offers advocates and why they utilize it despite its flaws.

The conclusion offers final thoughts, including avenues for further academic research related to the study of sexual violence and to the broader study of issue framing, norm development, and security concerns.

Epigraph

Margot Wallström delivered these remarks during the 6,722nd meeting of the United Nations Security Council on February 23, 2012.

Notes

1. I use both terms—"victim" and "survivor"—throughout the text to refer to those who have experienced sexual violence. The term "survivor" is more empowering and appropriate for a person who has experienced but survived an attack; we should not view these persons only as victims of violence but also as agents with voices and important stories to tell. References to policies, legal documents, and rhetoric in the text reflect the terminology used in the original source.

2. The discussion of the nonrecognition of sexual violence in chapter 1 explores historical efforts to regulate wartime sexual violence.

3. For acknowledgment and criticism of the centrality of the "weapon of war" frame, also see Kirby (2012), Davies and True (2015), and Meger (2016).

4. In her study of sexual violence in armed conflict, Janie Leatherman (2011, 116–48) addresses the linkages between the commission of sexual violence and the global political economy of warfare. Trafficking in arms and humans, involvement of peacekeepers in abuse and exploitation, wartime shadow economies, and global militarization all contribute to what Leatherman deems a "runaway norm" of sexual violence in war.

5. To this point, Brownmiller (1975) argues that sexual violence has long been a centerpiece of warfare. Recalling Brownmiller, Harrington (2010, 1) observes that the only remarkable aspect of sexual violence in the wars in the former Yugoslavia and Rwanda was that they received international attention.

6. For a discussion of US opposition to the treatment of women under the Taliban in Afghanistan, see Hirschkind and Mahmood (2002).

7. For an illustration of the effects of gender insensitivity on programmatic outcomes at the UN, see Roberta Cohen's (2000) account of her time working with a UN humanitarian agency as a consultant.

8. Elisabeth Jean Wood (2009) presents a compelling study of the armed conflicts in which rape is rare, offering a reminder that sexual violence is not an inherent by-product or constant strategy of war. Work by Dara Cohen (2013), and by Cohen and Ragnhild Nordås (2014, 2015), explore variation in the prevalence of sexual violence across armed conflicts and types of armed groups.

9. Chloé Lewis (2014) deftly discusses the silencing of male survivors and victims of sexual violence in international discourse on sexual violence.

10. Prostitution becomes a thriving industry near military bases and in areas surrounding conflict zones. Cases of rape may be viewed as prostitution if the perpetrator "paid" the victim afterward with money, food, or other goods, or if the victim was hired as a domestic employee or "live-in girlfriend." In essence, consent is highly questionable in cases of prostitution in conflict zones. For an explanation of regulated camp town prostitution, see Katharine H. S. Moon (1997). For an explanation of the link between prostitution and human trafficking, see Sarah E. Mendelson (2005).

11. "Survival sex" arises from conditions in which individuals may be coerced, compelled, or otherwise led to engage in sexual acts in exchange for basic necessities like food rations, water, medicines, shelter, or protection. Survival sex and sexual exploitation draw on similar power relations between perpetrator and victim-survivor.

12. To the extent that prior international conventions and military codes did seek to prohibit sexual violence, such documents discussed it indirectly and as an attack on familial and community honor; sexual violence was not considered an attack on autonomous human beings or a breach of the laws of war. The Lieber Code (1863, Section II, Article 37) and Geneva Convention IV (1949, Part III, Section 1, Article 27) are illustrations of such prohibition attempts.

13. In practice, resolutions are truly binding when they create an explicit obligation for member states and UN agencies. Article 25 states: "The Members of the United Nations agree to accept and carry out the decisions of the Security Council in accordance with the present Charter." Obligation does not

imply perfect compliance with resolutions, and as with any international agreement the degree of adherence will vary over time and across member states. As a measure of organizational acceptance of an issue, however, Security Council resolutions provide useful insights. See Öberg (2005). Dianne Otto contends that the reliance on institutions like the Security Council to advance feminist and progressive objectives can be problematic (Otto 2009); but with persistent engagement and scrutiny, feminist activists and scholars can create and build on "productive footholds" (Otto 2010, 121). In pursuit of a better understanding of the framing of human rights and gender-focused issues, the influential security-focused institution is an appropriate actor through which we have much to learn about the dominant frame for sexual violence and the impact of protection-focused discourse on the agenda's implementation.

Chapter 1

Defining the Weapon
Sexual Violence as a Security Issue

Yugoslavia. That was the real opener.
—*Roberta Cohen*

The broad acceptance and diffusion of the "weapon of war" frame has created a paradox for advocates wishing to shed light on and end sexual and gender-based violence in its myriad forms: The frame gets states and international organizations to take sexual violence seriously as an issue of peace and security; but, by the same token, it limits the range of possible political, humanitarian, and legal responses by focusing on strategic sexual violence.

Sexual violence was not always viewed through the lens of a weapon or tactic. Frames do not simply appear in international political rhetoric and discourse; rather, they are carefully constructed and strategically employed. After advocates broke the silence shrouding survivors and victims, the security frame was neither the only nor the dominant understanding among advocacy networks, states, or international organizations (IOs). Even as the "weapon of war" frame became the commonly held understanding of sexual violence, advocates and—to a more limited extent—agents of states and IOs continued to work with a broader understanding of sexual violence in practice, despite their reliance on the "weapon of war" frame in external communications and efforts to compel others to act. The development of the security frame alongside broader frames for sexual violence, and the emergence of the "weapon of war" frame as the central narrative, underlines the deliberate nature of advocacy and the importance of understanding the relationship between the way in which an issue is represented and the resulting policy and programmatic changes. The "weapon of war" frame "sells" the issue convincingly; it gets attention and triggers condemnation. The frame provides an effective rallying cry, but how is the cry answered?

To understand the "weapon of war" narrative and its legacy, we must consider the central roles of ideas and interests, and the relationship between advocacy and context. The conceptual framework I present here places these concepts and their respective literatures in conversation before examining the development and impact of the security frame on the international anti–sexual violence agenda.

Central Concepts: Ideas, Interests, and Intersections

The account of the "weapon of war" frame's impact is one of advocacy simultaneously enhanced and constrained by states' interests. The dominant narrative portrays sexual violence as an element of strategy that armed groups use against vulnerable civilian victims/survivors to achieve political-military goals. Before discussing the ramifications of the "weapon of war" frame for sexual violence, it is worth understanding the theoretical roots of the concept of a security frame.

Ideas: External Advocates and Issue Framing

Words and ideas trigger action. An issue's frame—how the issue is presented or defined by advocates—has a significant impact on its ability to resonate with existing norms and emerge onto the international political agenda (Price 1995). Ultimately, the goal of advocacy efforts is to create lasting change, principally through the adoption of new policies, laws, norms, or beliefs. The international community of states and organizations condemns certain actions that are proscribed by norms for or beliefs about what constitutes appropriate behavior. These norms and beliefs change over time through the work of advocates, or norm entrepreneurs, and adoption by and diffusion among states (Finnemore and Sikkink 1998).[1]

How and why do some issues motivate action and normative change? Issues do not become priorities on their own; nor do problems and their solutions "simply exist out there" before someone endows them with meaning (Joachim 2007, 19). A frame provides the imagery needed to convey the urgency and severity of the issue and to persuade individuals and groups to join the advocacy effort (Tarrow 1998). Given the persuasive power—or lack thereof—of an issue's frame, advocates devote considerable attention to promoting the right one. An effective frame makes an issue relatable, understandable, and generalizable. Michael Barnett's (1999, 15) study of the Oslo process addresses the deliberate nature of issue framing: "Actors strategically deploy frames to situate events and to interpret problems, to fashion a shared understanding of the world, to galvanize sentiments as a way to mobilize and guide social action, and to suggest possible resolutions to current plights."

Some rights violations, threats, and victims attract more attention and concern than others. Framers—the advocates who "pitch" the issue within a specific frame—work within the constraints imposed by an audience's priorities. In their work on the strategies and effects of transnational advocacy networks (TANs), Margaret Keck and Kathryn Sikkink (1998, 203–6) find that advocacy efforts pertaining to the protection of bodily integrity or the prevention of bodily harm for vulnerable populations and the promotion of legal equality are most likely to generate substantial international support. In each of Keck and Sikkink's cases, successful transnational advocacy efforts functioned as a boomerang: When domestic organizations' attempts to seek justice or obtain rights were denied by the state, the domestic groups turned to external nongovernmental organizations (NGOs) to take up their case; the external NGOs then solicited assistance from a state ally, and that state then pressured the rights-denying state directly or through an international organization to create policy—and eventually norm—change. The NGOs, states, and IOs working together to advocate for an issue or normative change form a TAN, and much of the pressure for change comes from outside the rights-denying state. The issue frame's persuasiveness and the sense of urgency derived from it are key elements of success at each stage of the process.

Richard Price's (1998, 619–23) work on the international prohibition of antipersonnel land mines, to take another example of successful transnational advocacy, suggests that the use of graphic images of bodily harm to vulnerable or "innocent" groups (namely, civilian children), effectively mobilized advocacy and secured state support for the prohibition of what was once considered an acceptable weapon. New issues must resemble or fit within well-established norms or issues that states and IOs already prioritize; the presence of existing prohibitions on specific weapons, such as the chemical weapons taboo, was an essential aspect of the international backdrop against which the land mine ban was adopted (Price 1998, 628–29). Price highlights the "combination of active, manipulative persuasion and the contingency of genealogical heritage," or "grafting," at work in the promotion and adoption of new norms. Advocates are strategic in their choice of frames (Price 1998, 617). When an issue's frame enables advocates to persuade the audience of the connection between the issue at hand and past crises, threats, or violations of rights, the issue gains recognition and support. Once advocates and the leaders of states and organizations began to discuss sexual violence in terms of a weapon or tactic of war, they overcame two conceptual obstacles that had previously prevented recognition and action: the assumption that sexual violence is an inevitable by-product of war and the view that sexual violence is a women's issue or complex human rights (and therefore domestic) issue rather than a security concern. Sexual violence used as a weapon of war can, in theory, be sanctioned and condemned like any other proscribed weapon.

Even when a frame is effective, and when the issue becomes accepted as a priority by states and international organizations, the resulting actions, policies, and perceptions of the problem may not be in line with advocates' initial goals and may even have perverse consequences. The civilian immunity norm—which has evolved over time from the protection of all individuals employed in specific vocations to the protection of women, children, and the elderly—demonstrates the impact of the constraints imposed by dominant frames.[2] Charli Carpenter (2005) argues that international humanitarian agencies are restricted by the "innocent women and children" frame for civilians, which leads not only to inefficiencies in the services these organizations provide to vulnerable populations but also to the reproduction of destructive and dysfunctional gender stereotypes in war. The very strategy that enabled the frame's success can lead to these constraints and unintended outcomes. Carpenter (2005, 297) observes that advocates for civilian protection "attempted to establish a 'frame' that 'resonates' with the moral language familiar to international donors, belligerents, and the media, and that is acceptable to political allies in the women's network." The persuasive frame, then, is not always the most comprehensive or realistic representation of the issue. Such is the case with the "weapon of war" frame. Sexual violence understood as a weapon of war is less a gender issue than it is a matter of wartime strategy and atrocities, and thus the issue becomes a matter of state and international security.

Interests: Embedded Voices and Shifting Security Priorities

It is through examination of the "weapon of war" frame's legacy that the intersection of the literature on TANs, framing, and new norms with the security studies literature becomes apparent. Securitization theory, one of the Copenhagen School's major contributions to security studies, shares with the literature on TANs, issue framing, and norm development the core premise that new interests and priorities emerge through persuasive framing efforts and—more broadly—social interaction.[3] Just as problems and their solutions need to be constructed by advocates, security issues must be defined as such before they can be elevated to the priority status accorded to threats and crises.

Securitization theory demonstrates how certain problems are deemed security issues, broadening or widening the range of what can be considered "security" and complementing traditional realist (i.e., military and state-centered) views on national interests (Buzan, Wæver, and de Wilde 1998; Hudson 2010; Donnelly 2013). Indeed, to "study securitization is to study the power politics of a concept" (Buzan, Wæver, and de Wilde 1998, 32). The process of securitization offers an explanation of how previously overlooked issues, like conflict-related sexual violence, might quickly emerge as state priorities through advocacy on the part of elites or policymakers embedded in government or international organizations. By "securitizing" an issue, advocates seek to place it above the fray of politics-as-usual and prioritize or expedite actions to address it (Buzan, Wæver, and de Wilde 1998, 23). The process unfolds in several stages: A securitizing actor identifies an existential threat to a referent object (a collective group with a legitimate claim to survival); the audience—the domestic public, IOs, NGOs, or other government sectors—accepts this "securitizing move" (security speech or the framing of an issue as a security issue); emergency actions are taken to address the threat; and, eventually and as conditions allow, the issue may be desecuritized and returned to the realm of normal politics (Buzan, Wæver, and de Wilde 1998; Balzacq 2005; Taureck 2006; Hirschauer 2014). Speaking "security," portraying an issue or an act as a threat, *does something* (Austin 1962); this is the central assumption on which securitization theory is built and a key assumption in this project. Acceptance of the issue as a matter of security is a necessary component of the securitization process. Thierry Balzacq (2005, 192) expands on the interaction between the audience, context, and securitizing actor in his approach to securitization as strategic or pragmatic practice: The audience must have some frame of reference regarding the issue, be prepared to be convinced by the securitizing actor, and be able to approve or deny a mandate to that actor; the issue must impact the audience's interpretation of the securitizing move; and the securitizing actor must have the capacity and willingness to use frames and language to win support. Because securitization is not complete until the audience accepts the securitizing move, but it is not always easy to determine when this acceptance has occurred, it is useful to identify which audience carries significant weight (Donnelly 2013, 64). In the case of conflict-related sexual violence, the "tough cases"—traditional security-focused agencies and states—are effective markers of the "weapon of war" frame's success. Whereas insights from the literature on TANs, framing, and norm development highlight the role of external actors in pressuring the state to prioritize new issues and effect normative change, securitization theory examines how the concept of what constitutes security can shift from *inside* the state (Hudson 2010, 30).

The process of securitization widens the range of security matters through the advocacy of embedded elites or policymakers, who are in a position of authority to convincingly frame the issue as one of security. Three interrelated key observations follow: Securitization is not inherently positive or beneficial; securitization can be strategic and permit co-optation; and not everyone is in a position to speak of security. Because securitization moves issues out of the participatory political process and into an emergency mode, it represents a failure of normal political functions to solve the problem at hand (Buzan, Wæver, and de Wilde 1998; Donnelly 2013, 45). By endowing the securitizing actor with the mandate to enact emergency measures, the usual constraints imposed by the democratic system are lost and opposition is effectively silenced; desecuritization, the return of the issue to politics as usual after a short period, thus may be the ideal outcome (Buzan, Wæver, and de Wilde 1998, 29; Wæver 1995). Beyond the issue of formal rules and political processes, it is also worth noting that the traditional, state-centered approaches to security threats—intervention, costly signaling, and sanctions—that are considered viable solutions to other weapons may not be appropriate responses to an issue like conflict-related sexual violence. Militarized responses often endanger the very civilians they aim to help, especially those civilians who are traditionally marginalized or vulnerable (Enloe 2010). This ties closely to the second point: that securitization is strategic, and securitizing actors may not be sincere.

In moving an issue outside the realm of everyday politics and into the realm of extraordinary measures, those who possess the mandate to make decisions will do so with far less accountability. Balzacq (2005, 176) notes that "political elites use discourse to win a target audience without necessarily attending to one of the basic rules of a successful speech act—sincerity." Buzan, Wæver, and de Wilde (1998, 29) warn that successful securitization is not "an innocent reflection of the issue *being* a security threat; it is always a political choice to securitize or to accept a securitization." Problems must be constructed as such, and "security threats" can be inflated for political gain or ulterior motives. Issues deemed to pertain to security can be co-opted and fenced off from normal political processes for the sake of interests other than those of the referent object, as studies of the factors leading to the United States' intervention in Iraq have demonstrated (O'Reilly 2008; Heck and Schlag 2012; Donnelly 2013; Rythoven 2015). The threat of co-optation is in line with realist predictions of state involvement in humanitarian and human rights agendas—a point to which I return later in this chapter—but the concept of expanding security issues provides a helpful bridge between ideational and realist scholarship. Co-optation is a particular concern of women's human rights advocates, and of those who take a broader approach to conflict-related sexual violence, and this leads to the third observation.

Not everyone is in a position speak of security, but the centrality of the speech act in the securitization process demands that securitizing actors have both the voice/capacity and influence to speak convincingly of security. Scholars examining security from a feminist perspective seek to identify and challenge the inequalities in security discourse, access to decision-making bodies, and the potential for securitization to have adverse consequences. Lene Hansen critiques securitization theory's lack of consideration of gender in the process—particularly regarding the securitizing actor's capacity and credibility and the difficulty of identifying a coherent referent object for gendered security issues—and highlights the disproportionate impact of certain advocates' voices (Hansen 2000b). Although the securitizing actor's social or political position is not an absolute guarantee of successful securitization—after all, the audience can scrutinize security claims (Balzacq 2005, 173)—influence derived from an elite position goes a long way (Joachim 2007, 26). This influence is not always benign. Dianne Otto's early reservations about the Women, Peace, and Security agenda and feminist advocacy at the UN Security Council highlight a potential threat in the midst of expanding possibilities for change: "As feminist ideas make their way into legal texts and places of power, they can become the tools of powerful actors committed to maintaining the gendered status quo, at the same time as opening new possibilities for progressive change" (Otto 2009, 26). In essence, ideas are reshaped to suit the institution to which they are presented. With the adoption of subsequent resolutions related to the Women, Peace, and Security agenda that strengthened the institutional framework for the broader empowerment-focused agenda and the anti–sexual violence agenda, Otto (2010, 121) has added that the feminist engagement with institutions of international law and power stands to create starting points or "footholds" on which activists can build with some degree of cautious optimism. To the extent that advocates can gain and use their voices, and proceed with caution, securitization may present a useful starting point for traditionally marginalized and gendered concerns (Hudson 2010), including conflict-related sexual violence (Hansen 2000a). Hirschauer makes the case that, even if securitization is a flawed approach to recognizing sexual violence, desecuritization is *not* the best outcome, as it stands to re-silence survivors and advocates (Hirschauer 2014, 188). The extent to which advocates are able to speak of sexual violence as a security issue relates to advocates' identities, political influence, and the gender composition and awareness of policymaking bodies and international organizations. When studying the success of a security frame, then, it is worth noting whose voices are heard and how these voices are employed.

Intersections: External Advocates and Embedded Voices

The literature on TANs, framing, and norm development presents a view of the relationship between transnational advocacy efforts, states, and changing ideas. In this view, change is characterized by long-term ideational shifts brought about by social pressure exerted (largely) from outside the state and in state-to-state interactions through international organizations and forums. Norm entrepreneurs and advocates introduce an idea in the context of a persuasive frame and work through transnational networks to exert pressure on states to change their behavior and adopt new norms. The securitization literature focuses more heavily on the articulation of security interests from inside the state; when elites speak of security, they bestow increased political importance on an issue and constrain debate in order to implement a more immediate response. Lasting change is not guaranteed through this process—and some theorists argue that it should be discouraged—given that securitization is an emergency response to a situation deemed a security threat. These two approaches offer complementary insights into the process through which previously silenced or marginalized issues become security priorities and the degree of change resulting from the portrayal of an issue as a security problem, and each stands to benefit from greater scrutiny of the strategic use of frames by advocates both within and outside the state and the extent to which framing indicates either a genuine concern for or co-optation of an issue. It is from these two views on changing ideas and interests that I explore potential outcomes stemming from the broad adoption of the "weapon of war" frame.

Theorizing the Response to Wartime Sexual Violence

To speak of sexual violence as a *weapon* of war (or of genocide or violent extremism) is to view it "as having a systematic, pervasive, or officially orchestrated aspect" (Buss 2009, 149) and to underscore the assertion that, unlike opportunistic sexual violence, such acts are "not random acts, but appear to be carried out as deliberate policy" (Niarchos 1995, 658). When sexual violence is a weapon of war, the violation of bodily integrity does not occur solely as a result of the chaotic state surrounding the war zone—on the contrary, it is intentionally committed by combatants against members of the enemy's community; and where strategic sexual violence against a member of the perpetrator's own community or group occurs, it is often due to the perception that the target is a traitor (Alison 2007, 79). When combatants use sexual violence as a weapon, they aim to "intimidate, degrade, humiliate, and torture the enemy" (Weitsman 2008, 563). The rationale behind and effectiveness of this tactic stem from gender norms and the intersecting identities and power relationships that are inextricably tied to them.

These understandings of sexual violence as a weapon form the basis of the "weapon of war" frame. There is no single motivation or formulation for sexual violence, although gender inequality—in war, as in peace—provides a common cue for those who actively orchestrate or passively tolerate such violence.[4] Subtle differences in the use of sexual violence as a weapon exist across conflicts despite cross-cultural similarities in gender norms in wartime (Wood 2012, 390). Patricia Weitsman (2008, 565), in her discussion of genocidal rape, argues that the motivations driving procreative sexual violence campaigns—cases of mass rape, ethnic cleansing through forced maternity, and the propagation of the perpetrators' race—and those that underpin campaigns of ethnic cleansing through forced migration, ought to be viewed as distinct, lest scholars and practitioners risk perpetuating the perpetrators' notions of gender and ethnicity. Unlike the perpetrators of genocide in the former Yugoslavia, for example, the perpetrators of the genocide in Rwanda used sexual violence as a weapon to kill rather than to procreate for the purposes of ethnic cleansing (Buss 2009, 150). Sexual violence may also be used as a reward for combatants, as a tool to motivate them to take up arms in pursuit of sexual encounters with formerly off-limits women and to engage in behaviors that social norms in peacetime would proscribe (Weitsman 2008, 573); this particular use of sexual violence by armed groups resonates with historical understandings of sexual violence as one of the "spoils of war" or a reward for the conquering army. The differences in the deployment of sexual violence as a weapon underscore the complexity not only of wartime sexual violence in general but also of the use of sexual violence as a weapon in particular.[5] Because a frame's primary purpose is to simplify a concept so that it motivates a response, the deeper roots of gendered violence are obscured within the horrified reactions to sexual violence as a weapon of war.

The frame in its compelling simplicity has the potential to elicit a range of outcomes, ranging from genuine normative change and increased recognition and devotion of resources to the issue to pure co-optation of the issue for other purposes without any real change in policies or programs. The first scenario depicts positive change brought about by the "weapon of war" frame and stems from observations in the literature on TANs, framing, and norm development. If broad acceptance of the security frame for conflict-related sexual violence has resulted in meaningful policy changes and a commitment of resources to efforts to assist survivors, hold perpetrators accountable, and prevent sexual violence in armed conflict, then it stands to reason that inclusive human rights and gender-focused policy and programmatic agendas *benefit* from greater attention and influence once advocates introduce a security frame. The image of sexual violence as a "weapon of war" grafts easily onto existing weapons taboos, suggests that sexual atrocities are not inevitable but

strategic and therefore punishable, and focuses on bodily harm perpetrated against civilians by armed actors; these are all crucial aspects of
successful issue emergence and should, in theory, generate normative
action and lasting change among states and IOs.

An alternative outcome is that only short-lived policy and programmatic changes have occurred as a result of the "weapon of war" frame. In
accordance with insights from the security studies literature, especially
securitization theory, this scenario is characterized by the dominance
of states' political, security, and economic interests such that the anti–
sexual violence agenda suffers setbacks with the introduction of the security frame. Given the ability of securitizing actors or elites to portray
an issue as a threat to the state's or an ally's security for political gain,
inclusive human rights and gender-focused policy and programmatic
agendas may experience adverse consequences once a security frame is
introduced. Essentially, the agenda may be constrained, exploited, or
rendered ineffective by the involvement of security-focused individuals,
agencies, and state powers.

The effect of the "weapon of war" frame's emergence as the central
narrative is more complicated than these neatly constructed alternatives
can show. Inclusive human rights and gender-focused policy and programmatic agendas are undeniably constrained once a security frame is
introduced, but they also benefit from greater attention and the influence of state-based norm leaders, who leverage their positions to expand
the agendas over time. Use of the "weapon of war" frame at the state
and international levels is not indicative of pure co-optation by elites
or the security sector; rather, well-placed advocates have used the frame
strategically to promote the agenda while working to expand efforts
beyond the frame's constraints. Each of the three cases presented in the
book offers a unique but complementary illustration of how embedded
advocates—elite norm entrepreneurs and security framers—working
from positions in powerful states have used the "weapon of war" frame
to appeal to their respective organizational and political audiences as
well as national interests.

Embedded advocates are motivated by a genuine concern for the
issue, and they filter it through the security frame to garner attention
and resources from strong states and the UN Security Council; these
individuals represent a midpoint between TAN agenda-setting efforts
and national or international political commitment rather than pas-
sive targets of advocacy efforts. At times, they work in partnership with

transnational civil society groups; at times, they do not, by virtue of their positioning within or links to their states. Like civil society advocates, however, embedded advocates use the "weapon of war" frame not because they believe it covers all aspects of the problem but because they know it works. The "weapon of war" frame has increased recognition of and commitments to end wartime sexual violence, but principally (albeit no longer exclusively) with respect to the forms of violence, conflicts, survivors/victims, and perpetrators that fit within the frame. The frame has kept wartime sexual violence on the agendas of strong states and the UN Security Council and has resulted in changes to foreign and domestic policies, financial assistance, humanitarian relief, and military and police training. Many of these changes have been criticized for their narrow focus on protecting (over empowering and including) women and girls, and the effects of this focus on the day-to-day experiences of civilians in conflict zones.[6] I contend, while acknowledging the shortcomings of political efforts to date, that the drastic shift from historical silence to states' and organizations' repeated and institutionalized condemnation of and efforts to address sexual violence is a phenomenon worthy of examination, especially within the context of International Relations research on framing and security studies. The process of implementing the anti–sexual violence agenda is one of persistent negotiations and give-and-take between transnational advocates, embedded advocates, and state interests (and, by extension, organizational mandates and priorities). The "weapon of war" frame gets advocates in the door—or through the gate—and enables them to speak to states' security concerns and political priorities while also building a foundation for long-term change. Although implementation of the anti–sexual violence agenda is not without gaps, neither is it just cheap talk.

Measuring Action and Implementation

What, exactly, constitutes a "response" to wartime sexual violence? How do we know what the implementation of the anti–sexual violence agenda looks like? Based on the literature on wartime sexual violence, including the creation of the ad hoc tribunals and organizations', states', and activists' efforts to point out where and what type of action is needed, I have designed a scale of possible state-level and IO-level responses to specific cases or the general issue of wartime sexual violence. Although some types of responses will not conform to the categories I provide, the scale is intended to help measure the evolution of rhetoric, policies, and resource commitments to ending wartime sexual violence. It offers one way of conceptualizing international efforts to address novel human rights and gender issues. The responses are categorized in stages, ranging from 0 (nonrecognition) to 5 (full normative change). Table 1.1 presents the stages of responses, the types of responses, and a description of potential international responses.

The scale provides an illustration of how an issue might evolve from marginalization and nonrecognition to a broadly accepted and internalized norm. Stage 0, nonrecognition, describes the lack of acknowledgment of wartime sexual violence *or* to a specific conflict in which sexual violence occurs. In this stage we would not expect to see discussion of sexual violence in general or within a particular conflict, which was the norm before the mid-1990s. In stage 1, documentation and learning occurs. Efforts are led by NGOs, IOs, state officials, advocates, or some combination thereof to understand the nature of sexual violence, whether as a global issue or as an aspect of a specific conflict, and—most important for this particular study—states and IOs take note of and use this information. At this stage, actors commit time and effort to fact-finding and raising awareness, whether internally or externally. The focus in stage 1 is on understanding the scope of the problem of conflict-related sexual violence, presumably to ascertain whether condemnation and commitment of resources are necessary next steps. Stage 2 entails a rhetorical response and implies that an individual leader or group of elites has become aware of sexual violence through the efforts at stage 1 and has deemed the issue sufficiently serious to warrant official condemnation through a public forum. Rhetorical condemnation could take the form of a press release or speech specifically addressing sexual violence, or it could occur in conjunction with the condemnation of another type of atrocity; the key is the public shaming element of the rhetorical response and the employment of anti–sexual violence rhetoric by an elite figure, such as a head of state or high-level official.

The first two action stages, 1 and 2, are essential precursors to the more intensive implementation efforts, and these are the stages in which frames develop—in choosing which atrocities to publicize and condemn, an actor effectively shapes an issue's frame. Documentation and rhetorical condemnation certainly carry costs, including time and personnel resources, as well as political capital; but stages 3 and 4 involve the greatest commitment on the part of states and IOs. Stage 3

Table 1.1 Stages of Potential International Responses to Sexual Violence

Stage	Type of Response	Description
0	Nonrecognition / no action	Sexual violence is not recognized as part of a specific conflict, or the conflict itself is not recognized. Wartime sexual violence as a general issue is not recognized. No action is taken, and no formal discussion occurs within or among states or IOs.
1	Documentation/ learning	Sexual violence, as an aspect of a specific conflict or as a general issue in armed conflict, is the subject of a report, publication, commissioned study, hearing, and/or conference launched, used, or attended by a state or IO. Information-gathering occurs.
2	Rhetorical response / condemnation	Sexual violence, as an aspect of a specific conflict or as a general issue in armed conflict, is the subject of a speech, unprompted remarks, and/or in a press release by a high-ranking state official or leader of an IO but no further commitment is made. Rhetorical action occurs but resources are not committed.
3	Initial commitment	An IO or a state issues a binding resolution or policy and/or devotes financial, material, or human resources to addressing or mitigating sexual violence as an aspect of a specific conflict or as a general issue in armed conflict. An initial expression of intent and commitment of resources occurs.
4	Implementation/ obligation	A state agency, transnational initiative, legal mechanism, state military training or deployment, or multilateral peacekeeping operation is established and/or instructed to address sexual violence as an aspect of a specific conflict or as a general issue in armed conflict; implementation of a previous commitments occurs. A long-term or institutionalized commitment of resources occurs.
5	Norm change	Sexual violence, as an aspect of a specific conflict or as a general issue in armed conflict, is considered unacceptable and perpetrators are consistently and effectively held accountable. Lasting normative and behavioral change occurs.

involves a commitment of resources—whether financial, material, or human—to ending sexual violence in a specific conflict or in general. The types of responses typical at this stage include UN Security Council resolutions or state policies condemning sexual violence and pledging attention or short-term action, as long as the pledge entails clear provisions for steps to be taken. Stage 4 describes the actual implementation of commitments and promises as well as the establishment of institutionalized mechanisms, and suggests longer-term involvement in the effort to address sexual violence. Responses at this stage include institutions with specific mandates related to ending sexual violence; advances in laws and legal mechanisms; training programs for state officials and military or peacekeeping personnel; mandates for military, peacekeeping, or humanitarian missions; and the creation of permanent offices or programs. Each of these actions is an element of a long-term effort, with at least some degree of institutionalization that is not easily overturned.

Stage 5 implies normative change to the extent that sexual violence is considered a taboo weapon and its use is rare and prompts decisive action. The international responses to nuclear proliferation, antipersonnel land mines, and chemical weapons illustrate the type of normative change that stage 5 describes. In spite of resolutions and declarations stating moral outrage and states' willingness to commit resources to eradicating sexual violence as a tool of war, civilians (and combatants) still endure sexual atrocities related to armed conflict. Although states have created institutions and programs devoted to ending wartime sexual violence, NGOs, advocates, and especially civilians in the midst of hostilities repeatedly ask for more accountability for perpetrators of sexual violence, more action from states and the UN, and more aid to survivors and the agencies committed to their well-being. To date, efforts to implement the agenda have not eradicated conflict-related sexual violence or created an environment in which states and IOs feel obligated to respond decisively—or in ways that are contrary to their own national interests—to each case of sexual violence that occurs; but I include stage 5 here as a logical goal toward which advocates strive.

Although nonrecognition was once the standard international (non) response to wartime sexual violence, states and organizations now engage in active documentation and learning, rhetorical condemnation, policy commitments and resolutions, and some implementation activities with active monitoring by NGOs, institutions, and advocates. The chapters that follow examine how the shifting understanding of sexual violence from a rights issue to a security issue has affected states' and IOs' willingness to make commitments and implement changes; and they discuss the implications of the "weapon of war" frame for concerted action and strong normative change. As the implications of the success of the "weapon of war" frame illustrate, the ways in which advocates understand and discuss issues have a considerable impact on the ability to create and implement political responses to them.

The Evolution of the International Response to Sexual Violence

Frames succeed when advocates combine well-timed strategies with ideal political and institutional contexts. I turn now to a brief discussion of two other approaches to anti–sexual violence advocacy—nonrecognition, and recognition of sexual violence as a women's human rights violation—to provide contrast for the "weapon of war" frame.

Recognition, or Nonrecognition, of Sexual Violence

The limited historical attempts to address the occurrence of sexual violence in wartime sought to preserve masculine honor and feminine purity. These efforts did not respond to sexual violence as an atrocity or crime in its own regard; instead, they condemned the disruption and degradation of masculine, familial, and community honor caused by sexual violence. The historical condemnation of sexual violence was about men who experienced the embarrassment of failure to protect "their" women, as Brownmiller observes:

> Defense of women has long been a hallmark of masculine pride,
> as possession of women has been a hallmark of masculine success.
> Rape by a conquering soldier destroys all remaining illusions of
> power and property for men of the defeated side. The body of a
> raped woman becomes a ceremonial battlefield, a parade ground for
> the victor's trooping of the colors. The act that is played out upon
> her is a message passed between men—vivid proof of victory for
> one and loss and defeat for the other. (Brownmiller 1975, 31)

The prohibition of rape in the Lieber Code, General Orders No. 100, is consistent with the notion of the woman's body as an important facet of the larger social order, something to be kept pure. This code, which was issued to Union troops in 1863 during the US Civil War, mandated the protection of civilians, calling for special protection of women and the "sacredness of domestic relations" (Lieber 1863, Section II, Article 37). Specific protection from sexual violence did not emerge in *international* legal discourse until the Fourth Geneva Convention in 1949.

The Fourth Geneva Convention, like the Lieber Code, framed wartime sexual violence as a threat to familial honor. Specifically, the convention calls for the protection of women "against any attack on their honour, in particular against rape, enforced prostitution, or any form of indecent assault" (Geneva Convention IV, 1949, Part III, Section 1, Article 27). As Inal (2013, 97) observes, the social and normative context at the time required advocates pushing for recognition of sexual violence to discuss it as an attack on women's honor. State delegations negotiating the conventions would not have accepted a reference to rape or sexual violence any other way because of the socially taboo nature of sex and sexual abuse. Additional Protocol I (1977), on international conflicts, and Additional Protocol II (1977), on civil conflicts, reiterated the legal prohibition of rape, forced prostitution, and indecent assault established in the Geneva Conventions.[7] Inclusion in the Geneva Conventions and Additional Protocols represented important steps toward legal prohibition of sexual violence against civilians, but their honor-focused approach ultimately failed to generate open international discussion of sexual violence, let alone political condemnation and financial or institutional commitments. Sexual violence as an attack on the family or the community is not a crime with an autonomous victim; this view of sexual violence suggests that sexual atrocities are simply regrettable but inevitable aspects of war. More important, however, the Geneva Conventions and Additional Protocols did not designate a mechanism or party responsible for the protection of women's honor, rendering this early recognition little more than the basis for future efforts that would strengthen legal recognition and prohibition of sexual violence (Inal 2013).

Recognition of Systematic Sexual Violence and Women's Human Rights Advocacy

Political efforts to address wartime sexual violence as a crime against autonomous individuals began in the 1990s. The systematic use of rape, forced pregnancy, and other forms of sexual torture and humiliation in the genocidal armed conflicts in the former Yugoslavia (especially in Bosnia) and Rwanda were widely publicized by the international media and human rights groups. Up to 60,000 women and girls were raped and forcibly impregnated in Bosnia as part of an ethnic-cleansing campaign. In Rwanda, an estimated 250,000 to 500,000 women and girls were raped and tortured, systematically targeted in an effort to humiliate victims before killing them or to leave them alive and scarred to convey a message of brutality.[8] The systematic nature of sexual violence in both conflicts prompted outrage and the perception of the brutality as unprecedented (Niarchos 1995, 650; Alison 2007, 82). After revelations of the atrocities in Bosnia-Herzegovina and Croatia, the world began to see the realities of sexual violence in war, in contrast to the collective blind eye that policymakers and publics alike turned toward accounts of rape in wartime throughout history.[9] Mobilization around broader issues of women's human rights at this time prompted advocates to call for recognition of the use of systematic sexual violence in both conflicts.

Advocates built on the momentum of several women's rights and human rights achievements and framed wartime sexual violence as a women's human rights violation and a systematic instrument of genocide and war. During the Cold War, NGOs had consultative status within the UN system and worked on matters such as women's status and domestic rights, women's participation in the UN, and women and development. Women's rights advocacy efforts maintained a focus on legal equality and economic rights as pathways to empowerment; violence against women was not central to the campaign for improvements in women's status (Harrington 2010, 90). Although the UN Decade for Women (1975–85) resulted in the legally binding Convention on the Elimination of All Forms of Discrimination against Women in 1979, violence against women remained on the margins of the movement. Indeed, the agreement did not mention violence against women or sexual violence as a violation of women's rights in any of its statutes; instead, this convention focused on the legal status of women, broadly conceived (Keck and Sikkink 1998, 166; Harrington 2010, 95).

Cold War politics stifled the discussion of human rights in general, and women's rights groups encountered difficulties in promoting the notion of women's rights as human rights, in large part because the two agendas were viewed within both the UN system and the human rights network as wholly separate spheres. Joachim observes that the Commission on Human Rights and the Commission on the Status of Women were ideationally, geographically, and institutionally separate within the UN system, with the former based in Geneva and the latter based first in Vienna and then in New York. Human rights violations were framed as widespread, systematic abuses that are perpetrated by the state, and this understanding conflicted with the perception of violence against women at the time; violence against women was understood to be a private form of violence that is perpetrated by family members and intimate partners without the state's involvement and is thus beyond the reach of international law and organizations (Joachim 2007, 122–23). The concepts of women's rights and human rights remained wholly separate until the early 1990s, when activists came together at a series of UN world conferences and began to address violence against women within the context of the human rights agenda (Askin 1997, 257; Copelon 2011, 239; Harrington 2010, 95–96).

The Second World Conference on Human Rights, held in Vienna in June 1993, provided a meeting place for women's rights groups to voice their concerns about violence against women and women's human rights through the Women's NGO Caucus and through related channels and forums at the governmental meetings (Copelon 2011, 240). It was not by chance that women's human rights groups formed a vocal and influential bloc at the conference. In preparation for the Vienna conference, the Center for Women's Global Leadership organized training events to bring women's rights leaders from around the world together to develop strategies to ensure that gender-based violence made it onto the agenda (Joachim 2007, 122). Both Amnesty International and Human Rights Watch, two of the human rights network's "hubs" (Carpenter 2011, 69–70), documented violence against women in the early 1990s, and both organizations' reputations for credibility and influence over governments helped women's NGOs gain support for their efforts in Vienna (Joachim 2007, 128).

During the Vienna conference, the UN Development Fund for Women, whose focus on women and economic development throughout the 1980s had excluded gender-based violence concerns, provided a forum for women's NGOs in Vienna, where groups assembled daily to establish lobbying strategies. To generate visibility for women's human rights concerns, the Center for Women's Global Leadership's International Coordinating Committee planned and staged an Eighteen-Hour Tribunal during the conference, at which women from twenty-five states testified on violations of women's human rights before a panel of judges. The tribunal's "verdict" held that the UN's human rights agencies and instruments were insufficient to protect women's human rights. The US secretary of state, Warren Christopher, communicated in his opening remarks to the conference that guaranteeing women's human rights was a "moral imperative," and he signaled that the United States would take a leading role in the effort to secure these rights (Joachim 2007, 128).

In 1993 the world's leaders could not help but witness sexual violence being used as a method of genocide. Reports of sexual violence in the former Yugoslavia preceded and continued alongside the conference in Vienna, which had an impact on states' willingness to hear the concerns of women's NGOs. Media and NGO reports publicized widespread sexual violence against women in Bosnia-Herzegovina and Croatia, and survivors of these atrocities mounted a formidable presence at the Vienna conference to press for recognition and condemnation (Copelon 2011). And calls for recognition were not limited to the genocide in the former Yugoslavia. Before the conference, in 1991, allegations of systematic sexual slavery orchestrated by the Japanese military during World War II—the "comfort women" system—resurfaced and led to coordinated demands for recognition and compensation for survivors.[10] These demands continued well into the next decade.

The combined efforts of women's rights activists and survivors of sexual atrocities at the Vienna conference resulted in the condemnation of war rape in the Vienna Declaration and Program of Action, which called for equality for women, condemned all forms of violence against them, and specifically demanded the cessation and punishment of systematic sexual violence against women in all conflict zones:

28. The World Conference on Human Rights expresses its dismay at massive violations of human rights especially in the form of genocide, "ethnic cleansing" and systematic rape of women in war situations, creating mass exodus of refugees and displaced persons. While strongly condemning such abhorrent practices it reiterates the call that perpetrators of such crimes be punished and such practices immediately stopped. . . .

38. In particular, the World Conference on Human Rights stresses the importance of working towards the elimination of violence against women in public and private life, the elimination of all forms of sexual harassment, exploitation and trafficking in women, the elimination of gender bias in the administration of justice and the eradication of any conflicts which may arise between the rights of women and the harmful effects of certain traditional or customary practices, cultural prejudices and religious extremism. The World Conference on Human Rights calls upon the General Assembly to adopt the draft declaration on violence against women and urges States to combat violence against women in accordance with its provisions. Violations of the human rights of women in situations of armed conflict are violations of the fundamental principles of international human rights and humanitarian law. All violations of this kind, including in particular murder, systematic rape, sexual slavery, and forced pregnancy, require a particularly effective response. (United Nations General Assembly 1993)

Although the Vienna Declaration called for an international response to systematic sexual violence in armed conflict, it did not provide a specific mechanism for doing so.

Two years later, the UN Conference on Women in Beijing in 1995 and the resulting Beijing Platform for Action condemned all forms of violence against women, including systematic rape in war, and confirmed that women's rights are human rights. That same year, the United Nations Human Rights Council institutionalized the response to gender-based violence by creating a special rapporteur on violence against women (Alison 2007, 83). The timing of the UN world conferences; the strengthening of the transnational women's rights network; news of the sexual atrocities in Bosnia-Herzegovina, Croatia, and Rwanda; and the more general awareness and acceptance of human rights and individual security issues—all these together created an international political and legal context in which the efforts to address violence against women as a threat to women's human rights could gain unprecedented momentum (a legal expert, in a discussion with the author, New York, June 2012).

Transnational civil society advocates joined forces and lobbied the UN Security Council for the inclusion of sexual violence in the statutes of the International Criminal Tribunal for the Former Yugoslavia (ICTY) and the International Criminal Tribunal for Rwanda (ICTR) (an ICTY/ICTR prosecutor, in a discussion with the author, telephone,

July 2012). The Security Council included rape as a crime against humanity (but not as a war crime or crime of genocide) in the ICTY statute in May 1993. The ICTR statute, which was adopted in November 1994, included rape as a crime against humanity and added the charges of rape, enforced prostitution, and any form of indecent assault as war crimes. As the ad hoc tribunals were in the process of hearing cases, the UN General Assembly commissioned a preparatory committee for what would become the permanent International Criminal Court (ICC) on the basis of a draft statute presented by the UN International Law Commission (Inal 2013, 134–35). NGOs formed the Coalition for the International Criminal Court, and they remained hugely influential in the creation of the Rome Statute, which was signed on July 17, 1998, and entered into force on July 1, 2002. In large part because of the continued advocacy by women's human rights NGOs, the Rome Statute enumerates sexual violence—framed as including not only of rape but also "sexual slavery, enforced prostitution, forced pregnancy, enforced sterilization, or any other form"—as a crime against humanity in Article 7 and as a war crime in Article 8 (United Nations General Assembly 1998). Legal recognition of sexual violence in wartime represented a major success for women's human rights advocates; the statutes and decisions would have looked very different if NGOs and survivors of sexual violence had not presented a vocal constituency at the Vienna conference and had not directed intensive lobbying efforts toward the Security Council, ICC preparatory committee, and the judges and staff of the ad hoc tribunals (Sellers 2009).

The international legal prohibition of sexual violence in wartime was cemented through the ad hoc tribunals and the ICC statute; but in the years that followed, political discussions became divided between two competing frames for sexual violence. Sexual violence framed as a violation of women's human rights suggests that wartime sexual atrocities are a continuation of the inequality and daily forms of violence that women and girls face in a world still guided by patriarchal influences, or the privileging of masculine bodies, roles, and identities at the expense of feminine bodies, roles, and identities.[11] To effectively address sexual atrocities, advocates, states, and organizations must seek to rectify the root causes of gender-based violence in wartime and in the absence of active armed conflict. States, however, are hesitant to delve into other states' human rights issues; sovereignty, with all its political and legal limitations, remains a strong norm in spite of an increasing focus on the security of individuals after the end of the Cold War. Wartime sexual violence framed as a women's human rights issue resonates with the historical perception that sexual violence is an inevitable aspect of war—in which all manner of terrible things happen to civilians—and that it is largely a domestic problem individual states must deal with through their own national institutions.[12] Human rights issues, broadly conceived, and women's rights issues fall outside the traditional security interests of states and are perceived to be beyond the scope of the UN Security Council's mandate, which itself is shaped by the interests of strong states.

To illustrate the development of the two different approaches, table 1.2 highlights major international responses to sexual violence from 1993 through 2013 and pairs each response with its primary frame.

Sexual violence as a "weapon of war," the frame that both emanated from and competed with the women's human rights frame, was motivated by the observation that systematic sexual violence was a powerful tool of war in Bosnia-Herzegovina, Croatia, and Rwanda, and that it was categorically different from "everyday" sexual violence, which is a matter for domestic justice systems.[13] Transnational women's human rights advocates brought these atrocities to light, but they did so as part of the long-standing struggle for gender equality; the idea of sexual violence as a systematic tool used by combatants resonated more profoundly with states than the idea that sexual violence was the manifestation of societal gender norms and ideas about identity and personhood.[14] Table 1.2 includes "systematic sexual violence" as a precursor to the more specific "weapon of war" frame. The "weapon of war" imagery began to emerge as a rhetorical tool for advocates within the UN leadership and among influential NGOs in 2000 through 2002. In his February 2001 report on the war in the Democratic Republic of the Congo (DRC), UN secretary-general Kofi Annan highlighted "the tragic fact that civilians—especially women and children—have been the principal victims of the fighting. Terrible crimes have been committed against women, including rape as a weapon of war" (United Nations Secretary-General 2000, 2001). The frame gathered strength in foreign policy discourse as transnational advocates and state policymakers recalled the situation in the former Yugoslavia when expressing their horror at the widespread sexual violence in the DRC beginning in 2003, as discussed with respect to US foreign policy in chapter 2 below and UN Security Council discourse in 2007–8 in chapter 3. To refer to sexual violence as a weapon

Table 1.2 Responses to Sexual Violence and Their Frames

Year	Response	Frame
1993	Media, academic, and political discussion of sexual violence in Bosnia-Herzegovina and Croatia	Women's human rights Systematic sexual violence
1993	International Criminal Tribunal for the Former Yugoslavia statute includes rape as a crime against humanity	Women's human rights Systematic sexual violence
1994	Media, academic, and political discussion of sexual violence in Rwanda International Criminal Tribunal for Rwanda statute includes rape as a crime against humanity; and this statute includes rape, enforced prostitution, and indecent assault as war crimes	Women's human rights Systematic sexual violence
1998	Rome Statute includes sexual violence as a crime against humanity and a war crime	Women's human rights Systematic sexual violence
2000	UN Security Council Resolution 1325 (October) calls for recognition of war's impact on women and need for women's participation in decision making, postconflict reconstruction, and conflict prevention	Women's human rights
2000–2002	UN secretary-general and Human Rights Watch cite "rape as a weapon of war" in the Democratic Republic of the Congo	Weapon of war
2003	The United States condemns sexual violence as a weapon of war in the Democratic Republic of the Congo for the first time	Weapon of war
2008	UN Security Council Resolution 1820 (June) condemns sexual violence as a weapon of war	Weapon of war
2009	UN Security Council Resolution 1888 (September) condemns sexual violence as a weapon of war and calls for appointment of a special representative to the secretary-general on sexual violence in armed conflict	Weapon of war
2010	UN Security Council Resolution 1960 (December) condemns sexual violence as a weapon of war and calls for annual reporting on sexual violence in armed conflict	Weapon of war
2012	The United Kingdom launches the Preventing Sexual Violence Initiative	Weapon of war

Table 1.2   (*continued*)

Year	Response	Frame
2013	UN Security Council Resolution 2106 (June) condemns sexual violence as a weapon (and includes men and boys as targets) and calls for greater implementation of Resolution 1325 and subsequent resolutions	Women's human rights Weapon of war
2014	The Preventing Sexual Violence Initiative's Global Summit to End Sexual Violence in Conflict (June) gathers leaders from an array of organizations and 123 states with the stated goal of ending impunity for the use of rape as a weapon of war	Weapon of war

and as something similar to the atrocities that shocked the international conscience in the mid-1990s was to convince others of the imperative to *do* something. When advocates, policymakers, and organizational leaders discussed sexual violence in the language of weapons and security, they created a sense of urgency within their institutions because the phenomenon and the rationale behind it seemed to be unprecedented.

As the literatures on TANs and securitization instruct, the words that advocates use to describe an issue matter. When advocates adopted a "weapon" frame instead of a "gender" or "human rights" frame, they increased the likelihood that states and IOs would respond to wartime sexual violence because they spoke of the issue in terms that members of political entities adopt and prioritize. The implementation of efforts to address wartime sexual violence improved over time as states and organizations began to conceive of the issue as one of security. Once advocates both within and outside states, NGOs, and IOs begin to discuss a given case of wartime sexual violence in terms of the "weapon of war" frame, or when they discuss the general issue of wartime sexual violence with reference to conflicts in which sexual violence has been used as a weapon in the past, they are more likely to evoke a response from the state or organization targeted by advocacy efforts. Before moving on, it is helpful to explore *how* the "weapon of war" frame came to dominate the narrative on conflict-related sexual violence.

The "Weapon of War" Frame in Context

The "weapon of war" frame became the dominant frame for sexual violence through a combination of four political or institutional factors that make it accessible and persuasive. First, the frame resonates with international humanitarian law (IHL) and the more general prioritization of state-based security issues—namely, war, militarization, and a traditional view of weapons as the primary threats that humans and states face—among powerful states and the United Nations. Second, advocates leveraged the international community's shock at the sexual atrocities perpetrated in Rwanda, Bosnia-Herzegovina, and Croatia to encourage action and to gain recognition of sexual violence in armed conflict. Third, increases in nonstate actors' influence and a shift from a state-centric notion of security to one more inclusive of individuals and groups made states more attuned to nontraditional security issues. Fourth and finally, the "weapon of war" frame struck a chord with influential individuals, who then helped call for action against sexual violence; these individuals in positions of power were shocked and motivated by the notion that rape could be a weapon of war, and they turned this shock into advocacy. I consider each in turn.

International Humanitarian Law

IHL places limitations on the conduct of armed forces engaged in warfare. As discussed above, before the explicit legal prohibition of sexual violence was established by the Rome Statute, the condemnation of wartime rape and other forms of sexual violence in treaties, conventions, and military codes placed primary concern on upholding honor (rather than physical integrity) and lacked a clear sense of obligation or responsibility for enforcing the (non)prohibition (Nalaeva 2010; Inal 2013). The extensive media and transnational advocacy coverage of systematic sexual violence in the conflicts in the former Yugoslavia served to "shock the international community into rethinking the prohibition of rape as a crime under the laws of war" (Meron 1993, 425). The shock led the International Committee of the Red Cross (ICRC), the authoritative voice on international humanitarian law, to observe that Article 147 of the Fourth Geneva Convention includes rape in theory, if not in writing. Article 147 prohibits belligerents from intentionally causing "great suffering or serious injury to body or health," and considers such actions to constitute a grave breach of IHL (Meron 1993, 426). The following year, 1993, the US State Department argued that "rape already was a war crime or a grave breach under customary international law and the Geneva Conventions and could be prosecuted as such" (Meron 1993, 427). Separately, the provisions in the Rome Statute and the statutes and decisions of the ICTY and ICTR explicitly addressed sexual violence as a war crime, crime against humanity, and an instrument of genocide, solidifying its prohibition under international law.

Sexual violence used as a weapon of war is a form of gender-based violence that, at least on its surface, can be *viewed* as a phenomenon that is bracketed within armed conflict. Although IHL overlaps significantly with IHRL (International Human Rights Law) (Cassimatis 2007), the former deals principally with acts of war and acknowledges the complex "balance between military necessity and humanity. . . . [The] law makes allowance in its provisions for actions necessary for military purposes" (Doswald-Beck and Vité 1993, 98). In essence, IHL is permissive of states' interests, to a point, and it shields states from condemnation and prosecution as long as they can demonstrate the military utility of an action. Its focus on acts of war makes IHL a more appealing legal regime for state policymakers who wish to maintain or defend their government's sovereignty. When international efforts focus on the broader scope of sexual violence and its roots in gender inequality and patriarchal norms, these efforts stray from the delimited period of active hostilities and conceivably threaten the state's autonomy. Such efforts may be unappealing and appear meddlesome at best or imperialist at worst. When advocates discuss sexual violence as a weapon of war, they engage states on a limited scope of issues concerning a very specific period of time and set of behaviors.

Traumatic Conflicts

Individual advocates and policymakers learn from history and reason that if conflicts are similar in some regards, they may be similar in nature and require comparable responses (Khong 1992). As the first conflicts to trigger a significant international response to the use of sexual violence, the wars in the former Yugoslavia and Rwanda serve as the first and most critical analogues or reference points for horrific sexual violence. These conflicts essentially set the standards against which the international community came to understand how, why, and to what extent sexual

violence could be used systematically as a weapon of war. More fundamentally, these conflicts made wartime sexual violence *visible*.

Much of what makes the use of sexual violence in a particular conflict
familiar is its comparability to the atrocities in these early wars. One
international legal expert aptly described the role of conflict analogies:
"We see a response to conflicts that are 'sexy.' It's about familiarity and
one good article or speech can make a *big* difference" (a legal expert, in a
discussion with the author, New York, June 2012). Sexual violence during armed conflict and continued postconflict instability in the DRC
was eventually cast in the "weapon of war" frame and compared with
the sexual atrocities in Bosnia-Herzegovina and Rwanda, which made
the international response to this particular conflict very strong. Sexual
violence is not recognized equally across all armed conflicts, and when
the international community condemns and commits resources, it is
because the atrocities fit within the "weapon of war" frame and resemble
those that occurred in Bosnia, Rwanda, or—more recently—the DRC.

Once advocates or policymakers make the comparison between a
specific conflict or the general issue of wartime sexual violence and these
analogue conflicts, they are able to generate a response from the state or
organization they wish to persuade. For example, in a speech delivered
during the launch of the Preventing Sexual Violence Initiative in May
2012, then–foreign secretary William Hague referenced the massacre
at Srebrenica, "the worst atrocity on European soil since the end of the
Second World War," and the "50,000 rapes committed during the war
in Bosnia" to illustrate how sexual violence has been used as a weapon
(Foreign and Commonwealth Office 2012a). Emphasizing the need to
continue to address sexual violence in conflicts, Hague then recalled
reports of rape against women, men, and children in Syria in 2012.
By linking sexual violence in Bosnia-Herzegovina to sexual violence in
Syria, Hague advocated for action in response to the latter. Highly visible accounts of systematic sexual violence in the former Yugoslavia,
Rwanda, and the DRC allow advocates to mobilize around familiar feelings of shock and outrage.

The Expansion of "Security" and Nonstate Actors

The concept of security in international relations and in the practice of
international affairs has traditionally encompassed threats to the state
as a political entity. In this view of a world of sovereign states, security

threats come from outside the state and threaten the sanctity of its physical borders, population, governing institutions, or norms and way of life (Ogata 2001). Along with the emergence of the state as the primary actor in international affairs and governance in the eighteenth and nineteenth centuries came the "monopolization of security by the state" and the bargain through which individuals traded their liberty for protection by the state against both internal and external threats (MacFarlane and Khong 2006; Kaldor 2007). The underlying assumption holds that the state itself does not pose a threat to its own citizens and that it can and will effectively mediate any conflicts between intrastate factions. At the close of the twentieth century, the international community shifted from the rigid political structure imposed by Cold War–era hostilities to the current system in which states and nonstate actors alike have the ability—albeit to wildly varying degrees—to influence international politics. The increasing acceptance of a broader range of issues as potential international priorities allowed the women's human rights movement, alongside other new human rights concerns, to flourish in the 1990s. TANs and movements could function with greater ease, utilizing the UN as a central platform to convey interests and pressure states or monitor their compliance with commitments. Although states are far from inconsequential, as I noted above in the observation that strong states remain the key targets of transnational advocacy, the notion that the state is the *only* political entity that can protect and represent the interests of individuals, groups, or entire populations was called into question. Nonstate actors became more influential, and traditionally marginalized issues took center stage.

As the mobilization around women's human rights and wartime sexual violence was gaining momentum, so too was the notion of human security. A product of the increased focus on human development and human rights, especially within the UN system, human security "means safety from the constant threats of hunger, disease, crime and repression. It also means protection from sudden and hurtful disruption in the pattern of our daily lives—whether in our homes, in our jobs, in our communities or in our environment" (United Nations Development Program 1994, 3). The inclusion of threats to individuals' lives and livelihoods extended the range of issues that states and IOs might reasonably address as international security concerns.

Sexual violence is an issue that fits comfortably within the range of human security concerns, but it still resembles traditional (weaponized) security concerns when framed as a *weapon* of war. Human security's emergence within the UN and among state proponents contributed to the acceptance of sexual violence as a "new" security issue that states should address. As human security became more institutionalized within the UN, the partner notion of "the responsibility to protect"—adopted at the UN's 2005 World Summit and reaffirmed by the Security Council through Resolution 1674 in April 2006—provided even greater justification for state and IO action in response to systematic atrocities targeting civilians. The responsibility to protect redefines the traditional notion of state-based security and argues, instead, for sovereignty as a responsibility to citizens. The state remains the primary provider of security for its population but is no longer considered the *sole* provider of security; if a state fails to uphold its responsibility to its citizens, then the international community must provide assistance or mediation, and if such efforts fail, they must intervene to reestablish security for the people.[15] Against this backdrop, it should be clear that political efforts to respond to sexual violence do not present a challenge to the redefined understanding of sovereignty or the broader concept of what constitutes a security concern. Such drastic revisions of the traditional political order do have staunch opponents; and for states and IOs that are loath to retire long-held notions of security and sovereignty, the "weapon of war" frame allows advocates to find a feasible middle ground on which to advance efforts to address sexual violence.[16] Still, sexual violence is not what we would consider a traditional security issue, an existential threat to the state, so even an incomplete acceptance of human security concerns as international policy priorities has provided space for advocacy around the issue of wartime sexual violence.

Powerful Allies and Embedded Advocates

For a frame to be compelling, it must appeal to someone who is in a position to make the issue a priority. Favorable issue attributes, prominent advocates, and existing norms onto which a new issue may be grafted can be present in the case of a nonissue as well as a successful or compelling one (Carpenter 2007a). Clifford Bob argues that NGOs engage in strategic calculations to determine which causes and claims they should advance (Bob 2005). I extend this reasoning to individual advocates, both within and outside states and IOs. In her study of the nonissue of children born of wartime rape, Carpenter finds that foundational accounts of norm development and transnational advocacy are insufficient to explain the mechanisms involved in issue emergence (Carpenter 2007b). Variation in issue adoption by advocacy networks is explained, then, by the agendas and decision-making processes of the most central organizations—the hubs—in the networks. Claims made by certain organizations—reputable, established organizations like Human Rights Watch and the ICRC—are taken more seriously by states. These central organizations can then use their agenda-setting and vetting capabilities to influence advocacy networks' agendas and construct (or constrain) entire issue areas (Carpenter 2011).[17] Of particular importance here are organizations and individuals working within or in conjunction with the UN system. Joachim (2007, 27) observes that additional allies of emerging issues include the media and wealthy foundations.

The source of advocacy matters; and capability, influence, and opportunity thus are significant factors that determine the success or failure of an issue's frame. A political actor's ability and willingness to leverage influence and financial or material resources to advance a given frame has a strong impact on that frame's success. When influential individuals with ties to strong states, the UN Security Council, and highly reputable human rights organizations began to discuss sexual violence as a weapon of war, this frame gained credibility and resonated with the broader international community. The continued use of the frame by influential individuals maintains pressure on states and IOs to honor their commitments to respond to wartime sexual violence.

Anti–sexual violence advocates, including policymakers and organization staff members, have leveraged political influence and legitimacy, positions in powerful or prestigious international organizations or alliances, and windows of opportunity to build support for the cause. Blurring the lines between politics and popular culture, celebrities have joined forces with political advocates to raise awareness and pressure decision makers to respond to sexual violence. Celebrity involvement and the mobilization of young adults played a significant role in referring the war crimes in Darfur to the ICC (a legal expert, in a discussion with the author, New York, June 2012). The actor and film writer and director Ben Affleck advocated on behalf of the victims of the conflict in the DRC during a US House of Representatives hearing in March 2011. Individual policymakers, functioning as embedded advocates or norm entrepreneurs within their states, make an impact on domestic policy, which in turn makes an impact on international efforts to address the

issue. During her tenure as US secretary of state, Hillary Clinton priori-
tized the response to sexual violence in the DRC, and in so doing she
also raised national and international awareness of the general issue of
wartime sexual violence (a legal expert, in a discussion with the author,
New York, June 2012; US State Department staff members, in a group
interview with the author, Washington, July 2012). William Hague's
personal commitment to addressing sexual violence in armed conflict
led to a renewed effort by wealthy and politically powerful states when
he leveraged the United Kingdom's presidency of the then–Group of
Eight and the UN Security Council to launch his government's initiative on preventing sexual violence (Foreign and Commonwealth Office 2012a). The presence and willingness of powerful allies to exert
political leverage within states and international organizations helped
the "weapon of war" frame emerge and shape implementation efforts.

Early advocacy by women's groups and human rights groups, which
predominantly relied on the women's human rights frame for sexual
violence, was essential to securing international recognition both during and after the wars in Rwanda and the former Yugoslavia, and for
encouraging the ad hoc tribunals and the ICC to take sexual atrocities
seriously. Still, attempts to address sexual violence that focus on gender
dynamics, particularly sexual violence as an impediment to women's
empowerment and agency in conflict and postconflict zones, situate
sexual violence within the broader context of gender equality and wom-
en's human rights and are not as compelling to states and state-led IOs.
When they began to discuss sexual violence as a weapon at the expense
of broader consideration of gender issues, advocates caught the attention of traditionally powerful international actors, including the United
States, the United Kingdom, and the UN Security Council. I return
now to the discussion of the frame and its effects.

The Implications of the "Weapon of War" Frame

To argue that the "weapon of war" frame for sexual violence became the
dominant frame is not to diminish the power of the transnational wom-
en's human rights movement. The competition between the women's
human rights frame for sexual violence and the "weapon of war" frame
does not begin or end with the advocates' affiliation; instead, it stems
from the particular aspect of advocacy around sexual violence that most
appealed to individuals and agencies with the capacity to adopt and

diffuse the frame. The "weapon of war" image of sexual violence took hold in spite of the fact that it is not necessarily in line with the aims of the women's human rights agenda, which makes the evolution of the international response to wartime sexual violence particularly intriguing. Advocates built on a hospitable political and institutional context and the momentum of international moral outrage to advance recognition of sexual violence, but the programmatic agenda that has evolved has strayed from concerns about women's human rights, empowerment, and gender norms. Implementation of the anti–sexual violence agenda has been shaped by both normative concerns and powerful political interests. If we ask why advocates chose—and continue to choose—the "weapon of war" frame, the evidence points to presumptions that the long-term benefits of increased awareness and implementation of political commitments outweigh the short-term risks of narrowing the agenda.

The benefits of the frame are not limited to the long term, however; acknowledgment that sexual violence is used as a weapon has assisted some advocates in their efforts to build a network. A group of UN staff members dedicated to efforts to prevent sexual violence remarked that their work has become significantly easier now that the "weapon of war" frame has helped security-minded agencies understand exactly how sexual violence relates to their goals and mandates: "We have managed to get this agenda on the security radar. Now the security folks try to get on *our* agenda. There is more interest now from the 'protection of civilians' people. The initial framing of sexual violence as a weapon of war helped with that—that's the feeling I get from a lot of informal conversations. This has become such a solid agenda and that helps" (UN staff members, in a group interview with the author, telephone, May 2013). The "weapon of war" frame does not simply bring efforts to end sexual violence into discussions of international politics and security; it also leads security-minded organizations and individuals to question the role of sexual violence in the issues central to their work.

The reliance on the "weapon of war" frame, though it has motivated international political action, has narrowed the international community's recognition of sexual violence. The implications for cases of sexual violence that do not fit within the frame or are not recognized as such are grave, and advocates continue to chastise states and IOs for their inattention to the broader scope of conflict-related sexual violence. To take only a few examples, the international responses to sexual violence occurring in Guinea, Colombia, Haiti, Mexico, Libya, and Syria have been weak—both in terms of rhetoric and material commitment—in comparison to the responses to the conflicts in Bosnia-Herzegovina and Croatia, Rwanda, the DRC, and other cases in which sexual violence is used as a weapon, including—but to a lesser extent—Darfur (a legal expert, in a discussion with the author, New York, June 2012). When policymakers are uncertain of the motives behind sexual violence and whether it is truly used as a weapon, the response is delayed or muted. Reports of sexual violence during the Libyan civil war beginning in 2011 perplexed decision makers within states and IOs, and also NGOs and civil society groups—none of whom were certain of how to classify sexual violence in this particular case. A US government official who specializes in gender issues conveyed her department's hesitation to respond to sexual violence in Libya in the following way: "At the time there were conflicting reports and we were not getting clear data. We saw evidence of some cases of rape in Libya, but we did not see evidence of systematic rape. I was very concerned that the issue would spiral out of control and lead to greater insecurity for women if we focused on systematic rape without proof, so when I advised on this topic I focused on standard efforts to protect women in the postconflict period" (a US government official, in a discussion with the author, Washington, September 2012).

The result of conflicting perceptions of sexual violence in Libya was a lack of concerted action from the international community, including NGOs. One international legal expert remarked with frustration: "No one is doing anything about sexual violence in Libya or Syria. Even human rights leaders say it's not happening or, if it is, we can't talk about it" (in a discussion with the author, New York, June 2012). The "weapon of war" frame has had a clear impact on not only the trajectory of the international anti–sexual violence agenda but also on the day-to-day decision making in response to sexual violence in particular conflicts.

Epigraph

Roberta Cohen—cofounder of the Brookings–London School of Economics Project on Internal Displacement and a specialist on human rights, humanitarian, and refugee issues—in a discussion with the author, Fairfax, Virginia, February 2012.

Notes

1. Finnemore and Sikkink (1998, 896) define norm entrepreneurs as individuals with "strong notions about appropriate or desirable behavior in their community."

2. For a full discussion of the etymology and evolution of the term "civilian," see Richard Shelly Hartigan's (1967) study of the noncombatant immunity principle.

3. The term "Copenhagen School" refers to research on security studies stemming from Barry Buzan's *People, States & Fear* (1983) and an examination of security by scholars at the Centre for Peace and Conflict Research in Copenhagen. See Bill McSweeney's (1996) review of Buzan and Wæver's works for the original use of the term "Copenhagen School."

4. Hudson et al. (2012) examine the everyday assumptions and interactions that fuel gender-based violence, inequality, and war in a global study of the gendered roots of international relations. Joshua Goldstein (2001) draws from biological factors and gender norms in his discussion of sexualized attacks and language in war. The centrality of gender in national and international politics is a core tenet of feminist international relations research, as articulated by J. Ann Tickner (1992, 23) in her observation that "a truly comprehensive security cannot be achieved until gender relations of domination and subordination are eliminated" and Cynthia Enloe (1990) in her claim that "gender makes the world go round."

5. For a comprehensive discussion of the choices armed groups make concerning types of violence (broadly conceived) used against civilians, see Hoover Green (2011).

6. The moving testimonies by Julienne Lusenge, Yanar Mohammad, and Alaa Murabit—activists, respectively, from the Democratic Republic of Congo, Iraq, and Libya—at the Security Council's annual open debate on Women, Peace, and Security in October 2015 discussed how focusing more on the protection of women from violence than on their participation in decision making and inclusion in peace processes inhibits full implementation of the goals laid out in Resolution 1325 (United Nations Security Council 2015d).

7. See "Protocol Additional to the Geneva Conventions of 12 August 1949, and Relating to the Protection of Victims of International Armed Conflicts (Protocol I) 1977, Chapter II, Article 76"; and "Protocol Additional to the Geneva Conventions of 12 August 1949, and Relating to the Protection of Victims of Non-International Armed Conflicts (Protocol II) 1977, Part II, Article 4."

8. In addition to table I.1, presented in the introduction, also see Alison (2007, 87), Heineman (2008, 5), and Weitsman (2008, 573).

9. Inal (2013, 9) uses the term "normative shock" to describe the impact of events, such as genocide, that have a transformative impact on international beliefs, norms, or laws; these shocks are "tragic situations or events that shock the public conscience into focusing on particular activities or institutions and change the core norms."

10. The campaign to secure official compensation, apologies, and prosecution for the offenses of the "comfort women" system continued into the twenty-first century. In December 2000 survivors presented evidence of rape and enforced prostitution during the Women's International War Crimes Tribunal. See Ellis (2007) and Copelon (2011).

11. For an excellent discussion of the continuum of violence, see Boesten (2014).

12. The response is consistent with Hansen's (2000b) observations about the absence of gender in securitization due to the view of women's and gendered security problems representing individual, rather than collective, security threats.

13. As Sam Cook (2009) cautions, advocates must take care not to normalize sexual violence and gender-based crimes in "peacetime" in the pursuit of implementation of efforts to eradicate sexual violence in war.

14. For a discussion of sexual violence and identity, see Weitsman (2008).

15. For a discussion of the responsibility to protect, see Bellamy (2009).

16. For more information on the human security agenda, its implications, and persistent colonial legacies, see Doty (1997) and Tadjbakhsh and Chenoy (2007).

17. Bob (2009) also confirms the influence of organizational gatekeepers on advocacy agendas.

Chapter 2

"Her Story Is Far Too Common"
The US Response to Sexual Violence in the DRC

> The United States condemns these attacks and all those who commit them and abet them. And we say to the world that those who attack civilian populations using systematic rape are guilty of crimes against humanity. These acts don't just harm a single individual, or a single family, or a single village, or a single group. They shred the fabric that weaves us together as human beings. Such atrocities have no place in any society.
> —*US secretary of state Hillary Clinton*

Condemnation of an armed group or regime for the use of rape, especially as a weapon of war or a tactic of political repression against women and children, is now one of the most powerful tools in the policymaker's or advocate's rhetorical toolbox. Precisely because advocacy efforts to highlight sexual violence have been so successful, waging a campaign of systematic rape against civilians is viewed as one of the most callous and barbaric forms of warfare. Condemnation may not follow exclusively from a decision maker's genuine concern for the victims and survivors of sexual violence; as the previous chapter suggests, state leaders have a variety of incentives to highlight an adversary regime's use of sexual violence. Such incentives range from preparing for military intervention to attempts to exert political pressure.

Regardless of the scale of the alleged abuses, making graphic references to sexual violence provides a powerful justification for political and military actions that would not otherwise gain domestic popular support. Such was the case in 1990, when President George H. W. Bush expanded his rationale for the Gulf War by citing the use of systematic rape against the women of Kuwait by Saddam Hussein's armed forces. Five years later, as the United States committed personnel to the peacekeeping operation in the former Yugoslavia, President Bill Clinton recalled Serb forces' use of systematic rape as a tool of war in Bosnia in an effort to justify the commitment of troops to a hesitant domestic public. President George W. Bush similarly condemned sexual violence by Saddam Hussein's regime after making the decision in late 2002 to wage war against Iraq; he cited the use of "rape rooms" and rape as a method of political intimidation and torture along with referring to other horrific abuses.[1] Graphic discussions of wanton sexual violence used against civilians can "sell" war or humanitarian intervention quite effectively to a hesitant domestic or international public; this type of condemnation serves a political purpose and, if it precludes more meaningful action to address sexual violence, it resembles the strategic use of securitization discussed by the Copenhagen School. Calling attention to sexual violence can serve a state leader's immediate political interests, but state and international responses to wartime sexual violence since the mid-1990s have also defied narrowly interest-based logic in many ways. Acknowledging US efforts to condemn adversaries' atrocities for the purpose of justifying belligerent policies or impending troop deployments, as explored elsewhere, this chapter examines the effect of the "weapon of war" frame on the recognition of and resources committed to programs addressing sexual violence in the Democratic Republic of the Congo (DRC).[2]

The US government began to acknowledge and document sexual violence in the DRC with increasing frequency over time, and its recognition became more consistent and comprehensive when the image of sexual violence as a weapon of war emerged as the dominant frame through which national policymakers and advocates viewed sexual violence. Changes in information about the scale and systematic nature of atrocities—due to improved mechanisms for documenting and reporting sexual violence, along with an increase in the frequency and brutality of sexual violence in some regions beginning in 2008—helped to solidify the image of sexual violence as a weapon of war and, with it, the US response to wartime sexual violence in that particular state. Political rhetoric and action concerning sexual atrocities in the DRC have followed a consistent pattern, emphasizing the systematic and brutal nature of wartime sexual violence used by combatants against civilians. This pattern of recognition indicates that both ideational shifts and national interests were at work as policymakers grappled with continuing violence in the DRC. Once policymakers were effectively persuaded of the strategic nature and large scale of sexual violence, they began to implement rhetorical and material responses to the situation. Construction of sexual violence as a weapon in the policy discourse created a clear threat to a referent object—Congolese civilians, and security in the Great Lakes region of Africa more broadly—and the "weapon of war" frame enabled embedded advocates in the United States to appeal to the state's interests in the Great Lakes region.

I focus on the period from 1990 through 2014, creating an account of the emergence and impact of the "weapon of war" frame with respect to one state's foreign policy rhetoric. The chapter proceeds with a discussion of the factors that motivate a state to highlight, condemn, and implement efforts to end sexual violence in another state. The subsequent section establishes the general trends in acknowledgment of sexual violence in the DRC and general conflict in the DRC within the US foreign policy discourse. The third section traces US action to address sexual violence in the United States, with a focus on two critical periods, 2003–7 and 2008–12. The final section offers reflections on the case study with respect to the roles of embedded advocates and state interests.

Understanding the US Response to Sexual Violence in the DRC

In recent years, policymakers in the United States have successfully securitized gender-based violence and oppression, justifying war in the name of defending women (Hirschkind and Mahmood 2002; Hunt and Rygiel 2006; Enloe 2010). In line with interest-based explanations of states' condemnations of sexual violence and other atrocities against civilians, US policymakers cited the oppression of women and the use of sexual violence as a tool of political repression as justification for the War on Terror. Before and after invading Afghanistan in 2001, the Bush administration worked to publicize the oppression of Afghan women under the Taliban to justify the military intervention. The "image of the Afghan woman shrouded in the burqa played a leading role" in the administration's public justification for military intervention in Afghanistan after the September 11, 2001, terrorist attacks on the United States (Ayotte and Husain 2005). In September 2002, while attempting to persuade the international community and the American public of the validity of invading Iraq, the Bush administration recounted the Iraqi regime's use of "rape rooms" and employment of sexual violence as a tool of political repression (Ben-Porath 2007, 194; Harrington 2010, 137–38). The administration's rhetoric condemning sexual violence faded after the exposure of the sexual abuse of Iraqi prisoners by US personnel at Abu Ghraib prison, and the troops' actions were condemned as the misdeeds of a few "bad apples" rather than the policy of an administration and the values of a nation (Ben-Porath 2007, 196). When it failed to serve US strategic interests, the administration abandoned its rhetorical condemnation of sexual violence in Iraq.

Strategic interests function as a mechanism driving states to respond to wartime sexual violence when doing so provides political cover or generates support for an existing interest or planned action. Interests also become a factor when the use of sexual violence threatens an object of national concern, such as an ally or a region that is host to economic interests or resources. Speaking about sexual violence in the language of security does not always reflect genuine concern for those who experience it. According to this explanation, a state's interests lie at the heart of any response; and the scale, nature, or egregiousness of the atrocities only provide a selling point for securitization attempts. In addition to justifying wars and sanctions waged for unrelated purposes or to satisfy other national interests, interest-based approaches suggest that states will be more likely to condemn sexual violence by adversaries than by allies or their own personnel. Highlighting the strategic use of sexual violence underscores a purported civilizational divide and makes an adversary appear barbaric. A state may also condemn systematic or politically motivated sexual violence within an adversary's borders in order to justify intervention or other domestically or internationally unpopular political maneuvers.

If a state's response to sexual violence is motivated purely by strategic concerns, two observable implications follow: States and the international organizations through which they act will be unwilling to bear costs tied to the response to wartime sexual violence, and they will not endeavor to institutionalize responses over the long term. The first implication assumes that a state's response to wartime sexual violence functions as cheap talk.[3] A state acting on narrowly defined national security interests alone will avoid references to sexual violence, especially graphic anecdotes that evoke sympathy for victims and anger toward the perpetrators, when seeking to avoid military engagement, regardless of the state's relationship with the perpetrator (Ben-Porath 2007, 192–94).

The second observable implication suggests that the state will not work to institutionalize the means to respond to wartime sexual violence and will respond only when doing so meets strategic or military ends. In other words, over time there would be little to no development or implementation of a programmatic agenda focused on sexual violence. To recall the typology of responses introduced in chapter 1 (in table 1.1), states motivated solely by strategic interests will not move beyond stage 2, rhetorical condemnation.

However, national interests and an earnest implementation of humanitarian initiatives are not mutually exclusive. When advocates and policymakers within the United States began to discuss sexual violence as a weapon or tactic of war, they merged genuine normative concern for sexual violence with foreign policy interests in the Great Lakes region. The issue-framing approach suggests that the "weapon of war" frame is compelling and that through it states have come to view sexual violence as a problem. The observable implication of the framing explanation is that states' implementation of anti–sexual violence efforts will generally increase or remain consistent over time, as long as reports of sexual violence in wartime continue. Within the United States, the response to sexual violence in the DRC grew consistently stronger from 2003— when policymakers widely recognized sexual violence as a weapon— through 2012. The US response to sexual violence in the DRC was motivated not only by domestic political actors but also by international nongovernmental organizations (NGOs), UN agencies and officials, and individual advocates from outside the United States—most notably, activists from or with direct ties to the DRC. Those transnational advocacy efforts that focused on ending sexual violence often targeted the United States, as an influential donor state with political and military influence, and much of the language used and reports written by transnational advocacy groups appear in the US political discourse on sexual violence in the DRC, reflecting policymakers' willingness and capacity to learn from advocates.

The "weapon of war" frame for sexual violence in the DRC emerged outside the United States, but it was quickly adopted by embedded advocates in Congress and the State Department. Use of the phrase "rape as a weapon of war" by the UN secretary-general in 2000 and 2001 in reports on the DRC (United Nations Secretary-General 2000, 2001) and a 2002 Human Rights Watch (HRW) report on sexual violence in the DRC preceded US policymakers' use of the "weapon of war" frame and shed light on the systematic nature of the sexual atrocities in the DRC (HRW 2002). Organizations such as HRW, the Open Society Justice Initiative, and the International Rescue Committee, as well as such individual advocates as the filmmaker Lisa Jackson and the Congolese physician Denis Mukwege, were involved in the developing US response to sexual violence in the DRC and elsewhere throughout the early 2000s. Their participation in congressional hearings provided the types of graphic testimonies and credible, valued institutional insights needed to draw attention to the issue. Conflict analogies made during such hearings and in public speeches supported the perception that sexual violence in the DRC fit within the "weapon of war" frame; policymakers and advocates emphasized the systematic and widespread nature of the sexual atrocities in the DRC and compared the atrocities with those in Bosnia and Rwanda.[4]

The US response to sexual violence in the DRC was driven at key moments by individual advocates' personal convictions and dedication to stamping out the use of sexual violence as a weapon. Influential US politicians—including Secretary of State Condoleezza Rice, Ambassador Zalmay Khalilzad, Secretary of State Hillary Clinton, and Ambassador-at-Large Melanne Verveer—were staunch proponents of committing US diplomatic efforts and financial resources to supporting survivors of sexual violence in the DRC (and elsewhere) and of addressing the dynamics of gender and identity that make sexual violence such a powerful weapon of war. The tremendous influence of Clinton, Verveer, Rice, and the State Department's Office of Global Women's Issues (which was itself staffed predominantly by women) also speaks to the importance of institutional gender sensitivity and equality for the success of gender-focused human rights agendas. The US government had documentation of the perpetration of sexual violence by security forces and nonstate armed groups in the region starting in the mid-1990s, but it did not take action until 2003, by which time advocates had successfully applied the "weapon of war" frame. The timing and nature of US efforts to address sexual violence in the DRC suggest that gender-sensitive embedded advocates used the frame to promote the issue in a way that appeared to support US foreign policy interests; this recognition of sexual violence as a security issue by such influential figures facilitated rhetorical condemnation, diplomatic outreach, financial assistance, and changes in military commitments.

Measuring the US Response to Sexual Violence in the DRC

The implementation of the anti–sexual violence agenda within the United States with respect to violence in the DRC has included documentation, rhetorical condemnation, and initial and long-term commitments, with the latter two occurring after state policymakers started to view sexual violence as a weapon used by nonstate militias. For the purposes of measuring shifts in implementation of the agenda, I consider discourse and rhetoric to include presidential speeches, executive orders, congressional hearings and records, State Department press releases, and speeches by officials. Initial commitments and long-term implementation efforts include financial support and troop or personnel commitments.

Data for this case study come from both documentary sources and interviews.[5] The State Department's country reports on human rights provide insight into the types of human rights violations and abuses recorded by the department and measure US awareness of sexual violence over a period of twenty-four years.[6] These reports indicate whether the US government has documented evidence of human rights violations and abuses, along with the State Department's perception of the credibility of initial reports and the scale of atrocities. The inclusion of a specific violation or abuse, such as sexual violence, in the country report suggests that US policymakers have knowledge of that atrocity. The country report cites isolated incidents of rape, sexual abuse, and violence against women beginning in 1990 but does not begin to cite rape or sexual violence consistently until the 1997 report, when sexual violence clearly occurs within the context of armed conflict. By including in the analysis country reports for the six years before the outbreak of active hostilities in the First Congo War (1996–97), I capture a baseline level of recognition of sexual violence in the DRC.

To assess the extent to which the US government has responded to sexual violence in the DRC, I analyze presidential, congressional, and State Department documents focused on the DRC or the general global issue of wartime sexual violence.[7] Given the sustained references to sexual violence in the DRC in the country reports from 1997 onward, but only on an intermittent basis before that year, I include State Department speech and press conference transcripts and press releases from 1997 through 2014.[8] These documents contain the policymakers' outwardly focused discussions of the DRC and wartime sexual violence and provide an effective measure of the development and implementation of political efforts to address sexual violence in this particular conflict.

The Development of US Action in Response to Sexual Violence in the DRC

The United States formally established diplomatic ties with the DRC (then Zaire) in 1960 after the state's establishment of independence from Belgium. Active diplomatic involvement in the DRC began in the midst of the First Congo War and Second Congo War (1998–2003), when the United States participated in mediation efforts in cooperation with the United Nations, the European Union (including Belgium, France, and the United Kingdom), and the Organization for African Unity, which resulted in the July 1999 Lusaka Ceasefire Agreement between the DRC and Angola, Namibia, Rwanda, Uganda, and Zimbabwe (United Nations Security Council 1999a; Autesserre 2010, 49). Active US involvement in the DRC increased in late 1999 with the deployment of the UN Organization Mission in the Democratic Republic of the Congo (MONUC), which was charged with a mandate to observe the cease-fire and combatant demobilization as well as to serve as the liaison between the parties to the Lusaka Ceasefire (United Nations Security Council 1999b). Hostilities did not end with the cease-fire or deployment of MONUC, and the conflict within the DRC involved armed groups and tensions related to neighboring states in the Great Lakes region, including United States–supported Rwanda and Uganda.

In light of persistent local-level conflicts, especially within the North and South Kivu and Orientale provinces, and the threats posed to national and regional stability, in July 2010 the UN Security Council replaced MONUC with the UN Organization Stabilization Mission in the Democratic Republic of the Congo (MONUSCO). MONUSCO's more robust mandate and larger contingent of military peacekeepers signaled changing understandings of the conflicts and a need to include civilian protection (including protection from widespread sexual violence) in the mission's mandate (United Nations Security Council 2010, 2012a). MONUSCO's mandate reflects the broader focus—within the UN and among major contributors to peacekeeping operations—on human security and civilian protection, which gives peacekeeping operations a more active, civilian-focused role in both conflict and post-conflict zones.

As a minor troop contributor and major financial contributor to both MONUC and MONUSCO, the United States has been involved in stabilization efforts in the DRC fairly consistently since late 1999.[9] Throughout its involvement in the DRC, however, US officials have expressed an unwillingness to launch any major US military engagement or humanitarian intervention in the Great Lakes region, preferring instead to support UN-led efforts to stabilize the region.[10] Despite consistent involvement in UN operations in the DRC during the period studied, the US response to sexual violence in the DRC varied over time and did not increase sharply during periods preceding or immediately following the deployment of the small numbers of US personnel attached to UN missions. It is also worth noting—as Séverine Autesserre (2010, 19–20) finds in her research on global peacebuilding culture—that involvement in mediation efforts and multilateral peacebuilding operations did not reflect strong national interests in the DRC but rather a broader concern about the potential for violence to spill over into neighboring states in the resource-rich Great Lakes region.

Sexual violence has been widespread and systematic during periods of active fighting at the regional, national, and local levels as well as during the peace and transition processes (HRW 2009). Although the ethical collection of reliable quantitative data on sexual atrocities proves to be a difficult endeavor, NGO and government reports indicate that the scale of sexual violence increased dramatically beginning in 2008.[11] Sexual violence has accompanied the conflict-related instability to varying degrees throughout the past two decades, and certainly for as long as the United States has been diplomatically and financially involved in the region. And though the narrative of weaponized rape targeting women and girls has painted a very specific picture of sexual violence in the DRC, academics and journalists have pointed to a more nuanced reality that includes sexualized violence against men and civilian-perpetrated abuse.[12] US recognition of and response to wartime sexual violence in the DRC reflects the "weapon of war" frame. Through the simplified view of sexual violence, US condemnation and commitments of financial assistance have become more consistent.

The State Department's annual country report cited sexual violence by government security forces in Zaire in 1990 and again in 1993. A single reference to rape by government forces in the 1993 report noted: "Undisciplined security forces also continue to beat, rob, rape, and kill citizens in their own homes. Hundreds of such cases occurred during armed forces' looting in January" (US Department of State 1994, section 1f).[13] References to rape by security forces and—later, with the onset of armed conflict—other combatant groups continued to appear in the country report, increasing steadily each year from 1993 through 2003. Recognition of sexual violence sporadically spiked in subsequent years in conjunction with the release of UN and HRW data on sexual violence, especially in the 2009 to 2011 period. Figure 2.1 illustrates the growing prevalence of references to rape and other forms of sexual violence in the country reports from 1990 through 2014.

The earliest reports referred only to "rape"; the broader term "sexual violence" did not appear in the country report on the DRC until 2002. After 2002, the country report used "rape" and "sexual violence" interchangeably. The reference counts include mentions of both rape and sexual violence from 1990 through 2014. It is important to note that the country report accounts for a broader range of sexual offenses than the foreign policy discourse suggests, including rape in prison, exploitation of children, domestic violence and marital rape, and harassment and violence on the basis of sexuality and gender identity, especially in the most recent reports.

Figure 2.2 demonstrates the relationship between increased awareness of sexual violence in the DRC, as measured by references in the country report, and US domestic political discussion of wartime sexual violence in the DRC. Overall, the increase in awareness of wartime sexual violence in the DRC correlates positively with the number of documents and speeches referencing and condemning wartime sexual violence in the DRC, but only *after* 2003. Before 2003 the US government did not make public political references to wartime sexual violence in the DRC outside the context of the country report. The steady increase, beginning in 2008—in both references to wartime sexual violence in the country report and the number of documents and speeches condemning wartime sexual violence in the DRC—appears to be related to a greater focus on wartime sexual violence in the DRC by advocates within domestic and international NGOs and the UN and the increased scale of wartime sexual violence, especially in North and South Kivu in the eastern DRC. As the violence escalated, it received more coverage and fit easily within the "weapon of war" frame.

Figure 2.1 State Department Country Report on Human Rights Sexual Violence Citations, 1990–2014

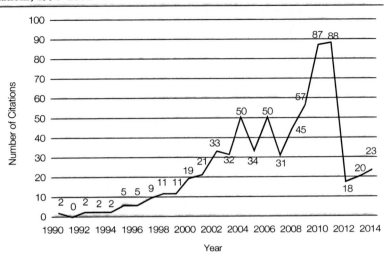

Figure 2.2 Knowledge and Discussion of Sexual Violence in the DRC within the US Government, 1996–2014

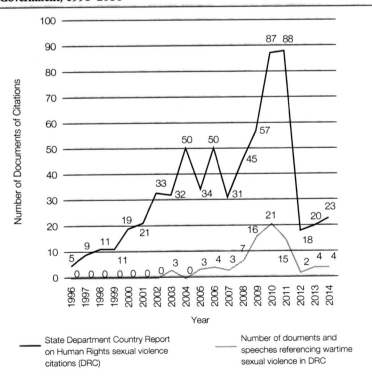

Figure 2.3   The US Political Discussion of Sexual Violence Relative to the General Discussion of the DRC, 1996–2014

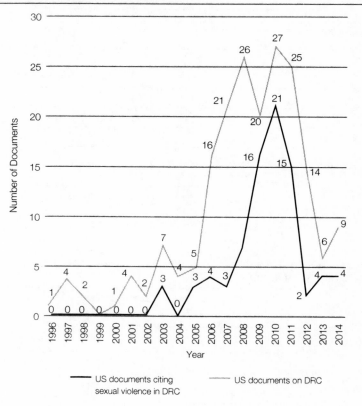

How has US political recognition of wartime sexual violence in the DRC compared with US political discussion of the conflict in the DRC in general? Figure 2.3 depicts the relationship between the frequency of discussion within the US government of the conflict in the DRC and the subset of that discussion focused on wartime sexual violence in the DRC.

US political discourse on the DRC excluded wartime sexual violence before 2003, but not for lack of attention to the conflict. Although consideration of the conflict in the DRC was comparatively less common from 1996 through 2002 than it was after 2003, the conflict did have a place in presidential, congressional, and State Department discourse. Wartime sexual violence in the DRC during the period from 1996 through 2002, however, was a nonissue on the foreign policy agenda. From 2003 onward, increased attention to the DRC in general is positively correlated with recognition of wartime sexual violence in the country, especially after 2008.

The sharp decline in documentation and discussion of sexual violence in 2012 occurs after a crucial period for US political recognition and response, the years from 2008 through 2012. This decline represents a return to the baseline (lower) level of recognition of sexual violence in the DRC because sexual violence in other situations, including in the Middle East and North Africa, has competed for political resources and recognition in recent years. The apparent drop in recognition is also indicative of streamlined reporting and discussion—the use of general references to a now-well-known conflict rather than repetitive and graphic discussions aimed at engaging a larger audience in paying direct attention to the conflict— and representative of a more institutionalized approach to responding to sexual violence.

Critical Points in the Development of the US Response to Sexual Violence in the DRC

As domestic political leaders became more aware of the scale, effects, and utility of wartime sexual violence, they were more willing to address it. Knowledge of wartime sexual violence alone is insufficient to explain the US response. Instead, effective framing of the issue by external advocates and policymakers with ties to the region and personal dedication to ending the use of sexual violence improved the strength and institutionalization of US political commitments. Despite consistent reports of rape and other forms of sexual violence from 1993 onward in the annual country report, US government documents and speeches did not include discussion of rape or other forms of sexual violence in the DRC until a decade later. House Resolution 239, a resolution on conflict diamonds introduced on June 26, 2003, observed that "rape was used as a weapon of war, a tactic of terror, and an act of revenge against scores of women and girls" in the DRC and Angola (US House of Representatives 2003a). The resolution was referred to committee, where its progress stalled, but it applied the "weapon of war" frame to the situation in the DRC for the first time in US congressional deliberations. House Resolution 4818, introduced on July 13, 2003, called for $5 million in programmatic funding for the DRC, Uganda, Burundi, and Liberia to address sexual and gender-based violence; the version that became law appropriated funds for programs addressing sexual and gender-based violence in Sub-Saharan Africa, and it too utilized the "weapon of war" frame (US House of Representatives 2003b). In the same year, 2003, the US Agency for International Development granted $500,000 to the International Rescue Committee to fund a program dedicated to helping rape survivors in North and South Kivu (US Department of State 2003). The initial recognition of the use of sexual violence as a tactic of war prompted both rhetorical condemnation and financial commitments to prevention and assistance programs in the DRC and, more generally, in Sub-Saharan Africa.

Framing Sexual Violence as a Weapon of War, 2003–7

The 2003 country report, issued in early 2004, made the report's first reference to sexual violence as a weapon of war in the DRC. The frame's inclusion in the 2003 country report and the congressional resolutions discussed above were not the first uses of this description of sexual violence in the DRC, but these were the first instances in which US public documents employed the frame in a discussion of conflict in the DRC. On December 6, 2000, and again on February 21, 2001, UN secretary-general Kofi Annan condemned the use of "rape as a weapon of war" by combatants in the DRC; US officials were present on both occasions (United Nations Secretary-General 2000, 2001). An HRW report, released in June 2002, focused on sexual violence against women and girls in the eastern DRC and described the use of sexual violence as a weapon of war in the region (HRW 2002). The 2003 country report cited both the 2002 HRW report and a statement by the UN's special rapporteur on the human rights situation in the Democratic Republic of the Congo, M. Iulia Motoc, charging that "armed groups used rape as a tool of war. . . . Between October 2002 and February 21, in the Uvira area, a women's association recorded 5,000 cases of rape, corresponding to an average of 40 per day" (US Department of State 2004b). The report also observed: "The use of mass rape and sexual violence as weapons of war intended to destroy the structure of the family has harmed Congolese society. Often rejected by their families or infected by sexually transmissible diseases or HIV, women have nowhere to turn for help. The climate of impunity continues unabated" (US Department of State 2004b). NGO advocacy and efforts by UN agencies to address wartime sexual violence allowed the "weapon of war" frame to make its way into

US foreign policy discussions and influenced the policymakers' willingness to respond.

Recognition of wartime sexual violence in the DRC and discussion of wartime sexual violence more generally, both within the United States and at the UN, lagged until the discovery of UN peacekeepers' complicity in sexual violence and exploitation in the DRC. During a 2005 US hearing on reforming MONUC to prevent further sexual misconduct by peacekeeping forces in the DRC, and on enhancing mechanisms to prevent and respond to such misconduct by peacekeepers in any operation, members of the US House of Representatives expressed concern that peacekeepers exacerbated wartime atrocities despite their intended role as agents of stability. During the hearing, HRW leveraged its influence as a reputable stakeholder to call on US officials to address but not limit their response to peacekeepers' misconduct; HRW urged Congress to take meaningful action to respond to the broader range of sexual violence and perpetrators in the DRC. Several speakers urged members of the House to recognize that far more women and girls are sexually assaulted by combatants in the DRC than by peacekeepers, and addressing both types of perpetrators and the occurrence of opportunistic sexual violence by all parties to the conflict is essential (US House of Representatives 2005). The United States' focus on strategic sexual violence as a weapon of war and preventing sexual violence by peacekeepers persisted, and recognition of the broader spectrum of sexual violence remained limited.

The Democratic Republic of the Congo Relief, Security, and Democracy Act of 2006—which was introduced on July 10, 2006, and became law on December 22, 2006—authorized $52 million in assistance for the DRC during fiscal year 2006. Among the act's motivations was the interest in "halting the high prevalence of sexual abuse and violence perpetrated against women and children in the [DRC] and mitigating the detrimental effects from acts of this type of violence by undertaking a number of health, education, and financial support measures" (US Senate 2005). The authorization represented a meaningful financial response to wartime sexual violence in the DRC. The act took concrete steps toward addressing the issue of wartime sexual violence in the DRC by committing financial resources to assistance programs rather than simply engaging in rhetorical condemnation. At about the same time, Executive Order 13413, which froze the assets of several key perpetrators in the DRC on October 27, 2006, cited the horrific scale of sexual violence as part of the rationale for the asset freeze. In remarks to the Senate Committee on Foreign Relations Subcommittee on African Affairs on October 24, 2007, the assistant secretary of state for African affairs, Jendayi Frazer, stated that the Bush administration considered the "epidemic of sexual and gender-based violence" to be one of the four critical areas in the US diplomatic approach to the conflict in the DRC (US Senate 2007). Policymakers perceived sexual violence used as a weapon not only as a morally repugnant form of violence against civilians but also as a factor in the continued instability in the Great Lakes region; given the Bush administration's emphasis on state stability as a factor in the prevention of terrorism, responding to widespread sexual violence fit within the overall approach to foreign policy.

Strengthening and Institutionalizing the Response, 2008–14

The most critical years for the development of the US response to wartime sexual violence in the DRC were 2008 and 2009, when US policymakers not only focused consistently on wartime sexual violence in the DRC in their domestic political rhetoric but also became more active in the effort to respond to wartime sexual violence at the UN level. On April 1, 2008, the Subcommittee on Human Rights and the Law of the Senate Committee on the Judiciary held a hearing titled "Rape as a Weapon of War: Accountability for Sexual Violence in Conflict." This hearing was the first congressional hearing dedicated solely to examining sexual violence in armed conflict, which Senator Dick Durbin (D-IL) deemed "a sad testament to our failure to take action to stop this horrific human rights abuse" (US Senate 2008, 1). Despite its presumed focus on sexual violence as a weapon of war in all armed conflicts, the hearing centered on the abuses perpetrated by combatants in the DRC. The DRC had begun to emerge as a highly salient example of sexual violence as a weapon of war. Senators made repeated references to the horrific scale of sexual violence and its use as a tactic of war. They drew on lessons learned from official visits to Goma, during which senators were personally moved by victims' stories and the efforts by a Congolese advocate and physician, Dr. Denis Mukwege, and his staff at Panzi Hospital to attend to the medical needs of rape survivors (US Senate 2008, 3). Apparently motivated by their personal connections to the horror in the DRC, as well as the presence of the influential Dr. Mukwege at the hearing, the senators emphasized a need to respond to sexual violence in the DRC in particular, despite evidence of widespread sexual violence in other conflicts at the time: "We have spoken of many countries where this use of rape as a tactic of war has been prevalent. We focused on the . . . Democratic Republic of Congo, and not to take anything away from the tragedy and genocide of Darfur, I hope that today's hearing will encourage people to look more closely at the sad, tragic situation in Democratic Republic of Congo" (US Senate 2008, 20). Senators asserted that the "use of rape as a weapon of war is at its worst in the Democratic Republic of Congo" (US Senate 2008, 2). The graphic discussion of sexual violence as a weapon of war in the DRC during this congressional hearing both galvanized US support for assistance to survivors of wartime sexual violence in the DRC and helped to inspire US leadership on UN Security Council Resolution 1820 two months later.

The US delegation to the UN Security Council used its council presidency to hold an open debate on wartime sexual violence, which led to the adoption of Resolution 1820 on June 19, 2008. As I discuss in greater depth in chapter 3, US leadership on this issue within the Security Council, under Secretary Rice and Ambassador Zalmay Khalilzad, was driven largely by personal appeals and extensive pressure from advocacy groups to address wartime sexual violence *as a weapon of war*, especially in the DRC (United Nations Security Council 2008a). Civil society advocates and United Nations personnel lobbied national delegations to the Security Council through the use of the documentary *The Greatest Silence*, victims' accounts, personal appeals, and— most important—a strategic narrowing of the scope of sexual violence to include only sexual violence as a weapon of war over the course of several months in 2008 (a UN Women official, in a discussion with the author, New York, June 2012; a UN Women official, in a discussion with the author, Washington, February 2013).[14] Resolution 1820 called for the immediate cessation of the use of sexual violence as a tactic of war. At the time, there were no imminent national security concerns that required the United States to use its Security Council presidency for national security or strategic concerns; the centrality of the issue of wartime sexual violence could have been limited if direct national security concerns had been at stake (a US State Department official, in a discussion with the author, Washington, August 2012).

During Hillary Clinton's term as secretary of state, global gender equality, women's political and economic empowerment, and violence against women became central issues in US foreign policy, coordinated by the Office of Global Women's Issues and the ambassador-at-large for global women's issues.[15] Discussion of sexual violence was not limited to the State Department but also continued to be a topic of debate within Congress. On May 13, 2009, a Senate Committee on Foreign Relations hearing, "Confronting Rape and Other Forms of Violence against Women in Conflict Zones, Spotlight: DRC and Sudan," focused on the issue of sexual violence as a weapon of war. As one senator observed: "Rape and other forms of gender-based violence are *not just outgrowths of war and its brutality, they can also be weapons of war*" (emphasis added; US Senate 2009). This particular description of "rape and other forms of gender-based violence" reflects an understanding that sexual violence as a weapon of war is not an inevitable by-product of war but a phenomenon to be condemned and prevented. The hearing also recalled Resolution 1820's focus on sexual violence as a weapon: "UN Security Council last year passed Resolution 1820, which condemns the use of rape and other forms of sexual violence in conflict situations and states that rape can constitute a war crime, a crime against humanity, or a constitutive act with respect to genocide" (US Senate 2009). At this point, politicians began to reiterate the language used by HRW reports, witness testimonies from prior congressional hearings, and UN discussions; policymakers discussed wartime sexual violence in the DRC as an intentional tactic of war rather than a regrettable consequence of a chaotic situation. Adopting the "weapon of war" frame facilitated more concrete responses and efforts to address and punish such atrocities, both in the DRC and elsewhere.

In August 2009 Secretary Hillary Clinton and the ambassador-at-large for global women's issues, Melanne Verveer, visited the DRC, held a roundtable discussion with NGOs and activists working to address sexual and gender-based violence, and announced that the United States would commit $17 million to efforts to prevent, respond to, and assist survivors of sexual and gender-based violence in the DRC (US Department of State 2009b). In her remarks, Clinton cited the US government's commitment to condemning *systematic rape*. Clinton recalled this visit to Goma, when she introduced UN Security Council Resolution 1888 on September 30, 2009, as president of the Security Council:

Last month, I travelled to Goma in the eastern Democratic Republic of the Congo. . . . I met with survivors of sexual violence, and the physical and emotional damage to individual women and their families from these attacks cannot by quantified, nor can the toll on their societies. The dehumanizing nature of sexual violence does not harm just a single individual, a single family, or even a single village or a single group; it shreds the fabric that weaves us together as human beings. It endangers families and communities, erodes social and political stability, and undermines economic progress. (United Nations Security Council 2009, 3)

Resolution 1888 established the position of special representative to the secretary-general for sexual violence in armed conflict, a human commitment to addressing sexual violence at the UN level. The adoption of Resolution 1888 and the creation of the new special representative ensured that the UN and its member states would begin to monitor and more effectively respond to wartime sexual violence used as a weapon. It also reaffirmed the US government's commitment to addressing wartime sexual violence in the DRC and demonstrated the centrality of the conflict in the DRC to US and international efforts to respond to wartime sexual violence.

The justification for the resolution and subsequent United States–led actions drew on statistics and personal stories from the conflict in the DRC, which Secretary Clinton cited in her speech to the Security Council: "In the Democratic Republic of Congo approximately 1,100 rapes are being reported each month, with an average of 36 women and girls raped every day. In addition to these rapes and gang rapes, of which there have been hundreds of thousands over the duration of the conflict, the perpetrators frequently mutilate the women in the course of the attacks" (US Department of State 2009a). Ambassador Verveer similarly recalled accounts from the Goma trip in her testimony before Congress:

Women and children are also at risk in zones of conflict, when legal and social norms fall away and armies and militias act without fear of accountability or judicial penalty. . . . At the Heal Africa Hospital we met a woman who told us she was 8 months pregnant when she was attacked. She was at home when a group of men broke in. They took her husband and two of their children in the front yard and shot them, before returning into the house to shoot the other two children. And then they beat and gang-raped her and left her for dead. Her story, unfortunately, is far too common. . . . Rape is used in armed conflict as a deliberate strategy to subdue and destroy communities. (US House of Representatives 2009)

Accounts of brutal, weaponized sexual violence cast the DRC as an analogue for sexual violence used as a weapon of war, like Bosnia and Rwanda, against which concurrent and future cases of wartime sexual violence would be compared and through which the "weapon of war" frame would persist in a mutually constitutive cycle: US political efforts to respond to sexual violence were motivated by the frame, which in turn grew increasingly influential through advocates' association of the frame with the conflict in the DRC.

The political momentum that had grown from 2008 onward ensured the inclusion of wartime sexual violence in much of the discussion surrounding US efforts in the DRC through 2014. Congressional Research Service (CRS) reports in June 2010, November 2010, and February 2011 all focused on the issue of sexual violence in African conflicts, and each focused in large part on the DRC, representing continued active recognition within the US government of wartime sexual violence in the DRC and elsewhere (Arieff 2010a, 2010b, 2011). Separately, the Dodd-Frank Wall Street Reform and Consumer Protection Act, a comprehensive financial reform measure signed into law on July 21, 2010, contains a provision requiring the disclosure of conflict minerals from within or near the DRC. The provision highlights a purported link between the artisanal mining of valuable minerals (including tungsten, coltan, tin, and gold) and the perpetuation of conflict and human rights abuses.[16] By linking conflict minerals to violence against civilians—including mass rape—Dodd-Frank and related advocacy efforts increased awareness of conflict-related atrocities in the DRC; but—much like the dominant "weapon of war" narrative—the conflict minerals narrative carried costs and unintended consequences for civilians on the ground (Autesserre 2014, 133–37). Less than a year after Dodd-Frank became law, on March 8, 2011, the House Committee on Foreign Affairs held a hearing, "The Democratic Republic of the Congo: Securing Peace in the Midst of Tragedy," to address the protracted conflict. Although this hearing was dedicated to consideration of all aspects of the conflict a significant portion of the testimony centered on sexual violence—particularly systematic sexual violence and its use as a weapon

(US House of Representatives 2011). In December 2011 the assistant secretary of state for African affairs, Johnnie Carson, testified before Congress on the necessity of ending sexual and gender-based violence in the DRC during a hearing on the election outcome and governance in the DRC (US Department of State 2011), indicating that the Obama administration and State Department under Hillary Clinton had come to view sexual violence as a persistent spoiler of security and good governance.

Although the frequency of discussion of the conflict and sexual violence in the DRC decreased in 2012 and afterward within the United States, the content of policy discourse maintained a focus on the severity of sexual violence and the link between persistent use of sexual violence and widespread instability in the region. The sharp spike in graphic references to sexual violence from 2008 until 2012 indicates strong advocacy efforts, the lessons from which appear to carry through government reports and foreign policy in subsequent years. CRS reports on US foreign policy related to the DRC from 2013 and 2014 and a Senate hearing on the ongoing conflict made references to rape and sexual violence by rebel armed groups, nonstate militias, and peacekeepers, citing both strategic and opportunistic attacks (Arieff and Coen 2013; Arieff 2014; US Senate 2013). The inclusion of opportunistic sexual violence and sexual violence perpetrated by peacekeepers marks a notable expansion of the range of recognized forms of sexual violence. The 2013 CRS report signals the political-military consequences that follow an armed group's tolerance of sexual violence:

> In 2010, State Department–funded contractors and military personnel from US Africa Command (AFRICOM) trained and provided nonlethal equipment to a "model" military battalion, now known as the 391st, using about $35 million in PKO [peacekeeping operation] funding. The battalion continued to receive US advisory support, including training on human rights and gender-based violence prevention, until March 2013. At that point, US support was suspended after a UN investigation found that members of the 391st, among others, had allegedly raped civilians near Goma during the M23 seizure of the town. Until then, the Administration had been exploring the possibility of training a second battalion; prospects for future US-funded train-and-equip missions are now uncertain. (Arieff and Coen 2013, 17)

Although there is not enough evidence to suggest that an internalized norm prohibits sexual violence and fundamentally changes the way in which armed groups behave or states respond to reports of sexual violence, the withdrawal of military funding and support is a strong signal of commitment to the issue and unwillingness to back armed groups that allow combatants to commit sexual violence.

The occurrence of systematic sexual violence and its use as a weapon of war in the DRC dominated much of the US political discourse on the issue of wartime sexual violence in general during the period from 2008 through 2014 despite awareness of its use in other active and recent armed conflicts. Sexual violence in the DRC has been widely publicized to the point of infamy because of the scale and brutality of the attacks in what came to be known as the "rape capital of the world."[17] The focus on the DRC in political discussion suggests that conflicts in which sexual violence appears to be used as a weapon of war are most likely to gain attention and evoke responses from states. Although references to opportunistic sexual violence by peacekeepers, members of armed groups, and civilians have increased in recent years, the primary focus in political discussion and action remains on systematic sexual violence as a weapon.

Advocacy, Interests, and the "Weapon of War" Frame

Advocates' successful framing of sexual violence as a weapon of war in the DRC established the issue as a security concern relevant to US interests in the Great Lakes region, which in turn facilitated the commitment of resources to address the problem. A total of sixty-nine documents, hearings, and speeches addressed wartime sexual violence in the DRC from 2008 through 2014. In the previous five-year period, from 2003 through 2007, only thirteen documents and speeches addressed the issue; before 2003, when the "weapon of war" frame emerged, none of the documents and speeches analyzed referenced wartime sexual violence in the DRC. Although the number of documents referencing any one policy issue is not a perfect measure of the issue's centrality, it is demonstrative of the issue's increased prominence in political discussion and the amount of time and effort devoted by policymakers. More important, the increase in financial and human commitments tied to the surge in references to sexual violence as a weapon of war in the DRC serves as a reliable indicator of the US government's growing commitment to addressing the issue during this period and its increased reliance on the "weapon of war" frame to make sense of whether and when to respond to cases of sexual violence.

Table 2.1 illustrates how the US response to sexual violence in the DRC moved through each of the first five stages of recognition. The most consequential moment is the first instance of political condemnation of sexual violence in the DRC in 2003, soon after the UN and HRW began to discuss sexual violence as a weapon in the conflict. Since 2008, there has been increased institutionalization of US efforts to respond to sexual violence, in the DRC and elsewhere, but not to the extent that we might consider the existence of a diffused and fully internalized international norm prohibiting sexual violence.

Discussing the issue of human rights norms in general, Julie Mertus (2008) argues that such norms have shaped the US presidency, military, and activist community but that the presumption of American exceptionalism prevents these norms from achieving full institutionalization within the government. Instead, US political actors view human rights norms as constraints on the behavior of others; nevertheless, civil society has an impact on presidential administrations, and the military (and—I add—the State Department, Congress, and other large domestic and international bureaucracies) and human rights norms represent available ideas that policymakers can reference. In the end, the US government recognizes human rights norms and has made some progress toward institutionalizing them, but not to the extent that they are taken for granted and fully internalized. This conceptual middle ground applies more easily to US recognition of wartime sexual violence in cases other than the DRC, cases in which the response to wartime sexual violence has been minimal, only rhetorical, or nonexistent. In these cases the government has not fully accepted the image of sexual violence as a weapon, and the response is therefore muted or entirely absent. Policymakers have clearly identified that wartime sexual violence—especially when used as a weapon of war—is a problem that merits attention, but it is unclear that the state will respond to wartime sexual violence if doing so directly clashes with its interests or if it is unclear that sexual violence is being used strategically in a given conflict.

Rather than serving an immediate strategic aim and then vanishing from political discourse, as was the case with references in earlier years to sexual violence in Iraq and Kuwait, condemnation of wartime sexual violence in the DRC persisted over a decade and grew stronger when

Table 2.1 The Evolution of the US Response to Sexual Violence in the DRC, 1990–2014

Stage	Type of Response	Description	Representative Event(s)
0	Nonrecognition / no action	Sexual violence is not recognized as part of a specific conflict, or the conflict itself is not recognized. Wartime sexual violence as a general issue is not recognized. No action is taken and no formal discussion occurs within or among states or IOs.	No demonstrated awareness, 1990–93 Inconsistent documentation, 1993–97
1	Documentation/ learning	Sexual violence, as an aspect of a specific conflict or as a general issue in armed conflict, is the subject of a report, publication, commissioned study, hearing, and/or conference launched, used, or attended by a state or IO. Information-gathering occurs.	Consistent documentation in Country Reports, 1997–2003 House hearing on reforming MONUC, 2005 Senate hearings on rape as a weapon of war, 2008–9 House hearing on DRC conflict, 2011
2	Rhetorical response / condemnation	Sexual violence, as an aspect of a specific conflict or as a general issue in armed conflict, is the subject of a speech, unprompted remarks, and/or in a press release by a high-ranking state official or leader of an IO, but no further commitment is made. Rhetorical action occurs but resources are not committed.	Public condemnation in addition to country report documentation, 2003–14
3	Initial commitment	An IO or a state issues a binding resolution or policy and/or devotes financial, material, or human resources to addressing or mitigating sexual violence as an aspect of a specific conflict or as a general issue in armed conflict. An initial expression of intent and commitment of resources occurs.	First US financial commitment to DRC that used sexual violence as justification, 2006 Sexual violence in DRC motivates US leadership on UN Security Council Resolution 1820 during its presidency, 2008 Clinton and Verveer visit DRC to discuss sexual and gender-based violence and commit funding to prevention and assistance efforts, 2009

Table 2.1 (*continued*)

Stage	Type of Response	Description	Representative Event(s)
4	Implementation/ obligation	A state agency, transnational initiative, legal mechanism, state military training or deployment, or multilateral peacekeeping operation is established and/ or instructed to address sexual violence as an aspect of a specific conflict or as a general issue in armed conflict; implementation of previous commitments occurs. A long-term or institutionalized commitment of resources occurs.	During the US presidency, UN Security Council Resolution 1888 establishes the office of the special representative to the secretary general on sexual violence in armed conflict and adds protection mandate to peacekeeping operations, 2009 US financial support for MONUSCO, 2009 onward US financial support and military training withdrawn from 391st battalion following reports of sexual violence, 2013
5	Norm change	Sexual violence, as an aspect of a specific conflict or as a general issue in armed conflict, is considered unacceptable and perpetrators are consistently and effectively held accountable. Lasting normative and behavioral change occurs.	

discussed in terms of sexual violence as a "weapon of war." However, national interests are still relevant to the story. Unlike the strategic rhetoric employed in response to sexual violence before the commitment of US troops in Kuwait, Bosnia, and Iraq, US interests in the case of the DRC center on peacebuilding and establishing regional stability. In addition to economic interests related to oil, minerals, and business opportunities in the region, instability in the DRC is relevant to post–September 11, 2011, US foreign policy efforts to curb protracted conflict and state instability and prevent the spread of extremism and international terrorism (Autesserre 2010, 236).

The destabilizing effects of systematic sexual violence make it a persistent spoiler of local, national, and regional stability, a view that is not limited to the foreign policy platforms of the United States and UN but is also held by conflict-affected states. The 2013 Peace, Security, and Cooperation Framework for the Democratic Republic of the

Congo and the Region cited sexual violence in the third paragraph, indicating the centrality of violence against civilians in the conflict and in efforts to resolve the conflict. Observing progress made in the region, the Framework continues on to emphasize the human cost of conflict: "eastern Democratic Republic of the Congo has continued to suffer from recurring cycles of conflict and persistent violence by armed groups, both Congolese and foreign. The consequences of this violence have been nothing short of devastating. Acts of sexual violence and serious violations of human rights are used regularly and almost daily as weapons of war" (Peace, Security, and Cooperation Framework for the Democratic Republic of the Congo and the Region 2013). Signed by (or on behalf of) the heads of state of the DRC, the Central African Republic, Angola, Burundi, Rwanda, Congo, South Africa, South Sudan, Uganda, Zambia, and Tanzania, the framework outlines commitments related to conflict resolution in the DRC and the region as a whole. Commitments within the DRC include security sector reform, consolidation of state authority, decentralization, economic development and improvements in infrastructure and social services, government reform, and reconciliation and democratization. Regional commitments include noninterference, cessation of support for armed groups, respect for sovereignty, improved regional cooperation and economic integration, respect for neighboring states' security concerns, refusal to shelter war criminals, and judicial cooperation. The international community is tasked with continued Security Council support and monitoring, support from bilateral partners, support for the Economic Community of the Great Lakes Countries, strategic review of MONUSCO to ensure support for the government of the DRC, and appointment of a UN special envoy to support implementation of the framework. The UN secretary-general's 2014 framework implementation report observes the persistence of sexual violence as an aspect of the conflict:

> Violations of international humanitarian and human rights law, including sexual and gender-based violence, have continued in the Democratic Republic of the Congo and in other States signatories to the Peace, Security and Cooperation Framework. There are strong indications that violations are being committed by all parties without exception. In the Democratic Republic of the Congo, armed groups and members of the Congolese defence and security Forces continue to commit rape as a weapon of war, along with

other forms of sexual violence and human rights violations, during and after rebel attacks on communities. (United Nations Security Council 2014b, 6)

The 2015 framework implementation report notes the continuation of human rights violations by armed groups in the region as well as programmatic efforts to address sexual and gender-based violence (United Nations Security Council 2015b). The US State Department notes that "regional stability and security is dependent on durable peace in the DRC, due to the country's size, resources and its location bordering nine nations" (US Department of State 2015). Given the interest in regional stability, the centrality of peace in the DRC to that stability, and the obstacles to peace posed by persistent sexual violence, we cannot extract national interests from the logic of US efforts to address sexual violence in the DRC.

By linking widespread strategic sexual violence to the broader foreign policy objectives of stability and reconstruction, advocates found an avenue through which to channel their efforts and justify condemnation and commitments of resources to the DRC and elsewhere. To align with foreign policy interests, advocates had to emphasize the weaponized nature of sexual violence, both within the DRC and more broadly, which presents a security threat and a spoiler of peacebuilding efforts. The frame also allowed embedded advocates to construct a form of violence that appeared wholly different from opportunistic violence and cases of nonstrategic abuse, which meant that the Bush administration could condemn systematic sexual violence without implicating US troops after the abuses at Abu Ghraib became public in the spring of 2004. More than a distraction from the unintended consequences of United States–led interventions, however, US foreign policy responses to sexual violence as a weapon indicate strategic rhetorical maneuvering by individuals—embedded advocates—with a genuine commitment to assisting survivors and reducing the prevalence of this atrocity in the DRC and elsewhere. Under President Barack Obama's administration, especially during Clinton's tenure as secretary of state, eradicating sexual violence formed part of a broader global push to address issues of gender-based violence and inequality.

Emphasis on the importance of securing evidence that suggests sexual violence is used as a tactic of war to justify action or condemnation leads to inefficient and incomplete implementation of the anti–sexual violence agenda. Looking beyond the DRC case, reluctance to respond to wartime sexual violence in both Libya and Syria—until the United Kingdom began to address sexual violence in the latter conflict in 2012—is suggestive of the power and limitations of the "weapon of war" frame, both within US political discourse and at the international level. States, the UN, and even NGOs were hesitant to recognize wartime sexual violence in both conflicts, citing limited evidence that sexual violence was being used as a *weapon of war* (an official of the US Agency for International Development, in a discussion with the author, Washington, September 2012; a legal expert, in a discussion with the author, New York, June 2012). Gathering evidence to prove that sexual violence is used as a weapon requires a great deal of information on combatants' intentions, which are often unclear in the midst of the conflict and may not become obvious until postconflict interviews or tribunals, as well as access to civilians who are willing to share their experiences. Such evidence and access can be extraordinarily difficult in a conflict environment that is hostile to journalists, humanitarian workers, UN officials, or state representatives trying to understand the nature of sexual violence. It is also ethically untenable and risks placing survivors in harm's way or retraumatizing them for the sake of data collection, if not done with extreme care. The reliance on the "weapon of war" frame as the basis for foreign policy responses to sexual violence in foreign conflicts suggests that there will be high levels of variation in the response to individual conflicts, especially when data and reports on the motives underlying sexual violence are unavailable or unclear.

Epigraph

This is a quotation from Clinton's remarks during a roundtable with NGOs and activists on sexual and gender-based violence issues in Goma, DRC, on August 11, 2009.

Notes

1. The examples of the Gulf War, the intervention in Bosnia, and the Iraq War come from Eran Ben-Porath's (2007, 189–94) discussion of the use of graphic rhetoric in presidential persuasion efforts.

2. See Hunt and Rygiel (2006) and Ben-Porath (2007).

3. For further discussion of "cheap talk" applied to similar contexts, see Hultman (2012), Sartori (2002), and Smith (1998).

4. See these public sources: "State Department on Refugee Crisis in Central Africa" (US Department of State 1996); testimony by Melanne Verveer (US Department of State 2009c); remarks by Hillary Rodham Clinton (US Department of State 2009a); and address by Hillary Rodham Clinton (US Department of State 2010b).

5. The US Department of State's website and the electronic archives for the State Department under George W. Bush and Bill Clinton give access to press releases, policy documents, and annual country reports on human rights.

6. The country reports are available at these URLs: for 1999–2014, www .state.gov/j/drl/rls/hrrpt/; for 1996–98, www.state.gov/www/global/human _rights/hrp_reports_mainhp.html; for 1993–95, http://dosfan.lib.uic.edu /ERC/democracy/hrp_index.html; and for 1990–92, http://archive.org /details/countryreportson1990unit.

7. I examined the following to compile data on political knowledge and discussion: transcripts of presidential speeches and government officials' remarks at the UN Security Council from 1992 through 2014; executive orders issued from 1993 through 2014 (for the full text of executive orders, see www .archives.gov/federal-register/executive-orders/disposition.html); and congressional hearings, debates, remarks, bills, and studies from 1996 through 2014. I include failed and engrossed congressional resolutions, in addition to successful resolutions, in the data as they contribute to our understanding of the presence of wartime sexual violence in political discourse and the success or failure of advocacy within Congress.

8. For the Clinton administration archive, see http://1997-2001.state.gov/; and for the Bush administration archive, see http://2001-2009.state.gov/p/af /ci/cg/prs/index.htm.

9. In December 2012 the United States was ranked fifty-seventh among countries contributing troops to MONUSCO, with a total of 128 troops and police. Public information is available through the UN Department of Peacekeeping Operations archive, www.un.org/en/peacekeeping/resources/sta tistics/. For troop and financial contribution statistics, see the mission sites for MONUC and MONUSCO.

10. See these public sources: remarks by Lee H. Hamilton (US Senate 1997); remarks by President Bill Clinton (US Department of State 2000); and press statement (US Department of State 2004a).

11. See HRW (2009, 15); and US State Department country reports for 2008–14 (see note 6 above).

12. See the coverage by Gettleman (2009), Kelly (2010), and Wolfe (2014).

13. A second reference to rape in the report relates to prison conditions, in Section 1c: "Human rights monitors report that controls are inadequate and rapes sometimes occur."

14. For a publicly available source, see Steinberg's (2011) discussion of WPS.

15. The Quadrennial Diplomacy and Development Review, 2010, emphasized the need to invest in the rights of women and girls as an element of improving development efforts (US Department of State 2010a). In 2012, Secretary Clinton's policy guidance included "promoting gender equality to achieve our national security and foreign policy objectives" as the third line item, noting that "countries are more peaceful and prosperous when women are accorded full and equal rights and opportunity" (US Department of State 2012).

16. The UN secretary-general's report on the implementation of the Peace, Security and Cooperation Framework for the DRC and the region notes the link between the exploitation of natural resources—specifically, minerals—and regional instability (United Nations Security Council 2015b, 15). The Dodd-Frank provision's effectiveness on the ground is a source of disagreement between policymakers, practitioners, journalists, and academics. Autesserre (2014, 133–37) argues that the causes of conflict in the DRC are more nuanced than the conflict minerals narrative implies and that measures like Dodd-Frank do not adequately address the sources of local conflicts and, as a result, fail to stop corruption and violence. Also see the debate between John Prendergast and Sasha Lezhnev (2015) and Lauren Wolfe (2015).

17. In a *New York Times* op-ed, Nicholas Kristof (2008) referred to the DRC as the "rape capital of the world." The special representative to the UN secretary-general on sexual violence in conflict, Margot Wallström, adopted this terminology during her reporting and advocacy efforts (UN News Service 2010).

Chapter 3

A Security Concern
Sexual Violence and UN Security Council Resolution 1820

As many here are aware, for years there has been a debate about
whether or not sexual violence against women is a security issue for
this forum to address. I am proud that today we can respond to that
lingering question with a resounding "yes."
—*US secretary of state Condoleezza Rice*

You seated around this table are the United Nations, and you
play an important role in ensuring that the United Nations and
the international community continue to intensify actions to end
violence against women and girls. We understand how many issues
are before you at this moment, each needing great care and attention. However, women and girls around the world are suffering. You
have the responsibility to protect them and to take real and effective
measures to put an end to this.
—*Major General Patrick Cammaert*

On June 19, 2008, representatives of the member states of the United
Nations Security Council rose to speak about their governments' condemnation of wartime sexual violence and the threat that this particular
weapon of war poses, not only to the civilian women and girls who
make up the majority of victims but also to international peace, security,
and stability. The fact that every member of the Security Council and
a host of UN member states would one day rise in support of a resolution explicitly condemning sexual violence would have been difficult
to predict just a few years earlier; in fact, it would have been a distant
prospect only a few *months* before the Security Council's 5,916th meeting.[1] The concept of a resolution condemning sexual violence faced opposition from Security Council members who raised concerns about

the appropriateness of such a resolution, including the perception that sexual violence is a women's human rights issue—rather than a security issue—and thus not within the council's mandate, the contention that acting on the issue would intrude on the UN General Assembly's mandate, and the fear that adding sexual violence to its agenda would draw the council into discussions of some members' own ties to conflict-related sexual violence or failure to protect civilians.[2] The unanimous adoption of Security Council Resolution 1820 was the result of advocates' skillful and deliberate efforts to frame wartime sexual violence as a weapon of war and therefore an issue of international security. By discussing sexual violence as a weapon or tactic of war, advocates narrowed the scope of offenses explicitly covered by the resolution to gain the Security Council's support, and they solidified the use of the "weapon of war" frame for sexual violence within the highest forum for international political action and advocacy related to international peace and security. Although discussion of systematic sexual violence began with the responses to Bosnia and Rwanda—particularly through the statutes and decisions of the International Criminal Tribunal for the Former Yugoslavia, the International Criminal Tribunal for Rwanda, and the International Criminal Court—Resolution 1820 represents the turning point, after which states and security-minded organizations began to refer consistently to wartime sexual violence as a weapon of war and a security issue. The adoption of Resolution 1820 also represents a critical moment for the Women, Peace, and Security (WPS) agenda, as it carved out separate space for the consideration of sexual violence as a tactic of war on the Security Council's agenda.

To give the "weapon of war" frame sufficient weight, advocates cited well-known conflicts involving systematic sexual violence used as a weapon, and they leveraged connections and opportunities for political influence. Through an intense lobbying effort, advocates were able to persuade Security Council delegates and their governments that the issue of systematic sexual violence in wartime affects prospects for international peace and security and is therefore within the council's jurisdiction. The resolution's rocky start demonstrates that persuading security-minded international actors to prioritize the issue of sexual violence was no easy task and accentuates the importance of strategic framing.

Resolution 1820 is the first Security Council action overtly and solely justified by the observation that sexual violence can be a deliberate tactic or weapon of war; this understanding of sexual violence compelled states to act in response to one aspect of gender-based violence. Transnational advocacy efforts to call attention to broader issues of gender-based violence and women's human rights brought about international legal prohibition nearly a decade earlier but had a more limited impact on states' willingness to make commitments to end sexual violence in wartime beyond the context of prosecuting war criminals through international courts. The narrower focus on its use as a weapon—a frame applied in this case by embedded advocates closely linked to the US delegation and supported, with some caveats, by transnational advocates—sparked multiple Security Council resolutions and laid the groundwork for state-led initiatives. An issue's frame, then, is not simply the wording used to discuss it; this frame can be the driving force behind states' and international organizations' political will and ability to act.

To trace the "weapon of war" frame's impact on the Security Council's response to sexual violence, the chapter proceeds as follows. The first section provides a brief overview of international recognition of wartime sexual violence through 2008. The next section turns to Resolution 1820 and analyzes the political processes leading to its adoption. The third section discusses the resolutions that followed Resolution 1820. And the fourth and final section offers concluding thoughts and outlines the implications of framing wartime sexual violence as a weapon for the implementation of an anti–sexual violence agenda and the WPS agenda.

Sexual Violence as an International Issue: Setting the Stage for Resolution 1820

A UN Security Council resolution condemning sexual violence as a matter of peace and security was a long time coming. The atrocities in Rwanda and the former Yugoslavia gave women's human rights transnational advocates a strategic opportunity through which they could convincingly articulate the gravity of sexual and gender-based violence. These wars were widely publicized, and media accounts described the systematic abuse, humiliation, and terror inflicted on civilians; in fact, genocidal sexual violence in Bosnia and Rwanda left such an imprint in the late 1990s that reporters "almost went head over heels to register this particular form of violence" in the Kosovo conflict, and the peacekeeping mission in East Timor was tasked with providing for the security and protection of women and girls (Skjelsbæk 2010, 29). The atrocities committed in the former Yugoslavia—particularly in Bosnia—and Rwanda resonated with and profoundly troubled individuals working in state agencies and international organizations, creating opportunities for cooperation between transnational advocates and the leaders of national governments and international organizations. The legal scholar Kelly Dawn Askin emphasized the historical significance of these events during a symposium on sexual violence in war:

> In the early 1990s, after five decades of impunity for mass atrocities committed around the world, a confluence of events generated renewed interest in holding international war crimes trials and in ensuring that gender crimes were taken seriously. There were many firsts that happened at the same time. A war was raging in the former Yugoslavia and experts and journalists reported on horrific crimes, including rape camps. . . . Atrocities were again happening on European soil, despite promises of "never again" after the Holocaust.[3]

As a result of the highly publicized atrocities, well-coordinated advocacy, and receptive women and men working with the ad hoc tribunals, a legal consensus emerged and sexual violence gained recognition as a war crime, a crime against humanity, and an act of genocide, setting precedents that previous international legal institutions had been unwilling or unable to accomplish.

Advocates for women's human rights built on the momentum of the ad hoc tribunals' decisions and the overall increase in international political attentiveness to war's gendered impact on civilians, initiating the WPS agenda through the adoption of UN Security Council Resolution 1325 on October 31, 2000. Resolution 1325 was the Security Council's first attempt to address the broad spectrum of challenges facing women in war, peacebuilding, and postconflict reconstruction, including sexual violence against women and girls in conflict zones. The resolution was unprecedented in its direct focus on gender dynamics related to conflict prevention and peace processes: Cora Weiss—president of The Hague Appeal for Peace, UN representative of the International Peace Bureau, and one of the drafters of Resolution 1325—remarked, "The Security Council finally uttered the word 'woman'" (Cora Weiss, in a discussion with the author, telephone, November 2015). The resolution was not only a landmark achievement because of its explicit recognition of women's suffering in war; its emphasis on women's *agency* and *capacity* to create positive change transformed the image of women from beings to be protected (by men and militaries) to autonomous agents with a valuable role to play in policymaking and peacebuilding at the national and international levels.

Resolution 1325's focus on women as agents stemmed from the tremendous transnational civil society influence on its development and adoption. The idea to lobby the Security Council for a resolution grew out of discussions among nongovernmental organizations (NGOs), through the UN Commission on the Status of Women, of the implementation of the 1995 Beijing Platform for Action's provisions on Women and Armed Conflict.[4] In early 2000 advocacy efforts became more formalized with the creation of the NGO Working Group on Women, Peace, and Security (NGOWG), and the network of advocates and NGOs lobbied the Security Council for a resolution. The NGOWG, the UN Development Fund for Women (UNIFEM), and individual transnational civil society advocates worked with representatives from Namibia to use the state's role as president of the Security Council in October 2000 to introduce and negotiate a resolution. Namibia was an ally to the movement and a recent host for the successful efforts to adopt the Windhoek Declaration and Namibia Plan of Action (May 2000) on mainstreaming gender in peace processes and operations. That the Security Council had recently begun to focus on issues outside its traditional focus on state-based security concerns enabled advocates to feel confident about the prospects of gaining the council's support, as one advocate for Resolution 1325 recalled: "In the lead up to the resolution the justification for bringing a 'soft issue' to the Council was that they had already had children in armed conflict debated by the Council. That was the opening that gave us the confidence to bring women to the Security Council" (Cora Weiss, in a discussion with the author, telephone, November 2015).

The resolution's central goal was—and remains—empowerment and equality; it was "drafted with the aim of ensuring that all efforts towards peacebuilding and post-conflict reconstruction, as well as the conduct of armed conflict itself, would entail sensitivity towards gendered violence and gendered inequalities" (Shepherd 2011, 505).[5] The resolution condemns sexual violence, but it does so within the context of a much broader effort to ensure women's full involvement and equal participation in peace and security efforts and the daily operations of the UN bureaucracy.[6] Although Resolution 1325 has met criticism for its essentialist representation of gender identity and roles—including its exclusion of gender-based violence against men, boys, and individuals who do not fit neatly within the male/female dichotomy—it is still considered a landmark international political achievement in its recognition of the need to increase women's input in matters of war and peace.[7] Resolution 1325 was an essential precursor to the Security Council's efforts in later years to grapple with sexual violence in armed conflict; the resolution's adoption enabled women's groups to maintain space on the Security Council's agenda through WPS—both conceptually and literally, because the council devotes a session to celebrating the resolution's anniversary each year.

Despite the adoption of Resolution 1325, international political recognition of wartime sexual violence remained inconsistent throughout the better part of the next decade. Nearly eight years passed between the passage of Resolution 1325 and the Security Council's next attempt to condemn wartime sexual violence through the WPS agenda. When it did revisit the issue, the international assembly trained its focus on sexual violence as a tactic of war and shifted the narrative on sexual violence from an issue of women's human rights or women's security to a weapon of war and therefore an issue of international security. In the months before Resolution 1820's adoption, advocates engaged in intense lobbying efforts that focused on the need to condemn sexual violence as a weapon of war, capitalized on opportunities for personal influence in the Security Council, and channeled policymakers' horror at the news of widespread sexual violence—primarily in the Democratic Republic of the Congo (DRC).

Resolution 1820 condemned the use of sexual violence as a tactic of war in modern armed conflict, called on perpetrators to cease their use of sexual violence against civilians, and charged the UN secretary-general with the responsibility of monitoring the occurrence of sexual violence in conflicts that are on the Security Council's agenda. Expanding its recognition of sexual violence as an atrocity, Resolution 1820 tied the systematic use of sexual violence to the severity of armed conflict and prospects for successful postconflict reconstruction. The resolution states that sexual violence used as a military tactic "can significantly exacerbate situations of armed conflict and may impede the restoration of international peace and security" (United Nations Security Council 2008b, 2). Sexual violence, then, is not only something regrettable that happens to civilians in wartime; it is also a phenomenon that degrades state, regional, and international stability and security. In June 2008 the Security Council adopted the "weapon of war" frame for sexual violence, and in so doing, it situated wartime sexual violence within the range of global security issues considered priorities for UN member states. Subsequent Security Council resolutions targeting sexual violence—Resolutions 1888, 1960, and 2106—added specific monitoring and shaming mechanisms to the UN's permissible responses to sexual violence used as a weapon of war, charging specific offices and individuals with the tasks of information gathering and reporting. The international community's political response to wartime sexual violence evolved from inconsistent recognition of sexual atrocities to a more focused, institutionalized effort to address sexual violence when it is used as or perceived to be a weapon of war.

The "Weapon of War" and the Adoption of Resolution 1820

US ambassador Prudence Bushnell, who also served as deputy assistant secretary of the State Department during the crisis in Somalia and genocide in Rwanda, summed up the logic of framing sexual violence as a "weapon of war" quite simply: "When sexual violence is used as a weapon of war, like using any other weapon, it gets attention" (Prudence Bushnell, in a discussion with the author, Fairfax, Virginia, March 2013). The "weapon of war" frame has allowed embedded advocates to establish wartime sexual violence as a threat to regional or international stability, a factor in the protracted nature of some armed conflicts, and a destabilizing force after active armed conflict. The perception of sexual violence as something more akin to land mines and less intimately tied to women's empowerment and societal gender dynamics—which require far more time, effort, and a consensus to change—has been crucial for increasing states' support for political commitments and resolutions. Still, we cannot divorce sexual violence used as a weapon from the broader landscape of gender norms; when sexual violence is used as a weapon, it is designed to terrorize, emasculate, and dishonor the enemy as an aspect of wartime strategy, and the perpetrators' ability to exact these effects depends on social understandings of masculinity, femininity, inequality, honor, and stigma (Weitsman 2008, 563). The justification for and effectiveness of sexual violence as a weapon or tactic of war stem from gender norms and the power relationships that are inextricably tied to them.[8] The *perception* that sexual violence is used as a weapon is as important in generating international condemnation as the actual strategic use of systematic sexual violence.

Advocates' use of the "weapon of war" frame in the months leading up to the discussion of Resolution 1820 facilitated the resolution's passage by allaying some member states' fears that the issue was too vaguely defined or politically costly for Security Council members to address. Sexual violence as a weapon of war appears, on its surface, to be less a women's, gender, or human rights issue than a discussion of wartime strategy and atrocities, even if the realities of sexual violence and the structural forces contributing to its prevalence are the same across each of these potential frames. Despite its deviation from the central emphasis on women's agency and empowerment in the WPS agenda, the text of Resolution 1820 still maintains a focus on women and girls, noting that they are "particularly targeted by the use of sexual violence" (United Nations Security Council 2008b, 2). The repetition of phrases such as "tactic of war," "deliberately target civilians," "systematic attack," and "systematic and widespread" throughout the text of Resolution 1820 underscores the council's focus on a particular subset of forms of conflict-related sexual violence. To understand why the "weapon of war" frame was so persuasive, we can return to the international political context in which the "weapon of war" frame evolved.

The frame offered an understanding of wartime sexual violence that was both feasibly and justifiably addressed within the Security Council's mandate to maintain international peace and security. To convince delegates that sexual violence can, in fact, be used as a weapon, advocates marshaled accounts from the DRC—reports of sexual violence reached peak levels in 2008—and more familiar references to mass rape in Bosnia and Rwanda. Instances of widespread and brutal rape by government forces and nonstate armed groups in the DRC became a rallying point; they were highly publicized by Western media outlets and bore all the markings of systematic abuse that had galvanized international advocacy and legal action just a decade earlier. Advocates who lobbied Security Council members' delegations in support of what would become Resolution 1820 emphasized the systematic and tactical nature of sexual violence in the DRC and the similarities in scale between sexual violence in the DRC and sexual violence in the Bosnian and Rwandan genocides. The historical, political, ethnic, and geographical ties between the latter and the conflict in the DRC made this analogy very strong. Sexual violence in the DRC became the focus of discussions on a potential Security Council resolution condemning sexual violence as a weapon of war. Advocates in New York made use of the heavy media coverage of widespread sexual violence in the DRC, arranged viewings of the documentary *The Greatest Silence* for council members and staff, and held events with activists visiting the United States from the DRC to raise awareness of the situation. By mobilizing delegates' shock and moral outrage at the mass sexual violence occurring in the DRC and—to a lesser degree—other conflicts on the council's agenda, advocates effectively recalled the systematic abuses in Bosnia and Rwanda and cast the issue within the "weapon of war" frame in Security Council discussions.

Resolution 1820 did not result directly from the mid-1990s mobilization around the issue of women's human rights or human rights more broadly conceived. The resolution was constructed on the WPS framework established by Resolution 1325, which was itself a direct result of mobilization in the mid-1990s, but Resolution 1820 was driven instead by embedded advocates with a keen eye for and vested interest in states' concerns and political limitations. As one UN Women staff member observed, "Resolution 1820 was not something that was necessarily driven by the women's international movement. Their Resolution was 1325—it was all about empowerment and agency. This [Resolution 1820] was one of those moments that resulted from individual norm entrepreneurs working with the UN. . . . International courts were already engaged; the Security Council was next" (a UN Women official, in a discussion with the author, New York, June 2012).

Transnational civil society advocates were involved in drafting Resolution 1820, but to a lesser extent than they were in the months preceding Resolution 1325's adoption. Part of the reason for this change was the fact that the US delegation was the central proponent behind the introduction of a resolution on sexual violence that would bolster protection efforts; many transnational civil society advocacy groups considered Resolution 1325 to be comprehensive enough and preferred to maintain a focus on women's agency and participation, especially because only seven member states had drafted national action plans (NAPs) in 2007 and only five more drafted NAPs in 2008.[9] Reflecting on transnational civil society groups' efforts to advise the Security Council on the draft resolution (United Nations Security Council 2008)—and on the tensions between the United States–led focus on protection and the broader goals of the WPS agenda—an advocate recalled the following:

> I would say there were reservations from civil society and some member states. The main question was: "Why do we need another resolution when the founding resolution [Resolution 1325] hasn't been implemented and less than twenty states had NAPs?" The national level implementation was still very slow. The good thing about our lobbying at that time is that all key stakeholders from governments and the UN were aware that Resolution 1325 was very much a civil society–led resolution. Civil society lobbied for it; civil society contributed to the drafting process. So the Security Council cannot just dismiss civil society. That created some pressure on the penholders (the United States and the United Kingdom—the United States primarily) to consult with civil society. So what happened was the US mission to the UN called civil society representatives in to two consultations to review the draft. As a result of our strong advocacy to highlight women's participation in decision making, conflict prevention and resolution became a strong element of [Resolution] 1820, even though its main focus is sexual violence. Basically, we in civil society told them "OK fine. Sexual violence is a scourge and it has to be stopped." But we emphasized to the US mission and the other member states in the Security Council that women will continue to be subjected to sexual and other forms of violence if they are not seen as key participants in decision making. Civil society groups did not have the same opportunity to participate on the same level of drafting [Resolution] 1820 as they did for [Resolution] 1325. However, the penholders did not draft it without consultation with civil society. On our part, we also reflected that international lobbying is a give-and-take [process]; it is not an all-or-nothing game. (the international coordinator of the Global Network of Women Peacebuilders, in a discussion with the author, Skype, February 2016)

The process leading to Resolution 1820 created some controversy within the context of the WPS agenda by focusing on protection from sexual violence without equally emphasizing conflict prevention and women's participation in peace processes and decision making, but the resolution cannot be divorced from its international political and normative roots in the women's human rights movement.[10] The concept of sexual violence as a weapon of war would have been a distant concern for decision makers if mobilization in the mid-1990s had not highlighted the systematic nature of atrocities in the former Yugoslavia and Rwanda and if women's human rights advocates had not secured Resolution 1325 in 2000 and continued to monitor states' and the UN's commitment to the WPS agenda. Although Resolution 1820 represents the securitization of sexual violence and the almost exclusive focus on its use as a weapon, the institutional space for any consideration of sexual violence was made possible by the WPS agenda, transnational advocacy, and dedicated agencies within the UN.

Capability, influence, and opportunity are significant factors that determine the success or failure of an issue's frame. Activists, policymakers, and organization staff both within and outside the UN leveraged political influence, reputation, and personal proximity to decision makers to build support for international efforts to address sexual violence as a weapon of war. Resolution 1820 was initially a United States–led effort, dependent on dedicated individual advocates and months of informal and formal lobbying tactics and awareness-raising public events in New York and the United Kingdom. When states hold a seat on the Security Council, whether as nonpermanent rotating or Permanent Five (P5) members, they assume responsibility for drafting resolutions and presiding over negotiations pertaining to the content of draft resolutions. After the Cold War ended, the number of issues on the Security Council's agenda increased and required a clear, systematic division of labor, which is still evolving. When Resolution 1325 was introduced, the council utilized the Groups of Friends method, whereby states with an interest in or expertise related to an issue could draft resolutions with other interested states (nonpermanent and P5 members alike); this allowed the NGOWG and UNIFEM to team up with Namibia's delegation to introduce and chair the negotiations for Resolution 1325. By the mid-2000s the division of labor shifted toward a system in which individual states took the lead on specific issues, with a "penholder" for each issue (though other member states can still act as cosponsors). Generally, one of the Permanent Three—the United Kingdom, the United States, and France—Security Council members would draft a resolution and informally negotiate the content of the text with the other four permanent members before introducing the text to the remaining members of the council. The penholder system creates a more efficient division of labor than when Security Council members would race to draft a resolution before another member state in order to preside over negotiations, but it has been criticized for its role in exacerbating the controversial hierarchy between permanent and rotating council members, given that the latter are discouraged from amending draft resolutions once they receive the text because negotiations among the P5 can be tense and agreements hard-fought (Security Council Report 2016). In April 2014 Nigeria held the Security Council presidency and issued a statement on the informal nature of the penholder system, clarifying the fact that any council member can act as penholder on an issue (United Nations Security Council 2014a). The United States is the penholder on WPS resolutions addressing sexual violence in conflict, a role that began with Resolution 1820 and continued through Resolutions 1888 and 1960.[11] The United Kingdom is the penholder on WPS resolutions addressing women's participation and protection but, as chapter 4 discusses, the United Kingdom took the lead on Resolution 2106—on sexual violence in conflict—in June 2013. Both the Groups of Friends and penholder systems underscore the importance of embedded advocates in advancing the implementation of human rights and gender-focused agendas; once individuals with the capacity to influence international political discourse and action become convinced of an issue's urgency, they can "sell" the issue to the relevant political and legal organizations.

Finally, we can also see where the "weapon of war" frame's close affiliation with humanitarian law came into play in the UN Security Council's consideration of Resolution 1820. The "weapon of war" frame for sexual violence suggests that the specific forms of violence under consideration are those occurring as a direct result of an armed group's strategy. Sexual violence as a weapon of war is not, by definition, the same phenomenon as sexual exploitation and abuse by peacekeepers or troops engaged in humanitarian intervention.[12] Advocates had to make clear to Security Council members that sexual violence was a security concern with ramifications for state, regional, and international stability; to do so, they had to present evidence that sexual violence could be threatened or used against civilian populations in ways similar to—or worse than—conventional weapons of war. Resolution 1820's final text notes the "obligations States have undertaken under international humanitarian law and international human rights law" and the "inclusion of a range of sexual violence offences in the Rome Statute of the International Criminal Court and the statutes of the ad hoc international criminal tribunals," making an overt connection between recognition of systematic sexual violence under international law and the council's ability to pass a binding resolution on the issue (United Nations Security Council 2008b, 1–2).

Frames result from deliberate, strategic maneuvering by advocates over time. To make the claim that advocates strategically discussed sexual violence as a weapon of war is not to say that sexual violence is *not* used as a tactic by armed groups or that advocates deliberately mislead; instead, the claim highlights advocates' political acumen and knowledge of their targets' preferences and institutional limitations. The "weapon of war" frame's impact on the Security Council's anti–sexual violence agenda owes as much to the political factors discussed here as it does to the realities of wartime sexual violence. The international response to any issue relies on the construction of that issue within an appealing, understandable frame that resonates with values, beliefs, and existing norms. The concept of sexual violence as a weapon of war allowed the international community to view as criminal, punishable, and preventable an atrocity that it had once ignored or believed to be inevitable. Even if the frame obscures the bigger picture of gender-based and sexual violence in conflict, it represents an important step in securing international political action.

A Matter of Security, a Matter of Scope: Advocacy and Resolution 1820

US secretary of state Condoleezza Rice, then president of the Security Council, opened the 5,916th meeting of the Security Council by alluding to the shifting frame for wartime sexual violence:

> Rape is a crime that can never be condoned. Yet women and girls
> in conflict situations around the world have been subjected to
> widespread and deliberate acts of sexual violence. As many here are
> aware, for years there has been a debate about whether or not sexual
> violence against women is a security issue for this forum to address.
> I am proud that today we can respond to that lingering question
> with a resounding "yes." This world body now acknowledges that
> sexual violence in conflict zones is, indeed, a security concern. We
> affirm that sexual violence profoundly affects not only the health
> and safety of women, but also the economic and social stability of
> their nations. (United Nations Security Council 2008a, 3)

The resulting resolution, number 1820, observes: "Sexual violence, when used or commissioned as a tactic of war in order to deliberately target civilians or as a part of a widespread or systematic attack against civilian populations" worsens armed conflict, threatens international security, and hampers peace processes (United Nations Security Council 2008b, 2). It was this observation that situated sexual violence in the range of security issues within the Security Council's mandate. Resolution 1820 condemns sexual violence beyond its use as a weapon of war by demanding that "all parties to armed conflict immediately take appropriate measures to protect civilians, including women and girls, from all forms of sexual violence" and—in much softer language—by *requesting* increased efforts to "implement the policy of zero tolerance of sexual exploitation and abuse in United Nations peacekeeping operations" (United Nations Security Council 2008b, 3). Sexual violence as a tactic of war nevertheless remains the focus of Resolution 1820, and of subsequent WPS-related resolutions that specifically address sexual violence.

By framing sexual violence as a weapon of war in 2008—rather than addressing the much broader spectrum of conflict-related sexual and gender-based violence—advocates narrowed the scope of situations that the Security Council would need to address, thereby alleviating some council members' fears of overreach and excessive involvement in domestic affairs or human rights issues. One UN staff member discussed the long-term positive impact of framing sexual violence as a weapon of war, noting:

> It has been really powerful as a means of convincing certain groups who did not previously think sexual violence was a concern to them, given the work they do. Peacekeepers, mediators, or UN Security Council members, for example. For a long time it was easy to say "that issue [sexual violence] is in a different camp and we deal with the real peace and security stuff." There was a very clever use of international criminal law and international humanitarian law and finding where sexual violence fits in with these laws. (UN staff members, in a group interview with the author, telephone, May 2013)

Sexual violence as a weapon of war is a potential threat to regional and international security; other forms of sexual violence may not fall under the Security Council's authority. Although the UN General

Assembly's responsibilities include human rights violations and social and domestic issues, potentially including the broad spectrum of sexual violence, only the Security Council's resolutions are binding on all UN Charter signatories. The adoption of Resolution 1820 created an obligation to monitor wartime sexual violence occurring in conflicts that are on the Security Council's agenda, and it established the precedent that sexual violence as a weapon of war is a matter of international security for member states to address.

Advocates working toward a resolution on wartime sexual violence were aware of the Security Council's priorities and limitations. In 2008 Cheryl Benard, the wife of the US ambassador to the UN, Zalmay Khalilzad, led an informal advocacy group of UN Security Council spouses and other advocates devoted to the passage of a resolution condemning wartime sexual violence.[13] She recalled very matter-of-factly that "Resolution 1820 would not have passed if it had not focused on sexual violence as a tactic of war. There are many grave issues in the world and the UN Security Council cannot take them all on" (Cheryl Benard, in a discussion with the author, McLean, Virginia, March 2013).

When Benard recounted her advocacy group's efforts, the impact of issue framing on the success of these efforts became clear:

> When [Resolution] 1820 appeared on the horizon and everyone was saying it would not pass, we tried to find out what could be behind this resistance. And we quickly understood that the issue wasn't that the ambassadors and their foreign offices didn't care about sexual violence against women or thought it was OK. Their concern was that the Security Council shouldn't take on matters that were outside of its mandate. In their view, this belonged to the general topic of violence against women, which was a social justice issue for which other agencies existed. It could also, in their view, be a topic for the General Assembly. They weren't dismissing it, but we saw that they were misunderstanding it. Their assumption was that terrible things happen in wartime, and that's just the way it has always been from time immemorial: people starve, lose their homes, soldiers get killed, children are orphaned, and women get raped. That's what war is. Our feeling, however, was that if rape was taking place as an act of war, then it was a Security Council matter. It would only be elevated to serious attention if the Security Council did pay attention to it, so our view was that [Resolution] 1820 was

quite essential. (Cheryl Benard, in a discussion with the author, McLean, Virginia, March 2013)

Although advocates believed that Resolution 1820 and the commitment it would elicit from the Security Council were essential, the resolution was not well received at first. The US delegation had made a previous attempt to pass a similar resolution less than a year before Resolution 1820's adoption, but the draft resolution was rejected in informal preliminary meetings and never reached the Security Council floor. Benard saw two reasons for the draft resolution's failure: The US delegation did not make an attempt to lobby for the resolution but assumed that the Security Council would adopt it based on the issue's merits and the US delegation's endorsement; and, similarly, the delegation was unaware of other council members' views on wartime sexual violence as a matter for Security Council debate and action (Cheryl Benard, in a discussion with the author, McLean, Virginia, March 2013).

The fight for what would become Resolution 1820 began again in the fall of 2007, and advocates were committed to ensuring the new resolution's adoption. Their efforts were met with a significant amount of pessimism; several ambassadors told advocates that there was no way their governments would support such a resolution (Cheryl Benard, in a discussion with the author, McLean, Virginia, March 2013). Help came in the form of media coverage of one particularly horrific conflict situation. On October 7, 2007, a front-page *New York Times* article by Jeffrey Gettleman graphically depicted the sexual atrocities carried out against women and girls in the DRC and the medical assistance provided to rape survivors by Dr. Denis Mukwege at Panzi Hospital in Bukavu. Gettleman's coverage linked the cases of mass rape to the complex political, social, and economic dynamics in the conflict-affected region:

> In almost all the reported cases, the culprits are described as young men with guns, and in the deceptively beautiful hills here, there is no shortage of them: poorly paid and often mutinous government soldiers; homegrown militias called the Mai-Mai who slick themselves with oil before marching into battle; members of paramilitary groups originally from Uganda and Rwanda who have destabilized this area over the past 10 years in a quest for gold and all the other riches that can be extracted from Congo's exploited soil. (Gettleman 2007)

The article, along with other news media and documentary portrayals of sexual violence in the DRC, captured the attention of the Security Council spouses' advocacy group and other civil society advocates and UN personnel. Appalled by the UN's apparent inaction in response to sexual violence in the DRC, the spouses' advocacy group went on to meet regularly, lobbying ambassadors and member states' delegations. Not inconsequentially, the group included the wives of some of the council members who had initially been difficult to convince, which meant that lobbying efforts were situated unusually close to home. Using the violence in the DRC as their primary example, the group capitalized on the media attention to the conflict at the time and compared the scale of sexual atrocities with the systematic sexual abuse that took place during the genocide in Bosnia in the 1990s. By not only comparing sexual violence in the DRC with the systematic sexual violence in Bosnia but also by making observations that the recent case could be *even more horrific*, advocates framed the issue of wartime sexual violence in terms that resonated with Security Council members and delegations. For this horrific situation to be "worse than Bosnia," one of the world's two original reference points for wartime sexual violence, was difficult to imagine—and the fact that such atrocities were occurring despite the presence of UN peacekeepers in the DRC was embarrassing.

The group's efforts fortuitously overlapped with the UN bureaucracy's efforts to address sexual exploitation and violence. In late May 2008 UNIFEM, the UN Department of Peacekeeping Operations, and the newly formed UN Action against Sexual Violence in Conflict (known as UN Action) joined forces with the governments of Canada and the United Kingdom to hold a conference at Wilton Park in the United Kingdom on the role of military peacekeepers in preventing sexual violence against women in armed conflict. The conference brought together military leaders, government representatives, UN staff members, civil society activists, and academics and moved the conversation from identifying the problem to enumerating potential solutions within the UN's reach (Goetz and Anderson 2008). Ambassadors and policymakers alike left Wilton Park with a greater sense of obligation to respond to wartime sexual violence (a UN Women official, in a discussion with the author, New York, June 2012).

Although advocates generated attention by comparing sexual violence in the DRC with sexual violence in Bosnia and Rwanda, they also set out to clarify the issue's scope. In discussions with national delegations to the Security Council, advocates lobbying for the resolution worked to convince council members that "this was not your everyday, some soldiers are going to behave badly sort of thing. This was systematic, on a large scale, and very severe, and that it was part of the Security Council portfolio" (Cheryl Benard, in a discussion with the author, McLean, Virginia, March 2013). Some Security Council members were unconvinced of the need for a new resolution specifically targeting sexual violence, owing to concerns about whether the issue was truly one of international peace and security and that the council would simply reiterate the condemnation expressed through Resolution 1325 and General Assembly Resolution 62/134, adopted in December 2007.[14] In informal discussions, some delegations expressed the opinion that sexual violence was a human rights issue that should be handled by the UN Human Rights Council, while others argued that there was insufficient evidence of large-scale sexual violence in conflict (Cook 2009, 133). But by drawing on analogies to Bosnia and the DRC, and by introducing the "weapon of war" frame to the council, advocates were able to persuade skeptical delegations that the type of sexual violence addressed by the proposed resolution would be on the scale witnessed in the former Yugoslavia, Rwanda, and the DRC, "where it was in the context of war and had a political purpose and was therefore in the context of what the Security Council dealt with" (Cheryl Benard, in a discussion with the author, McLean, Virginia, March 2013). Illustrating the systematic violence that the resolution's proponents aimed to address, seventy-one Congolese NGOs wrote an open letter in the week before the council's debate describing the devastation being caused by sexual violence in the DRC and urging UN member states to take concrete steps to address the problem. Most poignantly, however, the letter noted the Security Council's earlier inaction on sexual violence:

> While we applaud your recent condemnation of the sexual violence we suffer, and your actions in that regard, we remind you that we have suffered for decades without any notable action on your part. You must ensure that this situation will never repeat itself in Congo or elsewhere. The Security Council cannot keep silent while thousands of women suffer indescribable sexual violence. We urge you to insist that the Secretary-General provides you with information on the levels and patterns of sexual violence in all situations before the Council, to allow your analysis and action when required. (HRW 2008a)

The reminders of the scale and prevalence of sexual violence in conflicts on the Security Council's agenda, the clarification that council recognition would be limited to cases of sexual violence used as a weapon of war, and the assurance that the world was watching squelched remaining opposition to the resolution.

Recounting the shift from opposition to support, Benard noted: "We went from a situation in which no one believed this would pass to a situation where it took longer than any other resolution to pass because everyone wanted to speak out in its favor. It went on for an entire day. Ambassador after ambassador went to the podium to make a speech about how their country actually was at the forefront on this issue and it was important and thus they were supporting it" (Cheryl Benard, in a discussion with the author, McLean, Virginia, March 2013). Still, in their remarks, several member states' representatives—including those from China and Russia, both P5 members—noted that their states' support for the resolution and the issue of weaponized sexual violence was accompanied by concerns that sexual violence should not be treated as a stand-alone issue apart from the broader issues of violence against women, conflict prevention, and postconflict reconstruction—or the WPS agenda (United Nations Security Council 2008a).

By 2008 the United States had taken ownership of the issue, and its Security Council presidency in June provided the opportunity to negotiate the resolution's adoption. Because the United States had recently grappled with sexual violence in the scandal at Abu Ghraib prison during the war in Iraq, it came as a surprise that it would put forward a resolution that could further threaten its own interests and already-damaged credibility, and the US delegation's leadership on the issue contributed to the tense negotiating process (a UN Women official, in a discussion with the author, New York, June 2012). The behind-the-scenes work of the spouses' advocacy group at the Security Council and Ambassador Khalilzad's participation in the discussion at Wilton Park, however, make clear the US delegation's renewed interest in securing a successful resolution. Indeed, informal advocacy played a significant role in garnering support for the resolution. Detailing the grassroots strategy that the Security Council spouses' group employed almost daily in 2008, Benard recalled:

> Life became very uncomfortable for the Security Council members
> because with so many spouses now engaged on this issue, they
> could not escape. Every night there is a formal dinner and it's very

traditional—man, woman, man, woman—so the ambassadors were surrounded. As soon as they sat down, they would be harangued about mass rape; and forget the rules of polite dinnertime conversation—we spared no details. They heard about reconstructive surgery, women's uteruses punctured by bayonets. . . . It's not what they're used to, it's usually polite chit chat, but here they were, sitting next to the wives of their colleagues with no choice but to listen politely as they were barraged with, "Have you heard what's happening in the Congo?" (Cheryl Benard, in a discussion with the author, McLean, Virginia, March 2013)

If the advocates embedded in Security Council affairs had not had close ties to the US delegation, and if they had not leveraged these ties to table the new resolution for Security Council debate in June 2008, the resolution's fate—and renewed discussion of the WPS agenda as a whole—would have been less certain. The financial and political resources made available through advocates' ties to a member of the Security Council's P5, and the ability to point to particular conflicts in which sexual violence was used as a weapon of war, helped to secure Resolution 1820's unanimous adoption.

Building on the Framework of Resolution 1820

Two subsequent resolutions quickly followed Resolution 1820, each providing additional commitments and adding specific mechanisms that enabled the Security Council and the broader UN organization to monitor and respond to wartime sexual violence. The first, Security Council Resolution 1888—which was adopted in September 2009, with Hillary Clinton presiding over the debate at the Security Council—establishes the Office of the Special Representative of the Secretary-General on Sexual Violence in Conflict. This special representative is tasked with monitoring and reporting on cases of sexual violence in armed conflict and coordinating with UN agencies and member states to ensure an effective international response. Resolution 1888 clearly designates authority for monitoring and reporting to a UN appointee, signifying a commitment of personnel to the issue and institutionalizing the response within the UN bureaucracy. And the second, Security Council Resolution 1960, which was adopted in December 2010, cites the need for more effective monitoring of and greater accountability for wartime sexual violence. Resolution 1960 recognizes the all-too-frequent gap between Security Council resolutions and actual commitments by the UN and its member states, and it demonstrates frustration with combatants' continued use and tolerance of sexual violence. It tasks the secretary-general to produce an annual report documenting the prevalence of sexual violence in wartime and the perpetrators who commit it, effectively establishing a long-term monitoring and shaming mechanism with the ultimate goal of ending impunity for sexual violence. In addition, Resolution 2106, which was adopted in June 2013 and is discussed in more detail in chapter 4, expands the Security Council's recognition of sexual violence beyond the woman-as-victim trope, recognizing that perpetrators also target men and boys and that sexual violence is linked to concerns about gender equality and women's human rights. The broadening scope of who and what should be counted in resolutions and the attempts to improve the UN and member states' accountability in efforts to prevent and eradicate sexual violence are indicative of progress within the Security Council.

Where do these advances fall within the typology of international responses? Table 3.1 places each achievement within the response typology introduced in chapter 1 (in table 1.1).

When discussing Resolution 1820—and the follow-up Resolutions 1888, 1960, and 2106—the international political actors could not reasonably claim ignorance of sexual violence in war. Resolution 1325's reference to sexual violence made clear that the Security Council was aware of sexual violence and that it was considered one of the many terrible things that happen to civilians (particularly women and girls) in war. We can effectively eliminate the "nonrecognition" stage after Resolution 1325's adoption, even if little actual implementation followed between November 2000 and June 2008. Advocates' efforts to pressure the Security Council to adopt Resolution 1820 fall within the category of documentation and learning, especially given their emphasis on educating Security Council delegates about sexual violence in the DRC and persuading them of its resemblance to sexual violence in the former Yugoslavia and Rwanda. A great deal of learning occurred before the council adopted Resolution 1820.

Resolution 1820, with its binding obligation to condemn and work to prevent sexual violence used as a tactic of war, represents a commitment by the Security Council; this resolution moves beyond the rhetorical recognition stage, even if expectations for implementation were

Table 3.1 UN Security Council Resolution 1820 and Subsequent Resolutions as Demonstrations of Commitment

Stage	Type of Response	Description	Representative Event(s)
0	Nonrecognition/ no action	Sexual violence is not recognized as part of a specific conflict, or the conflict itself is not recognized. Wartime sexual violence as a general issue is not recognized. No action is taken and no formal discussion occurs within or among states or international organizations.	
1	Documentation/ learning	Sexual violence, as an aspect of a specific conflict or as a general issue in armed conflict, is the subject of a report, publication, commissioned study, hearing, and/or conference launched, used, or attended by a state or international organization. Information gathering occurs.	Lobbying effort at the UN Security Council, 2007–8
2	Rhetorical response/ condemnation	Sexual violence, as an aspect of a specific conflict or as a general issue in armed conflict, is the subject of a speech, unprompted remarks, and/or in a press release by a high-ranking state official or leader of an international organization, but no further commitment is made. Rhetorical action occurs but resources are not committed.	
3	Initial commitment	An international organization or a state issues a binding resolution or policy and/or devotes financial, material, or human resources to addressing or mitigating sexual violence as an aspect of a specific conflict or as a general issue in armed conflict. An initial expression of intent and commitment of resources occurs.	UN Security Council Resolution 1820 condemns sexual violence as a tactic of war, calls for cessation of attacks, requests that the secretary-general develop protection mechanisms, and pledges to remain seized of the matter

Table 3.1 (*continued*)

Stage	Type of Response	Description	Representative Event(s)
4	Implementation/ obligation	A state agency, transnational initiative, legal mechanism, state military training or deployment, or multilateral peacekeeping operation is established and/or instructed to address sexual violence as an aspect of a specific conflict or as a general issue in armed conflict; implementation of previous commitments occurs. A long-term or institutionalized commitment of resources occurs.	UN Security Council Resolution 1888 establishes the office of the special representative to the secretary-general on sexual violence in armed conflict, 2009 UN Security Council Resolution 1960 calls for reports on perpetrators of sexual violence in armed conflict, 2010 UN Security Council Resolution 2106 expands potential responses and consideration of persons targeted by sexual violence, 2013
5	Norm change	Sexual violence, as an aspect of a specific conflict or as a general issue in armed conflict, is considered unacceptable, and perpetrators are consistently and effectively held accountable. Lasting normative and behavioral change occurs.	

vague before the council adopted Resolutions 1888, 1960, and 2106. The most profound effect of Resolution 1820's adoption was that it fundamentally reshaped the WPS agenda, focusing on sexual violence as a tactic of war as a subtheme of the agenda. The subsequent resolutions designate specific actions to be taken and identify individuals and agencies that will implement the resolutions' provisions, placing both within the implementation category. Together, the three resolutions established a clear basis for action at the UN level (Vincent 2012, 3). However, fully internalized norm change, the highest level of potential international responses to sexual violence, remains elusive in light of gaps in the implementation of these resolutions in conflict-affected areas.

As the special representative to the secretary-general on sexual violence in armed conflict, Zainab Hawa Bangura observed in June 2013
during the Security Council's debate on Resolution 2106 that these resolutions together "affirm that this crime, when committed systematically
and used as a tool of war, is a fundamental threat to the maintenance
of international peace and security, and as such requires an operational,
security, and justice response."[15] The "weapon of war" frame proved to
be an effective tool that advocates could use to "sell" the anti–sexual
violence agenda to skeptical audiences; thus, each subsequent Security
Council resolution focusing on sexual violence reiterated the "weapon
or tactic of war" phrasing.[16] The political, legal, and conceptual framework that was established by Resolution 1820 and was upheld through
Resolutions 1888, 1960, and 2106 articulated the basis for future efforts
to combat wartime sexual violence—namely, the sweeping national and
international commitments elicited through the United Kingdom's Preventing Sexual Violence Initiative, which is discussed in chapter 4.

The "Weapon of War" Meets the Agenda on Women, Peace, and Security

Framing sexual violence as a weapon of war guaranteed the success of
Resolution 1820 and laid the foundation for subsequent resolutions,
national financial commitments, and future international political efforts to condemn wartime sexual violence—including the United Kingdom's Preventing Sexual Violence Initiative, which is discussed in the
next chapter. By clarifying the scope of sexual violence that they intended for the Security Council to recognize, advocates working on
behalf of Resolution 1820 made a complex issue more manageable and
more clearly relevant as an international security priority. Most important, adoption of the "weapon of war" frame ended all debate about
whether sexual violence was truly an appropriate matter for the Security
Council to consider. In 2008 the advocates' successful portrayal of the
DRC as an example of a situation where sexual violence was being used
as a weapon and the convincing comparison of this situation with the
atrocities in the former Yugoslavia and Rwanda allowed members of
the Security Council to view sexual violence in graphic, concrete terms
that were not only understandable but also profoundly disturbing and
highly publicized. Embedded advocates' ability to influence council
members through their positions in government or their personal ties

to ambassadors provided the necessary political connections to encourage council members to take the issue seriously. These individuals made a strategic move—a securitizing move, to borrow from securitization theorists—to speak about sexual violence in a way that appealed to this UN body that was most keenly focused on issues of traditional, "hard" security. In so doing, advocates did not situate the debate within the UN's more egalitarian, deliberative body, the General Assembly, or refer cases of abuse to the UN Human Rights Council, which was often politically contentious; instead, they targeted the Security Council in order to persuade it to make a decisive statement on the role of sexual violence in conflicts and vis-à-vis the other issues on its agenda.[17] The advocates who made this move were, and remain, genuinely committed to this issue; the security frame simply provided the most efficient and persuasive mechanism for convincing the council of its urgency.

One distinction—between tepidly opposing sexual violence with hollow security rhetoric and earnestly condemning sexual violence—is evident in the commitments made through Resolution 1820 and the subsequent resolutions, which have strengthened the mechanisms for monitoring and reporting on wartime sexual violence, both on the ground in conflict zones and within UN agencies. Although the Security Council's follow-up to Resolution 1820 and its overall implementation of commitments to end sexual violence have been imperfect, the resolution nevertheless established a framework for council and broader UN action on the issue of wartime sexual violence. The existence of a binding resolution places the signatories to the UN Charter under scrutiny and invites monitoring from advocacy groups and NGOs; this links back to advocates' need to clarify the resolution's scope—systematic sexual violence as a tactic of war—in order to convince skeptical ambassadors. The "weapon of war" frame narrowed the range of offenses that the Security Council was committed to keeping on its agenda, which is in line with the interests of states that are wary of interference in their political and military affairs.

Human rights NGOs and advocates who had worked toward and hoped for Security Council action on sexual violence celebrated Resolution 1820's adoption, deeming it "a historic achievement for a body that has all too often ignored the plight of women and girls in conflict," and applauding the council "for setting out in the resolution a clear path to systematic information gathering on sexual violence" (HRW 2008b). This sense of accomplishment was, however, neither universal nor without caveats. Some argued (and continue to do so) that the sin-gular focus on conflict-related sexual violence would "take away from the powerful breadth of [Resolution] 1325 and reduce its importance by reducing the focus of the WPS agenda to issues of sexual violence" (Women's International League for Peace and Freedom 2008).[18] Re-calling the months leading up to June 2008, one civil society advo-cate noted that several NGOs and women's human rights activists were concerned that Resolution 1820 "would change the dynamic of the Women, Peace and Security agenda. And it did" (a women's human rights advocate, in a discussion with the author, telephone, February 2016). The WPS agenda is effectively split into two camps in the Secu-rity Council's repertoire and the UN bureaucracy, although civil society advocacy groups lobby and work with both. One camp, centering on the WPS agenda, is rooted in conflict prevention and women's par-ticipation and empowerment; the other, emphasizing conflict-related sexual violence, is more heavily focused on the protection of civilians (especially women and girls) from sexual and gender-based violence as a tactic of war. The council holds an open debate on the WPS agenda every October to commemorate the adoption of Resolution 1325 and to discuss the current state of its implementation, and it also sponsors an open debate on sexual violence in conflicts every spring (generally between March and June, since 2008) to discuss the secretary-general's report on sexual violence in conflicts. Although there is some overlap, within the UN bureaucracy, the entity tasked with making progress on the WPS agenda writ large is UN Women, whereas UN Action focuses on efforts to address sexual violence. The NGOWG and many other civil society groups, including the Global Network of Women Peace-builders and the Women's International League for Peace and Freedom, attempt to bridge the divide and engage with the Security Council and member states to provide recommendations for incorporating gender considerations and WPS provisions in all matters before the council. For the past decade, each of the council's resolutions that has focused on sexual violence in wartime has been followed by another resolution calling for implementation of the WPS agenda's broader objectives.[19]

At its core, the WPS agenda is about conflict prevention, gender equality in peace processes and decision making, and improving wom-en's agency and participation in order to create a more peaceful world; in short, it strives to end the structural forces that lead to violence against women, in both wartime and peacetime, and to violence in general.

But because they had focused on sexual violence as a stand-alone aspect of Resolution 1325 and the WPS agenda, advocates worried that those longer-term, more difficult changes would be neglected in favor of efforts to address the more widely publicized violations of (women's) physical integrity in war. In her assessment of the evolution of WPS on the fifteenth anniversary of Resolution 1325's adoption, Cora Weiss observed: "Prevention has given way to protection. It looks on paper like governments want to make war safe for women, which is anathema to me. We can't make war safe for women, we have to get rid of war. . . . The focus [on sexual violence] diverts attention from a broader focus on WPS. It also gives countries an excuse not to quit using violence. If you can promise violent activity without raping your women, lucky you" (Cora Weiss, in a discussion with the author, telephone, November 2015). But advocates must be strategic in pressing for change, as illustrated by the letter from the seventy-one Congolese NGOs calling for Security Council action, and the "weapon of war" frame and a separate focus on sexual violence are avenues toward increasing the resources and attention given to the issue.[20]

This increasing attention is also not without costs. Focusing on sexual violence in wartime as a phenomenon separate from the daily forms of sexual and gender-based violence perpetrated in "peacetime" risks normalizing the latter and—perversely—increasing the notoriety of those who commit wartime offenses.[21] Framing sexual violence as a weapon of war also has profound implications for the international community's ability and willingness to respond to sexual violence in its various forms. When cases of conflict-related sexual violence do not fit within the "weapon of war" frame, states and organizations find it difficult to determine what constitutes an appropriate response. Deployment-related opportunistic sexual violence and exploitation by peacekeepers and members of states' armed forces, for example, are issues that remain overlooked because of the dominant narrative's focus on sexual violence as a weapon of war. Certain groups of victims and survivors are left out of the Security Council's discourse on wartime sexual violence. These others who have experienced sexual violence—men and boys, female combatants, children born of wartime rape, and civilian women and girls who are members of the aggressor's ethnic, religious, or political group—are rarely discussed. The WPS agenda intentionally emphasizes the obstacles to women's agency and participation because women and girls have historically been overlooked and have faced gender-based threats and abuses in both war and peace. The rationale for the focus on women's participation and empowerment is that achievement of the WPS goals will lead to a more peaceful and secure world for people of all genders. The risk run by Security Council resolutions and other WPS efforts that specifically name women and girls as the primary targets for sexual violence used as a tactic of war, however, is that victims and survivors who fall outside the designated category remain effectively invisible. In their strategic deliberations, advocates must weigh their measure of progress in the fight against conflict-related sexual violence against efforts to implement broader goals related to gender in conflict prevention, decision making, and peacebuilding. The expansion of the WPS agenda in recent years to include some consideration of silenced victims and survivors and obscured perpetrators suggests that the narrow "weapon of war" frame, though limiting at the outset, does indeed provide a wedge to enable advocates to bring other voices and experiences into the discussion.

Epigraphs

The epigraphs are from Rice's and Cammaert's statements delivered during the UN Security Council meeting on June 19, 2008 (United Nations Security Council 2008a, 3, 9).

Notes

1. In June 2008, these UN member states had Security Council seats: the United States (president), Belgium, Burkina Faso, China, Costa Rica, Croatia, France, Indonesia, Italy, Libya, Panama, Russia, South Africa, the United Kingdom, and Vietnam. In addition to the Security Council members, these UN member states requested and received permission to participate in the council meeting (on a nonvoting basis): Afghanistan, Argentina, Australia, Austria, Bangladesh, Benin, Bosnia and Herzegovina, Brazil, Canada, Colombia, the Democratic Republic of the Congo, Ecuador, El Salvador, Germany, Ghana, Iceland, Iraq, Ireland, Israel, Kazakhstan, Liberia, Liechtenstein, Mexico, Myanmar, the Netherlands, New Zealand, Nigeria, the Philippines, Rwanda, Slovenia, South Korea, Spain, Switzerland, Tonga, Tunisia, and Tanzania.

2. These insights are drawn from interviews with Cheryl Benard (McLean, Virginia, March 2013) and UN staff members (telephone, May 2013). It is important to note that sexual violence was already part of the Women, Peace, and Security agenda but was not a stand-alone issue at the time. For a detailed

firsthand account of the trade-offs in advocating for a resolution specifically addressing sexual violence in 2008, see Cook (2009).

3. Askin delivered these remarks to the Missing Peace Symposium—a gathering of academics, advocates, and practitioners focused on sexual violence in armed conflict—Washington, February 14, 2013.

4. Carol Cohn, Helen Kinsella, and Sheri Gibbings (2004, 131) present a roundtable discussion of the factors leading to the NGOWG's creation and Resolution 1325's adoption.

5. Also see Puechguirbal (2010).

6. Articles 10 and 11 state the following: "10. *Calls on* all parties to armed conflict to take special measures to protect women and girls from gender-based violence, particularly rape and other forms or sexual abuse, and all other forms of violence in situations of armed conflict; 11. *Emphasizes* the responsibility of all States to put an end to impunity and to prosecute those responsible for genocide, crimes against humanity, and war crimes including those relating to sexual and other violence against women and girls, and in this regard *stresses* the need to exclude these crimes, where feasible from amnesty provisions" (emphasis in the original; United Nations Security Council 2000).

7. For a discussion of gender and UN Security Council Resolution 1325, see Shepherd (2008, 2011).

8. See, e.g., Meger's (2010) discussion of sexual violence in the DRC.

9. For access to all current NAPs, see the Institute for Inclusive Security's National Action Plan Resource Center, https://actionplans.inclusivesecurity.org/.

10. US leadership on a WPS resolution was also politically controversial because the fundamental objectives of WPS include conflict prevention and demilitarization. The United States was involved in wars in Afghanistan and Iraq in 2008, having unsuccessfully appealed to the UN Security Council for authorization for the war in Iraq in March 2003, and the focus on protection was viewed by some advocates as a way to focus on protection of women (something the Bush administration had frequently emphasized in its foreign policy) rather than prevention of war.

11. A total of fifty member states were cosponsors of the draft resolution, S/2008/403 (United Nations Security Council 2008c), many of which are also members of Friends of 1325. Notably, the DRC also cosponsored Resolution 1820.

12. For an analysis of the UN's efforts to address sexual offenses by peacekeepers, see the studies by Crawford, Lebovic, and Macdonald (2015) and by Karim and Beardsley (2016).

13. The spouses' advocacy group was a separate entity from the NGOWG, which is a formal advocacy network of NGOs that lobbies the UN Security Council on all matters related to WPS.

14. UN General Assembly resolutions are not binding on UN member states and require a vote of 50 percent plus one to pass. General Assembly resolutions can make recommendations on peace and security, but these are not binding. General Assembly Resolution 62/134, adopted on December 18, 2007, takes a broader approach to sexual violence in armed conflict and recognizes a range of actors tasked with addressing it, including the International Criminal Court.

15. United Nations Security Council, June 24, 2013, 6,984th meeting, S/PV.6984, 4.

16. UN Security Council Resolution 1889 (October 5, 1009), Resolution 2122 (October 18, 2013), and Resolution 2242 (October 13, 2015) take a broader approach and reaffirm the full WPS agenda by recounting the commitments made in Resolution 1325. Although they recognize sexual violence, these resolutions, like Resolution 1325, do so within the broader context of WPS issues and priorities.

17. For a discussion of the politics of the UN Human Rights Council and its predecessor, the UN Commission on Human Rights, see Voeten (2009) and Lebovic and Voeten (2006).

18. Also see Cook (2009, 129).

19. The Repertoire of the Practice of the Security Council provides further evidence of the divide and includes references to resolutions and meetings on WPS. For studies by agenda item, see www.un.org/en/sc/repertoire/studies/overview.shtml.

20. Otto (2009, 2010) offers a thorough discussion of the tensions surrounding WPS advocacy, appeals for the Security Council to take action on human rights and gender-focused issues, and feminist critiques of gendered power structures.

21. For discussions of these potential implications of the dominant narrative on sexual violence in armed conflict, see Cook (2009); Crawford, Hoover Green, and Parkinson (2014); and Meger (2016).

Chapter 4

Expanding the Agenda
PSVI and State-Led Advocacy

> Now that we have put war zone rape on the international
> agenda, it must never slip off it again and must be given even
> greater prominence.
> —*British foreign secretary William Hague*

On May 29, 2012, British foreign secretary William Hague announced the launching of his government's effort to combat sexual violence in war, the Preventing Sexual Violence Initiative (PSVI). In his public comments on PSVI, Hague often cited the use of sexual violence as a weapon of war in Srebrenica and Darfur and referred to "chilling reports" of rape in Syria (Foreign and Commonwealth Office 2012a). In the first of his many speeches that conveyed a deep personal, moral connection to the issue and his eagerness to eradicate the use of sexual violence in war, he declared: "I am appalled by the scale of sexual violence against women, men and children in situations of conflict and repression—ranging from opportunistic acts of brutality to deliberate torture and systematic campaigns of ethnic cleansing" (Foreign and Commonwealth Office 2012a). Throughout the following year, under Hague's foreign policy leadership, the United Kingdom established a seventy-member, government-funded, and readily deployable Team of Experts; committed roughly £1.4 million to United Nations agencies dedicated to tackling sexual violence; pledged (along with the United States and Japan) £23 million to the Group of Eight's (G-8's) efforts to end impunity for perpetrators; and capitalized on its positions of influence in the G-8 and the UN Security Council to call for international legal agreements and additional funding from other strong states. In 2013 the United Kingdom held the G-8 presidency, and in April of that year the G-8 declared sexual violence a grave breach of the Geneva Conventions, strengthening the consensus on the legal prohibition of sexual violence in wartime (Foreign and Commonwealth Office 2013a). Also,

121

in an unprecedented political achievement, in June 2014 the United Kingdom hosted a global summit in London at which representatives of 120 states discussed and condemned the use of sexual violence in war.[1] As the most recent of the cases I examine here, the launch of PSVI promised a shift toward clear and long-term material, institutional, and human commitments in response to wartime sexual violence as a general issue at its outset. The initiative's future remains uncertain at the time of writing, given changes in political leadership—most consequentially, Hague's departure from the foreign secretary post—but PSVI stands out as a case of skillful framing and a key development in the international community's recognition of sexual violence.

The initiative's transition from a national to an international effort uncovers the importance of effective framing and the ability of embedded advocates to use the "weapon of war" frame as a wedge to expand the anti–sexual violence agenda within states and international organizations. This chapter examines the role of the "weapon of war" frame in United Kingdom–led advocacy on sexual violence. PSVI's emergence, like the adoption of UN Security Council Resolution 1820, bolsters the claim that advocates are able to convince security-focused states and organizations to make commitments by using the "weapon of war" frame for sexual violence, especially when their use of the frame draws on compelling historical cases and capitalizes on moments of political influence. This chapter's first section outlines the role of the "weapon of war" frame in PSVI's launch, rhetoric, and accomplishments. The second section examines PSVI's key developments and outcomes from its launch in May 2012 through the Global Summit to End Sexual Violence in Conflict in June 2014, concluding with a brief assessment of the initiative. And the third section offers conclusions on the influences of principled advocacy, state interests, and the "weapon of war" frame.

Framing PSVI

When the UK Foreign and Commonwealth Office announced the launch of PSVI in May 2012, the initiative's architects did not aim to duplicate the UN's mechanisms that were already in place or to obscure the work of humanitarian and human rights organizations to prevent and condemn sexual violence. Rather, PSVI involved providing financial resources and deploying personnel to address sexual violence in conflict and postconflict zones, and improving investigative techniques and, by extension, prosecution rates. The initiative's core objective is to end impunity for those who commit sexual violence by increasing the number of perpetrators successfully prosecuted by international, national, and local courts; by strengthening international responses through improved coordination among nongovernmental organizations (NGOs), state agencies, and international organizations; and by building states' capacity and political will to respond to sexual violence. The centrality of legal accountability links PSVI and embedded advocates' goals with international humanitarian law; one of PSVI's early successes was recognition by the G-8 that sexual violence can constitute a grave breach of the Geneva Conventions. With its emphasis on investigation, medical care, and documentation, PSVI contributes to the overarching international effort to hold perpetrators of wartime sexual violence accountable for their crimes and reinforces the work of Office of the UN Special Representative to the Secretary-General for Sexual Violence in Conflict, UN Women, and UN Action against Sexual Violence in Conflict. The assumption underlying PSVI's emphasis on ending impunity is that greater accountability for perpetrators of sexual violence will alter the strategic calculus through which armed groups (of any form or persuasion) arrive at the decision to use sexual violence as a weapon.[2] The assumption is not unique to PSVI; the interest in eradicating sexual violence by reducing its appeal to perpetrators is apparent in UN Security Council resolutions on sexual violence and is a common feature in civil society advocates' and NGOs' rhetoric and reporting.[3] PSVI has built on the findings, accomplishments, and continuing goals of previous international efforts to address sexual violence and in many ways has contributed to expanded recognition of the different manifestations of sexual violence before, during, and after conflict. In promoting PSVI publicly, however, Hague and the Foreign and Commonwealth Office have largely adhered to the established "weapon of war" narrative.

Despite the fact that PSVI's programmatic work includes sexual violence committed outside of the context of wartime strategy and victims and survivors who do not fit the "women-and-girls" mold, the language used by UK government officials when they lobbied the G-8 and UN Security Council and engaged in public awareness-raising efforts in the international media suggests that the "weapon of war" frame remains the dominant international view of wartime sexual violence. It became imperative, then, to pitch PSVI within this frame to persuade heads of state, as well as domestic and international publics, to sign on to the effort. In his appeal for domestic popular support in the *Huffington Post*'s UK edition on May 30, 2012, Hague cited the unsettling sexual violence statistics from recent high-profile armed conflicts and reiterated that sexual violence is an effective weapon of war: "The grave and regrettable reality is that rape and other forms of sexual violence have been inflicted upon women as weapons of war in battlefields the world over. In Rwanda alone, it is estimated that more than 300,000 women were raped during the 100 day Genocide. In Darfur, Liberia, and the DRC [Democratic Republic of the Congo], levels of sexual violence have been extremely high too, and horrific reports are emerging of abuses in Syria" (Hague 2012a).

Throughout PSVI's first year, the foreign secretary's speeches and articles reiterated the "weapon of war" language and focused in particular on the use of sexual violence as a weapon against women.[4] When cast in the language of the "weapon of war" frame, an initiative to address and prevent sexual violence is more compelling, especially for states and security-focused international organizations that might otherwise hesitate to participate in human rights and gender-focused advocacy agendas. The "weapon of war" frame guaranteed PSVI's initial success and provided a gateway through which advocates could broaden its agenda and consideration of survivors, perpetrators, and forms of sexual violence that do not readily fit within the frame.

The rhetoric surrounding PSVI's launch drew extensively from analogies, as the excerpt above demonstrates, emphasizing the weaponized nature of sexual violence in recent conflicts to underscore the urgent need for international action. As US policymakers focused on violence in the DRC and advocates lobbying the UN Security Council in 2008 found ways to personalize the issue when speaking of illustrative conflicts, Hague spoke of the personal experiences that led to his own conviction to stamp out sexual violence: "Rape and other forms of sexual violence have been used as weapons against women in conflicts the world over. This was brought home to me most starkly when I met women in refugee camps in Darfur who had been viciously assaulted when collecting firewood to cook for their children, and the survivors of Srebrenica—the worst atrocity on European soil since the end of the Second World War" (Foreign and Commonwealth Office 2012a).

The conflicts in Darfur and Bosnia carried great significance for the foreign secretary because of his firsthand experience speaking with women in both places and, in the case of Bosnia, the experiences of his special adviser, Arminka Helić, who fled the war.[5] Perhaps just as important for the purposes of persuasive advocacy, each of the conflicts Hague cited in his speeches and written statements about PSVI was familiar to the national and international audiences he intended to reach, and equating the situation in Syria with better-known and long-substantiated cases of sexual violence legitimated the efforts to address sexual violence there.

PSVI-related advocacy efforts also—and uniquely—involved frequent references to the movement to abolish the slave trade. Although conflict analogies recalled horrific wars in which the international community witnessed systematic sexual violence, the slave trade analogy suggested that the seemingly insurmountable task of abolishing wartime sexual violence is akin to past efforts to right an established wrong. The historical analogy came easily to Foreign Secretary Hague, given that he is a biographer of the British abolitionist William Wilberforce, and it remained a key feature of his rhetorical efforts to promote PSVI, as these excerpts show:

> In the past, slave trading was seen as a problem that was much too complex to be tackled. But eventually the groundswell of public outrage and efforts from powerful countries led to its abolition. I will have that example in mind in April, when I urge our G-8 partners to redouble their efforts against another scourge the world has put up with for far too long. (Hague 2013b)

> There comes a time in each generation when it's possible to make progress on ending great injustices or tackling vast global problems. We saw this in the 18th century, for instance, with the historic campaign to abolish the slave trade and drive it from the seas. And in many of our lifetimes the world has come together to ban cluster munitions, to tackle the trade in conflict diamonds, and to outlaw the use of land mines. Foreign policy has always to be about these things, it has to be about more than dealing with the immediate crises. (Foreign and Commonwealth Office 2013b)

If Great Britain led the world to abolish the slave trade and end slavery, then it stood to reason that the United Kingdom should emerge the leader of the effort to end the current generation's humanitarian scourge. The analogy asserted a moral imperative to stamp out sexual violence in armed conflict, just as there was a moral obligation to abolish the international slave trade and outlaw antipersonnel land mines, cluster munitions, and conflict diamonds. The rhetoric of morality is consistent with Hague's approach to foreign policy, as he articulated it early in his tenure as foreign secretary: "We cannot have a foreign policy without a conscience. Foreign policy is domestic policy written large. The values we live by at home do not stop at our shores. Human rights are not the only issue that informs the making of foreign policy, but they are indivisible from it, not least because the consequences of foreign policy failure are human" (Hague 2010). The notion of "foreign policy with a conscience" was apparent in all of Hague's PSVI advocacy, especially in the initiative's early days.

PSVI's mandate includes a focus on women's rights and enjoyment of full equality, noting that impunity for wartime sexual violence is an obstacle to these goals. Like UN Security Council Resolution 1820, PSVI's advocates used the "weapon of war" frame to attract national and international support by lobbying for the program using the frame that resonates most effectively with security-minded states and organizations. To a greater extent than Resolution 1820's provisions, PSVI's framework includes recognition of sexual violence in relation to the more complex dynamics of human rights and women's equality (Foreign and Commonwealth Office 2013d, 90–92). In addition to recognizing that sexual violence and women's human rights (or a lack thereof) affect one another, the Foreign and Commonwealth Office's efforts to survey the issue's landscape and determine how best to begin implementing PSVI's agenda included outreach to international civil society groups focused on sexual violence and women's human rights (Foreign and Commonwealth Office 2012c). Hague's advocacy on behalf of PSVI frequently emphasized the fact that sexual violence is both a security issue *and* a women's human rights issue: "It is my firm conviction that tackling sexual violence is central to conflict prevention and peacebuilding worldwide. It must be as prominent in foreign policy as it is in development policy, for the two cannot be separated. And it also cannot be separated from wider issues of women's rights" (Foreign and Commonwealth Office 2012a). The attempt to reconnect with the original aims of the women's human rights movement that first ushered the issue of sexual violence onto the international agenda distinguishes PSVI from prior state-led advocacy efforts, including Resolution 1820. It also indicates that the "weapon of war" frame, though initially constraining, creates space where advocates can expand the agenda to include the wider range of survivors, perpetrators, and forms of sexual violence. Once advocates created an international political context in which nontraditional security issues could become serious security concerns, subsequent efforts like PSVI were free to broaden the scope of sexual violence and suggest more nuanced international responses if they first used the "weapon of war" frame to gain entry into the dominant discourse.

Just as in previous efforts to address sexual violence, influence and power are central to the account of PSVI. Not only did Hague and his colleagues mobilize the UK government's international political influence throughout PSVI's first year, but they also explicitly and repeatedly stated their intention to do so. For example, in his May 30, 2012, publicity-building article introducing the new initiative, Hague wrote:

> "Our government is determined to bring new energy and leadership to this task. We want to use Britain's influence and diplomatic capability to rally effective international action, to help find practical ways to ensure that survivors feel confident to speak out, and regain the dignity, rights, and restitution that is their due. . . . We will use Britain's Presidency of the G-8, starting on 1 January 2013, to highlight the need for stronger international action to deter and prevent sexual violence in conflict. We will use these crucial seven months before our Presidency to build real momentum around this initiative and to encourage other countries to work with us on this vital issue" (Hague 2012a).

In the case of PSVI, the timing was both fortuitous and intentional. The Foreign and Commonwealth Office seized the opportunity to leverage the United Kingdom's G-8 presidency in 2013, understanding that the annual media spotlight trained on the G-8 meetings would improve international awareness of sexual violence and the government's new initiative to combat it. When asked about the Foreign and Commonwealth Office's decision to use the G-8 presidency to build support for PSVI, one UK foreign policy official remarked:

> We saw the opportunity to really raise the issue because at times it seems like sexual violence gets discussed in side meetings and isn't always seen as being central to the agenda. This is such a priority to the Foreign Secretary himself and he saw the chance to put this out on a big stage [through the G-8]. I think also in terms of generating more financial support, the thought was that this was the right forum. And then in terms of getting the acceptance of the breach of the Geneva Conventions and the Additional Protocol, he saw the

G-8 as a good group from which to start out and get those people aligned so it can expand further. (a British official, in a discussion with the author, Washington, April 2013)

The ability to use political leverage in the case of PSVI stems in large part from Hague's great personal interest in the issue. PSVI's development demonstrates that principled advocacy using a compelling frame is a powerful tool in the hands of an advocate who is embedded within the state.

At PSVI's launch, Hague stated his wish to "publicly renew the British Government's commitment to tackling sexual violence in armed conflict" (Foreign and Commonwealth Office 2012a). He also used that venue to announce that Britain's 2013 presidency of the G-8 would be devoted to a "year-long diplomatic campaign on preventing sexual violence in armed conflict" (Foreign and Commonwealth Office 2012a). Between the summer of 2012 and the summer of 2014, advocates for PSVI not only renewed the United Kingdom's commitment to the issue but also reenergized discussion and action in international forums. The Foreign and Commonwealth Office gathered a range of organizations and individuals from international civil society for a conference at Wilton Park (which is the office's venue for strategic discussion) in November 2012. And building on the recommendations made at Wilton Park, the British delegation to the G-8 capitalized on the United Kingdom's 2013 presidency of the organization to secure a declaration on preventing sexual violence in conflict in April 2013. During its presidency of the UN Security Council in June 2013, the British delegation introduced Resolution 2106 to strengthen the UN's efforts to address wartime sexual violence. At the start of the 2013 UN General Assembly session, more than half the UN's member states endorsed the Declaration of Commitment to End Sexual Violence in Conflict, which the United Kingdom put forward as part of PSVI. And in June 2014, London hosted the largest gathering to date of state representatives and members of civil society to address sexual violence in armed conflict.

From National to International Effort, May 2012 to June 2014

To accomplish its goal of making sexual violence an unattractive and useless weapon, PSVI focuses on eliminating the culture of impunity surrounding perpetrators of sexual violence and on reversing the traditional stigmatization away from survivors. In theory, this applies equally to the leadership and rank-and-file of armed groups. The threat of accountability and prosecution should alter the calculation whereby commanders come to view sexual violence campaigns as rational means to achieve strategic ends, and it should raise the cost of opportunistic violence committed by individuals. Ending impunity, however, requires a long-term normative shift that rests on effective, consistent, and highly publicized legal mechanisms, not just at the international level but also at the state and local levels, as appropriate. Such a shift requires a broad global consensus, action, and the provision of resources.[6] Recognizing the need for international support—and especially the support of other states—PSVI comprises three interrelated efforts: establishing and maintaining a rapidly deployable Team of Experts specializing in medical care, legal processes, and security; building an international consensus that wartime sexual violence is a violation of the Geneva Conventions and therefore a serious international legal matter; and securing financial commitments for existing and proposed UN and domestic initiatives addressing wartime sexual violence.

PSVI's Launch, May 2012

In his speech marking PSVI's launch, Hague described an initiative that would go beyond political discourse and rhetoric to make a very powerful and truly human commitment to ending conflict-related sexual violence. In the months that followed Hague's initial announcement, the Foreign and Commonwealth Office engaged in an intense national and international campaign to raise awareness of and support for PSVI. From the summer of 2012 through the summer of 2013, Hague and his colleagues gave speeches, made blog posts, published editorials, and made remarks to international political assemblies that emphasized the use of sexual violence as a weapon of war, citing statistics from recent salient conflicts and remarking on the fact that the international community, in spite of its promises and commitments, had not done enough to end the culture of impunity surrounding these atrocities.

Building on the political foundation set by previous efforts to frame sexual violence as a weapon of war and a matter of security—including UN Security Council Resolution 1820 and subsequent UN resolutions and efforts—the campaign to internationalize PSVI consistently recalled that sexual violence is a peace and security issue and a threat to postconflict stabilization efforts:

> The grave and regrettable reality is that rape and other forms of sexual violence have been inflicted upon women as weapons of war in battlefields the world over. . . . Such crimes, especially if they are not addressed or punished, affect the victims and their families as well as their communities for years to come. This feeds anger, distrust, and continuous cycles of conflict. It creates long-lasting enmity between peoples, and makes it hard to bring peace. Degrading the dignity of women in such a way reduces their essential role and crucial ability to help build peace and holds back development. As a community of nations, we will not succeed in preventing conflict and building sustainable peace unless we give this issue the centrality it deserves; alongside the empowerment and participation of women at every level in all societies. (Hague 2012a)

From its outset, PSVI has been built on the assumption that sexual violence is a security issue in addition to a women's human rights issue, a stance that would have been tenuous just five years before its launch. Given the consensus reached by UN member states—beginning with Security Council Resolution 1820, and reiterated through Resolutions 1888 and 1960 before PSVI's launch, that sexual violence constitutes an international security issue—the Foreign and Commonwealth Office's efforts to lobby the international community for support emphasized the strategic nature of sexual violence using the "weapon of war" frame and focused on the moral imperative to end impunity and the specific mechanisms whereby such a goal is attainable.

Hague's initial speech on the motivations for and goals of PSVI demonstrated the utility of the "weapon of war" frame; cited the use of sexual violence as a weapon in Darfur, Bosnia, Liberia, and the DRC; and likened wartime sexual violence to the Atlantic slave trade (Hague 2012a; Foreign and Commonwealth Office 2012a). By linking the persistence of wartime sexual violence to the international slave trade, Hague suggested that the issue is a despicable entrenched institution—but one that is possible to eradicate with sufficient political will. The slave trade analogy emerged in no small part because of the foreign secretary's deep personal admiration for Wilberforce.[7]

The impact of embedded advocacy is clear in the developments during PSVI's first year, and Hague's experience demonstrates how multiple factors lead advocates to adopt and use a specific frame. Hague's leadership on the issue was motivated in part by his personal interactions with survivors of sexual violence in Darfur and Bosnia, both through site visits and daily professional interactions. Speaking of his travels to Darfur and Srebrenica, he recalled: "All these women told me of the unspeakable violence perpetrated against them. They talked to me of their rights unfulfilled and violated; their desire for justice for themselves, for their children and families, and above all their desire for peace" (Foreign and Commonwealth Office 2012a). In addition to Helić's influence, Hague was inspired by a film made by the special envoy of the UN high commissioner for refugees, Angelina Jolie Pitt, *In the Land of Blood and Honey*, about the Bosnian War and the atrocities committed against women throughout the conflict (a British official, in a discussion with the author, Washington, April 2013). Finally, political relations between the United Kingdom and the United States—especially, Hillary Clinton's influence as US secretary of state, her focus on Security Council action to address sexual violence in conflict, and her push for National Action Plans on Women, Peace, and Security during the US presidency of the G-8 in 2012—directed Hague's attention to the potential for UK leadership on the issue (a British official, in a discussion with the author, Washington, April 2013).

The "weapon of war" frame has been utilized by embedded advocates—that is, principled individuals working within or linked to states and international organizations—but the strategic use of framing is not limited to these advocates. PSVI is one case suggesting that celebrities and members of civil society can also have great influence over international political issues when they are personally motivated to support the cause and speak about the issue in the language of security; Jolie Pitt was one of Hague's crucial allies in the effort to internationalize PSVI through mass public appeal. To make more than a superficial endorsement of PSVI, Jolie Pitt reportedly worked with Hague and the Foreign and Commonwealth Office on "nitty gritty details" throughout the initiative's development and diffusion (a British official, in a discussion with the author, Washington, April 2013). The alliance between Hague and Jolie Pitt began with PSVI's launch, which included a screening of *In the Land of Blood and Honey*, and continued after the Global Summit to End Sexual Violence in Conflict. Celebrity involvement in human rights and human security issues is not unique to wartime sexual violence, but the question of whether such alliances help or hinder progress frequently arises.[8] One UK government official observed: "I think this is one of those cases in which you really see individual motivations. . . . I see a lot of cases where celebrities get involved in issues. I haven't always thought of that as helpful, but in the case of sexual violence Angelina Jolie Pitt has been very involved and that has helped. Her involvement helps to get the message out more broadly, not just to politicians" (a British official, in a discussion with the author, Washington, April 2013). The alliance between Hague and Jolie Pitt came about through Hague's personal connection to women's experiences of sexual violence in Bosnia-Herzegovina. Expanding on the emergence and effectiveness of the Hague–Jolie Pitt partnership, the official recalled:

> I think because of the movie being set there [Sarajevo] it was some-
> thing that generated a conversation between [William Hague] and
> Angelina Jolie Pitt. When he started to think about how to move
> forward with the broader initiative she seemed like a sensible person
> to work with. I'm personally quite impressed with her in the sense
> that she has been involved in the nitty-gritty details. We hosted
> a conference on this at Wilton Park in November 2012, . . . and
> Angelina Jolie Pitt attended that. She has been on visits with him;
> she went to Rwanda recently and to the G-8. She's put in quite a lot
> of time and it has been quite helpful in this case. (a British official,
> in a discussion with the author, Washington, April 2013)

Celebrity endorsements and involvement generate media coverage; where celebrities go, the cameras follow. In this sense, celebrity advocacy serves to advance agendas regardless of the individual's involvement in the daily management of an initiative, and it is especially helpful at the outset of a new policy effort when raising awareness is crucial. Through skillful advocacy, PSVI quickly became a high-profile initiative in 2012.

The Wilton Park Conference, November 2012

Between November 12 and 14, 2012, the Foreign and Commonwealth Office partnered with its executive discussion forum, Wilton Park, to host a high-level meeting on preventing sexual violence in conflict and postconflict situations. The Wilton Park Conference built on the international community's "increased understanding and awareness of sexual violence as a tactic and weapon of war" and the "increased momentum from the international community to break the silence of sexual violence in conflict, combat a culture of impunity and shift the balance of shame from the survivors to the perpetrators" (Vincent 2012, 1). The gathering of state delegates and civil society experts served as a "brainstorming" session to guide the Foreign and Commonwealth Office's efforts during the crucial months leading up to the United Kingdom's presidency of the G-8, by identifying "where global leadership on this issue could make a difference" in establishing a new "culture of deterrence" (Vincent 2012, 1).

The conference included Hague; Jolie Pitt; Zainab Bangura, the UN special representative to the secretary-general on sexual violence; former UN special representative Margot Wallström; and an array of government personnel, NGO staff members, and academic experts. State participants included representatives of the G-8's members (Canada, France, Germany, Italy, Japan, Russia, the United Kingdom, and the United States), and several conflict-affected states working to eradicate sexual violence (Sierra Leone, Liberia, Sudan, and the DRC). Representatives from the International Criminal Tribunal for the Former Yugoslavia, the Women's International League for Peace and Freedom, UN Women, Amnesty International, the International Committee of the Red Cross, the International Rescue Committee, and the Women's Media Center, among others, attended the conference to offer lessons learned and advice on best practices for responding to sexual violence. Given PSVI's focus on ending impunity through effective prosecution, at its outset the meeting emphasized the need to improve investigation and prosecution mechanisms, and then those in attendance shifted the conversation back to *preventing* sexual violence by recognizing the early warning signals in conflict and the increasing implementation of the international initiatives and policies already in place (Foreign and Commonwealth Office 2012c; Wolfe 2012; Anderlini 2012).

The Wilton Park Conference's agenda included sexual violence in conflicts worldwide, but the worsening conflict in Syria emerged as a focal point, and civil society participants expressed frustration at the lack of a high-level international response to sexual violence in that conflict. Lauren Wolfe, representing the Women's Media Center, was asked to present findings from the Women Under Siege Project on sexual violence in Syria, but in addition to presenting facts and figures, she appealed to the group to make concrete recommendations asking Hague and his government to do something real in response to the situation in Syria and the diplomatic impasse that prevented the UN Security

Council from taking serious action in light of council members' lack of political will and Russia's political ties to the Assad regime. The group held an impromptu session on Syria and presented Hague with the following goals to meet using his political influence as foreign secretary and soon-to-be president of the G-8: Urge the United Kingdom and the G-8 to provide funding to humanitarian efforts focused on sexual violence; "make diplomatic overtures toward Russia on intervening with the Assad regime specifically about the use of sexualized violence with a view toward ending it"; support a referral of Syria to the International Criminal Court and encourage other G-8 members to do the same; given Russia's interest in making progress on UN Security Council Resolution 1325, "seek a window of opportunity to create a relationship with Russia on ending sexualized violence in Syria" through the United Kingdom's ambassador to NATO; review the efficacy of the European Union's sanctions and their link to trafficking in Syria; and "work with international civil society initiatives that are aimed at raising the profile of Syrian women's perspectives and voices" (Wolfe 2012). Wolfe concluded that "Hague received our recommendations well. Now it's up to him to figure out what he and the other G-8 countries can do as the UK takes up the G8 presidency in 2013." In his November 16, 2012, speech after a meeting with the Leaders of the National Coalition of Syrian Revolutionary and Opposition Forces, Hague integrated many of the Wilton Park group's insights. He stressed the importance of the coalition's commitment to opposing violence—including rape and other forms of sexual violence—against Syrians, "upholding high standards of human rights, of international humanitarian law, preventing sexual violence and . . . abuse of prisoners" (Foreign and Commonwealth Office 2012b). In 2013 the United Kingdom also partnered with Physicians for Human Rights to run two projects on Syria's borders and deployed members of the Team of Experts to assist with the documentation of sexual violence and other crimes and human rights abuses (Foreign and Commonwealth Office 2014e).

The Wilton Park discussion's core themes demonstrated the pervasiveness of the "weapon of war" frame while also referencing the broader issues of development and human rights. The final report on the meeting lists first among the themes arising during the group's discussion the following observation: "Sexual violence in conflict is a security, development and human rights issue. Violations perpetuate an atmosphere of insecurity and instability and provide a major challenge to sustainable development and peace. Such crimes require an integrated and coordinated response which addresses all three aspects of the problem" (Vincent 2012, 2). In the report's section on international frameworks, the first observation is that "sexual violence is a highly effective weapon of war; it humiliates, dominates, instills fear and creates enduring ethnic, religious, family and community divides. Some compare this to extending the battlefields in wartime to the bodies of women, men, and children" (Vincent 2012, 2). The discussion at Wilton Park, just like the broader PSVI, recognized the use of sexual violence as a weapon but also conceded that sexual violence is more complex than the frame suggests, as there are "a number of types of sexual violence in conflict; these may be tactical and strategic or opportunistic" and men and children are victimized by sexual violence but remain silenced (Vincent 2012, 2). The nuanced picture of sexual violence that became common in PSVI-related discussions and outcomes represents a turning point in the development of the international anti–sexual violence agenda; the "weapon of war" frame remained the core of any "pitch" for the effort, but actual recognition moved beyond the frame's simplistic view.

Foreign Secretary Hague used the Wilton Park Conference both as a means to gain insight from key players in the international community into what would make PSVI and the UK government's efforts most effective and also to announce his government's progress on and commitments through PSVI. In other words, Wilton Park served as a venue to communicate PSVI's goals to the international community *and* to incorporate other states' and international civil society's insights into the Foreign and Commonwealth Office's approach. In a speech that again claimed that "shattering the culture of impunity for those who use rape as a weapon of war is the next great global challenge of our generation," Hague announced two landmark commitments: the Team of Experts, and financial support for UN peacekeeping reform (Foreign and Commonwealth Office 2012c). The UK government would finance, maintain, and deploy the Team of Experts "to conflict areas to support UN missions and local civil society to investigate allegations of sexual violence, gather evidence and help build the capabilities of other nations" (Foreign and Commonwealth Office 2012c). By November 2012 the Team of Experts had enrolled seventy individuals (Foreign and Commonwealth Office 2012c). The team included lawyers, police, psychologists, doctors, and forensic specialists as well as experts in gender-based violence. In its first year of operation, the team deployed

to Bosnia, Libya, and the Syrian border to build capacity for investiga-
tions, medical assistance, and prosecution—ultimately working toward
PSVI's core goal of ending impunity by enhancing the capacity of local,
national, and international justice mechanisms. One official described
the response from host countries as generally accepting of the assistance:
"There has been great receptivity. Obviously there has been some sensitivity towards being labeled as a country that suffers from this. But I
don't think we've had objection from any countries, or a sense that they
do not want to work with us, so I think they see the value in some of
the things we are trying to do, like improving investigative methods and
evidence collection" (a British official, in a discussion with the author,
Washington, April 2013).

The deployments were not intended to be shaming maneuvers but
instead aimed to build capacity within conflict-affected areas (whether
at the local or state level, or among NGOs working in conflict and
postconflict zones) to collect evidence, render assistance to survivors of
sexual violence, and ensure the successful prosecution of sexual violence
crimes or facilitate international efforts to prosecute these crimes. The
second commitment involved a contribution of an additional £250,000
to the UN Department of Peacekeeping Operations and Department of
Field Support over a period of three years to "develop policies, guidance
and training for use by UN peacekeepers as first responders to incidents of sexual violence" (Foreign and Commonwealth Office 2012c).
As Sanam Anderlini, cofounder of the International Civil Society Action Network and a Wilton Park attendee, wrote of the conference, "the
overwhelming message was: enough policy and rhetoric, let's 'just do it'"
(Anderlini 2012). And as they entered 2013 and the United Kingdom's
G-8 presidency term, that is what Hague and his colleagues set out to
do.

The United Kingdom's G-8 Presidency, 2013

Hague kicked off the United Kingdom's presidency of the G-8 in 2013
by recalling the slave trade analogy, citing the regrettably small number of successful prosecutions of sexual violence in international courts,
emphasizing that sexual violence in Syria was exacerbating the conflict
there, and calling on fellow leaders of influential states to take action and
make concrete commitments to end impunity for sexual violence used
as a weapon of war. In the four months leading up to the G-8 foreign

ministers' meeting in the United Kingdom in April 2013, Hague and British diplomats lobbied broadly for international legal and financial support for PSVI and other existing efforts to combat wartime sexual violence. The lobbying techniques centered on the "weapon of war" frame, discussing sexual violence as a military tactic, as a security and foreign policy issue, and as a destabilizing element in well-known and protracted conflicts.

A core strength of the Foreign and Commonwealth Office's—and particularly Hague's—international advocacy efforts lay in the consistent emphasis on the foreign secretary's personal investment and sense of urgency in tackling the issue. Hague's calls for international support conveyed the expectation that other state officials ought to feel similarly driven both by a normative sense that wartime sexual violence is wrong and that ending it constitutes sound foreign policy. The following excerpt from an appeal for support to the US domestic public encapsulates the normative and strategic angles of Hague's lobbying approach:

> As eight of the world's leading nations, we have a responsibility to confront vast global issues as well as immediate crises. My personal priority during the UK's presidency of the G-8 this year is to secure new international action against the use of rape and sexual violence as a weapon of war. Just as it fell to our forebears to eradicate the slave trade, tackling rape in war zones is a challenge for our generation. We have to deter perpetrators, bring people to justice for crimes, and provide long-term support to survivors. Sexual violence is abhorrent in any setting, and all countries have a responsibility to tackle it at home. But its prevalence in war makes it a foreign policy issue, not just a national concern. (Hague 2013b)

As discussed above, frequent references to the slave trade are indicative both of Hague's personal belief that the international community is capable of ending the use of wartime sexual violence as a weapon and of his sense that there is a moral imperative to do so. The efforts to secure the adoption of UN Security Council Resolution 1820 demonstrated the effectiveness of lobbying for action against sexual violence at the international level through the use of the "weapon of war" frame, and the United Kingdom's efforts in the lead-up to the G-8 foreign ministers' meeting similarly employed both normative and strategic appeals, as this excerpt indicates:

This is violence used as a military tactic: to degrade and humiliate the victims themselves and undermine the ethnic, religious, or political group to which they belong. It perpetuates divisions and fuels conflict. Survivors are left traumatised, often ill and unable to work, and shunned by society. But if you orchestrate or commit mass rape today the chances are you will still get away with it. Only thirty convictions resulted from the tens of thousands of rapes perpetrated during the Bosnian War. Of the 14,200 cases reported in 1998 in the DRC's South Kivu province, ninety-eight percent were not pursued at all. The international community must do better than this. We have to shatter the culture of impunity for those who commit rape and sexual violence in conflict and extend the hand of support to survivors. (Hague 2013b)

To lead the effort to do better, Hague outlined his intentions for the G-8 presidency. Beyond establishing and maintaining the nationally financed Team of Experts, PSVI's first year included two internationally focused goals: eliciting from G-8 member states "practical commitments to help victims on the ground, and support for a new international protocol on the investigation and documentation of sexual violence in conflict" and appealing for financial support (for existing UN efforts) and action from the broader international community, including member states of the EU, UN, NATO, and the Organization for Security and Cooperation in Europe (Hague 2013b).

At its foreign ministers' meeting in April 2013, the G-8 formally recognized that "rape and other forms of sexual violence in armed conflict are war crimes and also constitute grave breaches of the Geneva Conventions and their first Protocol" through the Declaration on Preventing Sexual Violence in Conflict (Foreign and Commonwealth Office 2013a, 2). NGOs, most notably among them the International Committee of the Red Cross—the arbiter of international humanitarian law—had already recognized sexual violence as a grave breach, but *states* had neither explicitly nor formally done so before the G-8 summit. The assembly also pledged £23 million ($35.5 million) in funding to address sexual violence in wartime (Amnesty International 2013; Foreign and Commonwealth Office 2013c).

By declaring wartime sexual violence to be a grave breach of the Geneva Conventions, the G-8 member states pledged to take on the responsibility of finding perpetrators and holding them accountable. Through their understanding of sexual violence as a weapon of war, the delegates to the G-8 summit were able to reach a consensus that this type of atrocity violates international humanitarian law in the most serious ways, contending that "there should be no safe haven for perpetrators of sexual violence in armed conflict" (Foreign and Commonwealth Office 2013a, 1). The declaration also committed the G-8 member states to develop an International Protocol on the Documentation and Investigation of Sexual Violence in Conflict, which the UK government led in collaboration with civil society, and renewed efforts to train national military and police personnel deployed to conflict and postconflict zones to recognize and understand the implications of wartime sexual violence. Through the declaration and its attendant outcomes, PSVI's emphasis on eradicating sexual violence in the long run by eliminating impunity is visible, as is the general sense that sexual violence in wartime constitutes a security and stabilization issue, especially when it is used systematically as a weapon.

In a notable departure from past international rhetoric, however, the declaration includes men and boys explicitly in its discussion of sexual violence as a weapon of war, noting the "importance of responding to the needs of men and boys who are victims" and the need to "provide comprehensive support services to victims, be they women, girls, men or boys" (Foreign and Commonwealth Office 2013a, 2). The declaration expanded the range of affected individuals included within the "weapon of war" frame and called more generally for international action in response to sexual violence during the first phases of humanitarian intervention and assistance. According to the declaration, sexual violence is not only a security issue, as established by UN Security Council Resolution 1820 and subsequent Security Council resolutions, but also one that must be considered a top-priority security issue when the international community responds to conflict situations. Continuing to lead the charge against wartime sexual violence through his government's positions of international influence, Hague announced during the G-8 foreign ministers' meeting that he would utilize the United Kingdom's presidency of the Security Council to open further discussion of sexual violence within that body.

Britain's Advocacy in the UN Security Council and General Assembly, 2013

Two months after the annual UN Security Council debate on sexual violence in armed conflict, Hague—as representative of the United Kingdom and president of the Security Council—chaired a ministerial-level open debate on sexual violence.[9] On June 24, 2013, the Security Council unanimously adopted Resolution 2106, the sixth resolution on Women, Peace, and Security and the fourth of those six to address wartime sexual violence as a stand-alone issue under the umbrella of Women, Peace, and Security. Resolution 2106 was cosponsored by forty-six UN member states, indicating broad acceptance of its provisions and of the urgency of addressing sexual violence in war.[10] An international effort, the resolution still bears the hallmarks of—and makes explicit references to—Foreign Secretary Hague's advocacy and PSVI's central goals.

Resolution 2106 builds on previous resolutions on women, peace, and security; adds specificity to previous resolutions' stated goals and mechanisms; and urges the UN's member states and agencies to take action in response to wartime sexual violence. Although Resolution 2106's preamble maintains the Security Council's focus on sexual violence as a weapon or tactic of war, it also broadens the scope of sexual violence to observe that men and boys are affected (even though women and girls still stand out as *disproportionately* affected), includes language about "vulnerable groups" that are targeted, acknowledges the impact of secondary trauma on those who witness acts of sexual violence, and recognizes that women's human rights and empowerment are inextricably linked to the root causes and long-term consequences of wartime sexual violence (United Nations Security Council 2013b; UN Women 2013). The call for action and expanded recognition of previously overlooked survivors and victims of sexual violence in Resolution 2106 are both traceable to the efforts made under PSVI's auspices during its first year, especially the active involvement of civil society in discussions about the initiative's scope.

On June 7, 2013, in preparation for the open debate, the permanent representative of the United Kingdom circulated a concept note on addressing impunity for sexual violence in conflict. This note provided background information on sexual violence and actions that the Security Council had taken in response in recent years, noting that "sexual violence in conflict is a fundamental peace and security concern" (United Nations Security Council 2013a, 2). In 2013, almost exactly five years after the Security Council resolved to consider sexual violence a security issue, the security frame was still a necessary aspect of advocacy within that body, as in other efforts targeting states. In broadening the scope of sexual violence beyond the image of the "weapon of war," the note emphasizes that opportunistic sexual violence and intimate partner violence in conflict zones still jeopardize stability and security (and therefore fit within the Security Council's mandate):

> Sexual violence in conflict has a number of manifestations. It is sometimes used as a deliberate tactic or strategy by one group against another with the intention of destroying, degrading, or humiliating political opponents or members of ethnic and religious groups. It is sometimes the result of the individual behaviours of poorly trained and ill-disciplined armed forces. Often, it can be invisible, opportunistic assaults by acquaintances or family members, which can escalate when society breaks down. Yet, the result remains the same: a devastating effect on individuals and their communities and the collapse of established social norms and structures, leading to detrimental impacts on future opportunities for peace and security. (United Nations Security Council 2013a, 2)

By referencing sexual violence as a tactic of war alongside opportunistic violence and intimate partner or family violence, and linking all forms to diminished prospects for societal stability, the note expands the security frame for sexual violence. The concept note also reiterates the Security Council's previous efforts to address wartime sexual violence and observes that impunity for such atrocities continues despite the "solid framework to prevent and address conflict-related sexual violence" put in place through Resolutions 1820, 1888, 1960, and 1325 (United Nations Security Council 2013a).

The objectives for the open debate were indicative of the United Kingdom's influence and the intention to garner Security Council and broader UN support for PSVI-related efforts. That the objectives for the Security Council debate included not only international and national courts but also truth and reconciliation commissions and mobile courts demonstrates the progress that has been made toward recognizing the mechanisms developed and maintained by NGOs and states in the Global South, two groups from whom Foreign Secretary Hague sought input when determining the best way to implement PSVI and the broader international efforts to end wartime sexual violence.

Resolution 2106 expands the scope of conceivable responses established by previous Security Council resolutions and establishes clear political and legal mechanisms whereby the council, the UN secretary-general, the UN agencies, and the UN's member states should act in response to wartime sexual violence. At the outset of the debate, Secretary-General Ban Ki-moon made note of the need to expand the definition of "victims" of sexual violence, but he maintained the focus on sexual violence as a weapon: "Sexual violence occurs wherever conflict rages. It has devastating effects on survivors and destroys the social fabric of whole communities. Although women and girls suffer disproportionately from these vicious crimes, men and boys are also targeted. Sexual violence is a crime under international human rights law and a threat to international peace and security. When used as a weapon of war, it can significantly exacerbate conflict and seriously hamper reconciliation" (United Nations Security Council 2013c, 3).

The resolution dispels the "myths that sexual violence in armed conflict is a cultural phenomenon or an inevitable consequence of war or a lesser crime," building on the precedent set by the ad hoc tribunals, the International Criminal Court statute, and Resolution 1820 (United Nations Security Council 2013b, 1). Where Resolution 2106 broadens the potential for recognition of wartime sexual violence is in both its recognition of men and boys as primary and secondary targets of sexual violence and its emphasis on addressing the root causes of sexual violence by promoting "women's political, social and economic empowerment" and gender equality (United Nations Security Council 2013b, 1). By maintaining the Security Council's preferred focus on sexual violence as a "method or tactic of war or as a part of a widespread or systematic attack against civilian populations" (United Nations Security Council 2013b, 2), but linking the issue back to the women's human rights framework that initially motivated transnational advocacy in the mid-1990s and resulted in Resolution 1325, Resolution 2106 improves the chances of a strong and successful international response to wartime sexual violence.

In addition, Resolution 2106 gives the UN and its member states a clearer mandate to respond to sexual violence and adds specificity to the mechanisms outlined in the previous resolutions on sexual violence as a weapon of war. The resolution recognizes the G-8's Declaration on

Preventing Sexual Violence in Conflict, thereby upholding the agreement reached by the G-8 member states that sexual violence as a weapon of war constitutes a breach of the Geneva Conventions and that states must make actual commitments to eliminating the use of sexual violence as a tactic of war. Resolution 2106 calls on "Member States to comply with their relevant obligations to continue to fight impunity by investigating and prosecuting those subject to their jurisdiction who are responsible for such crimes" and to "include the full range of crimes of sexual violence in national penal legislation to enable prosecutions for such acts," obligations made feasible through the agreement that sexual violence as a weapon of war constitutes a breach of the Geneva Conventions (United Nations Security Council 2013b, 2). The resolution builds on the mechanisms established by Resolutions 1820, 1888, and 1960, calling specifically for more "systematic monitoring"; "review of peacekeeping and political mandates, public statements, country visits, fact-finding missions, international commissions of inquiry, consultations with regional bodies and in the work of relevant Security Council sanctions committees"; "timely, objective, accurate and reliable information as a basis for prevention and response"; and cooperation on existing commitments and implementation efforts among "all relevant parties" (United Nations Security Council 2013b, 3–4). As is clear from the efforts at Wilton Park, the G-8, and the UN Security Council, a key strand of PSVI was "not duplicating work but complementing and building on existing efforts and taking all [the international community's] efforts to the next level."[11] Resolution 2106, in addition to making prior Security Council commitments more explicit, attempts to bridge or consolidate the efforts of the Security Council, UN bureaucracy, states, and NGOs already working to eliminate wartime sexual violence. The attempt to improve international collaboration and avoid duplication of efforts is in sync with the Foreign and Commonwealth Office's endeavor to strengthen the international response to sexual violence in armed conflict by reducing redundant efforts and focusing on established best practices.

PSVI advocacy at the UN continued through the summer, concluding with an event at the opening of the Sixty-Eighth General Assembly session on September 24, 2013. Hague presided over a gathering of state representatives and members of civil society at which the Declaration of Commitment to End Sexual Violence in Conflict received the endorsement of 113 states. By the first week of October, 122 member states had endorsed the pledge, committing to contribute to efforts to "do more to raise awareness of these crimes, to challenge the impunity that exists and to hold perpetrators to account, to provide better support to victims, and to support both national and international efforts to build the capacity to prevent and respond to sexual violence in conflict" (United Nations General Assembly 2013). Integrating the same principles as the G-8 declaration and Resolution 2106—most essentially, the recognition of sexual violence as a grave breach of the Geneva Conventions, as a form of violence that affects men and boys as direct and indirect victims, and as a dynamic linked to gender inequality and a lack of respect for human rights—the declaration acknowledges that sexual violence exacerbates conflict and threatens stability and efforts to restore peace. The nonbinding agreement specifies states' intentions to fund efforts to prevent and respond to sexual violence; provide better medical and psychological care to survivors and their families; integrate recognition of sexual violence in peace processes and exclude amnesty provisions for perpetrators from peace agreements; promote women's participation in decision-making processes related to governance and peace processes; support and strengthen UN and regional efforts to address sexual violence in conflict; support conflict-affected states' efforts to prevent and respond to sexual violence; support the deployment of national and international experts when conflict-affected states request assistance; integrate prevention and response tactics in police and military training and policies to improve the handling of sexual violence cases; promote and support the ethical collection of evidence on sexual violence; protect and support civil society organizations working to monitor and document cases of sexual violence; and encourage the development of the International Protocol on the Documentation and Investigation of Sexual Violence in Conflict (United Nations General Assembly 2013). Of particular importance, the declaration's provisions highlight the need for better coordination between states, international organizations, and civil society (including NGOs and researchers already working to monitor and recommend best practices for responding to sexual violence).

The declaration is a nonbinding pledge; its importance lies in the momentum signaled not only by the document's contents but also by the sheer number of states willing to endorse it. The declaration represents a rhetorical response, given that it lacks specific and binding commitments. But it marks an important moment in international discourse; at this point in time, several major international decision-making bodies became engaged in the effort to condemn sexual violence and went on record acknowledging that it is a breach of international law and an issue requiring state action. Zainab Bangura, the UN special representative to the secretary-general on sexual violence, optimistically observed that "when the history books are written, they will say that this is the date, time, and place when countries came together to stop this crime" (International Campaign to Stop Rape & Gender Violence in Conflict 2013). By continuing the discussion of sexual violence within the UN's larger, more representative assembly, Hague bolstered PSVI's appeal and continued to push for implementation of the anti–sexual violence agenda.

The Global Summit, the National Action Plan, and the New Protocol, June 2014

In June 2014 an unprecedented global assembly of state leaders and representatives of international organizations and civil society groups came together for four days in London to condemn sexual violence in armed conflict and discuss ways to eradicate it. The Global Summit to End Sexual Violence in Conflict, cochaired by Hague and Jolie Pitt, was PSVI's largest and most widely publicized milestone to date. The speeches given and discussions led by high-profile political leaders and celebrities reiterated that sexual violence is not an inevitable aspect of war; that it is a threat to peace, security, and development; and that the international community must come together to end impunity for perpetrators. The summit focused on the four themes common to the G-8 Declaration and the Declaration of Commitment to End Sexual Violence in Conflict: improving accountability and eliminating impunity for perpetrators; providing better support for survivors and their families; integrating responses to sexual and gender-based violence and efforts to improve gender equality in peace processes and security-sector reform; and enhancing international coordination to make responses more effective (Foreign and Commonwealth Office 2014c).[12] That the summit conveyed on a larger and more visible scale the messages and goals transmitted through each of the initiative's previous stages suggests that the gathering represented a capstone of sorts; the gathering was intended to send a message of global solidarity and build momentum for international, state, and local efforts to eradicate sexual violence.

At the summit, the United Kingdom released its third National Action Plan (NAP) on the implementation of UN Security Council Resolution 1325, with goals and indicators through September 2017, pointing to the institutionalization of PSVI's principles and objectives within the UK government. NAPs are intended to address the whole of the Women, Peace, and Security agenda; but in its coverage of sexual violence, the revised NAP presents the same broadened focus on conflict-related sexual violence that characterized PSVI advocacy efforts up to that point—the NAP recognizes that men and boys can be survivors and perpetrators of sexual violence, as can women and girls. The NAP also, in keeping with the dominant discourse and PSVI's strategic advocacy, emphasizes the link between sexual violence, security, and political stability. Planned foreign policy efforts described in the NAP include promotion of PSVI's goals in Afghanistan, Burma, DRC, Libya, Somalia, and Syria, among other states (Foreign and Commonwealth Office 2014f). The Foreign and Commonwealth Office, the Department for International Development, and the Ministry of Defence followed the NAP with a separate implementation plan centering on the six focus countries in December 2014, detailing activities and indicators of progress in each of the conflict-affected states (Foreign and Commonwealth Office 2014c, 2014d). The NAP provides a measure of accountability for the United Kingdom in keeping with its commitments made through PSVI and through Resolution 1325, more broadly.

In conjunction with the summit, the governments of the United Kingdom, Cameroon, Chad, Niger, Nigeria, Benin, France, Canada, and the United States, as well as the EU and UN, committed to an expanded military partnership to end Boko Haram's operations in Nigeria (Foreign and Commonwealth Office 2014b). Boko Haram gained global infamy through its April 2014 abduction of 276 girls from the Government Secondary School in Chibok, and the group's gender-based atrocities featured prominently in the June 2014 communiqué, which made several direct references to ending sexual violence in conflict.

The most portable and broadly applicable outcome of the summit, however, was—and remains—the International Protocol on the Documentation and Investigation of Sexual Violence in Conflict. This nonbinding protocol, the beginnings of which we can trace to the Wilton Park Conference in 2012, combines insights from civil society members, international organizations' staffs, practitioners, and survivors of sexual violence with the goal of creating internationally applicable standards to establish and improve legal mechanisms for investigating and prosecuting perpetrators. Noting the limitations imposed by the dominant narrative and by international political and legal constraints, the protocol's introduction contains an important caveat:

> This Protocol does not aim to tackle the entire sphere of crimes of sexual violence; its aim is focused on the specific subject matter of documentation and investigation of crimes of sexual violence under international criminal law. It should be clear, however, that the survivors of crimes of sexual violence outside this context are also in dire need of justice, support and remedies; it is hoped that this Protocol will be the catalyst for increased action on both preven-tion and accountability for all forms of sexual violence in conflict. (Foreign and Commonwealth Office 2014a, 6)

The protocol serves as a practical manual or tool kit for document-ing, investigating, and prosecuting sexual violence as a war crime, a crime against humanity, or an instrument of genocide. The protocol is designed for human rights, criminal justice, and humanitarian practi-tioners both within and outside state governments, and thus it contains clear guidelines for the implementation of international commitments on a local level; it provides definitions of sexual violence and relevant international law as well as ethical considerations and step-by-step guid-ance for navigating legal processes. The protocol translates international political rhetoric on ending impunity into a handbook for organizations and agencies positioned to implement lofty international commitments on the ground in conflict and postconflict zones and humanitarian crises.

PSVI's central logic holds that to eradicate conflict-related sexual vio-lence, a coalition of states, international organizations, and practitioners must end impunity for perpetrators; by improving the legal response to sexual violence, would-be perpetrators will reevaluate the rationality of strategic rape campaigns and will no longer view the "spoils" of war as cost-free—so the motivating theory holds. This core goal is a long-term one, which is brought about through an internalized international norm prohibiting sexual violence that drives states to act with such consis-tency and to such an extent that the effects trickle down to combatants. As Paul Kirby argues, the goal of ending impunity depends on a logic of deterrence; and, though the logic itself is clear, the evidence support-ing it is sparse—combatants may not weigh the "distant prospect of a trial in The Hague" as heavily as more immediate strategic aims, and, even if they do, it is difficult to root out the exact causal mechanism that triggers such a choice (Kirby 2015, 464–65). The practicalities of ending impunity, the protocol aside, are even more daunting. Convictions through international tribunals and courts are slow and expensive; and local justice mechanisms, despite the fact that they are promising, lack the resources and capacity to investigate and prosecute widespread sexual violence (Seelinger 2014; Kirby 2015). Still, ending impunity remains a powerful rallying cry, and after centuries of unquestionable impunity for perpetrators of sexual violence, there is good reason to focus attention on improving accountability.

The caveat in the protocol marks an important transition in the rhetoric on sexual violence; the excerpt from the protocol given above explicitly acknowledges that "the survivors of crimes of sexual violence outside [the context of crimes of sexual violence recognized by international law] are also in dire need of justice, support, and remedies" (Foreign and Commonwealth Office 2014a, 6). Presumably, this includes those affected by opportunistic violence and intimate partner and family violence. PSVI has pushed the boundaries of the dominant narrative, the "weapon of war" frame, since its inception, and the protocol is no exception. The stated hope "that this protocol will be the catalyst for increased action on both prevention and accountability for all forms of sexual violence in conflict" (Foreign and Commonwealth Office 2014a, 6) brings the effort to address sexual violence closer to the gender- and empowerment-focused advocacy of the mid-1990s and beyond.

PSVI and the Impact of the "Weapon of War" Frame

PSVI made an impact on the dominant international (especially interstate) discourse on sexual violence, securing commitments from states and international organizations to implement an anti–sexual violence agenda and expanding that agenda by using the "weapon of war" frame. The frame not only spoke to security-focused state leaders and members of international bodies in ways that meshed with existing priorities, but also created a wedge through which embedded advocates could work to expand the persons and forms of violence recognized by international efforts. Table 4.1 revisits the accomplishments discussed above, placing them within the typology.

Table 4.1 Progress through the Preventing Sexual Violence Initiative

Stage	Type of Response	Description	Representative Event(s)
0	Nonrecognition	Sexual violence is not recognized as part of a specific conflict, or the conflict itself is not recognized. Wartime sexual violence as a general issue is not recognized. No action is taken and no formal discussion occurs within or among states or international organizations.	
1	Documentation/ learning	Sexual violence, as an aspect of a specific conflict or as a general issue in armed conflict, is the subject of a report, publication, commissioned study, hearing, and/or conference launched, used, or attended by a state or international organization. Information-gathering occurs.	Wilton Park Conference, November 12–14, 2012
2	Rhetorical response/ condemnation	Sexual violence, as an aspect of a specific conflict or as a general issue in armed conflict, is the subject of a speech, unprompted remarks, and/or in a press release by a high-ranking state official or leader of an international organization, but no further commitment is made. Rhetorical action occurs but resources are not committed.	Announcement of the Preventing Sexual Violence Initiative, May 29, 2012 Declaration of Commitment to End Sexual Violence in Conflict endorsed by UN member states during the 68th session of the General Assembly, September 25, 2013 Global Summit, June 2014

(continued next page)

Table 4.1 *(continued)*

Stage	Type of Response	Description	Representative Event(s)
3	Commitment (initial)	An international organizations or a state issues a binding resolution or policy and/or devotes financial, material, or human resources to addressing or mitigating sexual violence as an aspect of a specific conflict or as a general issue in armed conflict. An initial expression of intent and commitment of resources occurs.	Additional commitment of £250,000 from the United Kingdom to the UN Department of Peacekeeping Operations and Department of Field Support, 2012–15 Declaration on Preventing Sexual Violence in Conflict issued by the G-8, consensus that sexual violence is a grave breach of the Geneva Conventions and Additional Protocol I, April 2013 The United Kingdom pledges £20 million and the United States pledges $10 million to address sexual violence in war, April 2013 The United Kingdom pledges £6 million to support survivors through the UN Trust Fund to End Violence Against Women, the International Criminal Court's Trust Fund for Victims, and the International Organization for Migration, June 2014

(continued next page)

Stage	Type of Response	Description	Representative Event(s)
4	Implementation (long-term obligation)	A state agency, transnational initiative, legal mechanism, state military training or deployment, or multilateral peacekeeping operation is established and/or instructed to address sexual violence as an aspect of a specific conflict or as a general issue in armed conflict; implementation of previous commitments occurs.	Team of Experts—financed, maintained, and deployed by the United Kingdom—2012
			UN Security Council Resolution 2106 adopted, June 24, 2013
			International Protocol on the Documentation and Investigation of Sexual Violence in Conflict, June 2014
		A long-term or institutionalized commitment of resources occurs.	Revised UK National Action Plan on Women, Peace, and Security, June 2014
			Expansion of military commitment to defeat Boko Haram in Nigeria, citing sexual atrocities, June 2014
			National Action Plan Country-Level Implementation Plan for six focus states released, December 2014
			House of Lords Select Committee on Sexual Violence in Conflict releases report on the Preventing Sexual Violence Initiative's achievements and work remaining, March 2016
5	Norm change / taboo	Sexual violence, as an aspect of a specific conflict or as a general issue in armed conflict, is considered unacceptable, and perpetrators are consistently and effectively held accountable.	
		Lasting normative and behavioral change occurs.	

The placement of each aspect and outcome of PSVI within a corresponding response category demonstrates the often nonlinear process of moving from documentation through long-term implementation. Implementing the anti–sexual violence agenda requires some back-and-forth between rhetorical condemnation and actual commitment of resources as advocates work to appeal to new audiences. As PSVI illustrates, the political response to sexual violence includes efforts corresponding with multiple stages at the same time in a process of learning, acting, and convincing others to join the effort or abide by normative concerns.

Shortly after the Global Summit, on July 14, 2014, Hague stepped down from his position as foreign secretary to become leader of the House of Commons. That same day, Prime Minister David Cameron appointed Hague as his special representative on preventing sexual violence in conflict, leaving PSVI's most central advocate at the forefront but prompting concerns about its long-term future. Indeed, less than a year later, in July 2015, Baroness Joyce Anelay assumed the appointment of special representative in Hague's place.

A report by the House of Lords' Select Committee on Sexual Violence in Conflict, released in March 2016, cites the important work undertaken by PSVI and calls for greater transparency and integration of the initiative's objectives within the Foreign and Commonwealth Office, the Department for International Development, and the Ministry of Defence. Noting PSVI's accomplishments in raising awareness among states and within international organizations of sexual violence in conflict, the report urges the UK government to provide support and resources for PSVI as a whole and for the prime minister's special representative on sexual violence in conflict. It stresses the need to coordinate efforts across all relevant sectors of the government, and cautions against focusing on conflicts in the Middle East to the exclusion of the many other conflicts in which sexual violence occurs. Conceptually, although PSVI is the most inclusive state-led effort to date, the report makes the case for tailoring responses to specific groups of survivors, noting that men, women, and children do not have identical needs—the broader scope of recognized survivors is only as useful as the recognition afforded to each group in its own right (UK House of Lords 2016, 3–4). Baroness Anelay responded to the report with assurances that the United Kingdom would continue to lead international efforts to "end the scourge of sexual violence in conflict" (Foreign and Commonwealth Office 2016).

Skepticism about PSVI's future without Hague and disappointment with the persistence of sexual violence in conflict, despite the lofty promises made at the Global Summit have called PSVI's value and impact into question (Townsend 2015; Wintour 2016). Recognizing the need for international support, PSVI was initially constructed by advancing three interrelated efforts: establishing and maintaining a rapidly deployable Team of Experts specializing in medical care, legal processes, and security; building an international consensus that wartime sexual violence is a violation of the Geneva Conventions and therefore a serious international legal matter; and securing financial commitments for existing and proposed UN and domestic initiatives addressing wartime sexual violence. Regardless of PSVI's future successes or shortfalls, what is clear is that, as a diplomatic endeavor, it has made important strides in institutionalizing efforts to recognize and respond to wartime sexual violence, both internationally and within the UK government. In responses to criticism of PSVI, civil society groups have asserted PSVI's true value: It marks an *entry* point (Wilton 2015; Rees and Chinkin 2015). The commitments and promises made by states, the G-8, and the UN Security Council through PSVI give NGOs and advocates— including both those embedded in states and those that apply pressure from outside states—a platform on which they can hold these political entities accountable. Ending impunity for sexual violence and ultimately working to decrease the utility and prevalence of sexual violence in war, as in "peace," requires long-term shifts in deeply entrenched norms. State-based consensus and commitments represent a strong step forward in this process.

The "Weapon of War" Frame, Power, and Principled Advocacy

The legal consensus and funding commitments made at the UN Security Council and G-8, the establishment and funding of the United Kingdom–based Team of Experts, the deployment of additional battalions to Nigeria in response to Boko Haram's use of sexual violence, and the publication of the International Protocol on the Documentation and Investigation of Sexual Violence in Conflict are some of the clearest examples of the implementation of the anti–sexual violence agenda undertaken by states and multilateral organizations to date. PSVI is a compelling case of skillful advocacy employing the "weapon of war" frame. Rather than securing commitments by selling the issue strictly within the confines of the frame, however, embedded advocates in this case used the "weapon of war" frame to appeal to security-focused states and international organizations but then pushed to broaden the dominant narrative. The frame provided a platform, not a constraint. The G-8 declaration, the Declaration of Commitment to End Sexual Violence in Conflict, and UN Security Council Resolution 2106 all contain more inclusive language that addresses the complexity of sexual violence in armed conflict, noting its use as a weapon and its threat to peace and security but observing that the ingrained image of the vulnerable female rape survivor is not all-encompassing. Much of the credit for PSVI's initial success goes to Hague's influential role and his approach to "foreign policy with a conscience," but it is also undeniable that the initiative's focus beyond the "weapon of war" (against women and girls) is due to the active dialogue with civil society representatives.

The rhetoric and advocacy surrounding PSVI still draws heavily from the security frame because the frame provides a necessary rhetorical foundation when targeting other states in appeals for support. As the securitization and feminist security studies literatures contend, the authority and identity of the person speaking about security matter. Remarks and interviews on PSVI have highlighted Hague's personal motivation and strong leadership in this particular case, noting that much of PSVI's initial success is attributable to his advocacy and coalition-building efforts, both at home and in the international arena.[13] A UK government official posited that the fact that Hague is a *man* also makes a contribution to international efforts to address wartime sexual violence because it challenges the assumption that only female leaders and advocates are concerned about the issue:

> I think it's helpful that the Foreign Secretary is a man. Secretary Clinton has put so much effort into this issue and to women's issues in general. Given that most of the people put in these positions tend to be women, I think it's very important that we have a man. . . . At least for us having the Foreign Secretary so taken with the issue has helped others who may not have taken the issue seriously take the issue seriously. That was one of the things as the

G-8 approached. The US emphasized quite often that we need to understand that this is not just a women's issue, in terms of who the victims are. (a British official, in a discussion with the author, Washington, April 2013)

By taking up the issue of wartime sexual violence, Hague may have provided greater legitimacy to sexual violence as a security issue and affirmed that it is not limited to female leaders' priorities. Of course, Hague is not alone as a man in speaking out against sexual violence; Dr. Denis Mukwege has often risked his life to improve his patients' lives and to speak on behalf of survivors of sexual violence, leaving his indelible mark on the international anti–sexual violence agenda as a civil society advocate and medical professional (Amnesty International 2012). Dr. Mukwege's advocacy was key in the successful effort to convince the UN Security Council delegations of the urgency of addressing sexual violence in the DRC. Regarding PSVI, and consistent with feminist approaches to security studies, Hague's identity as a man in a position of political influence within a wealthy Western state contributed to his ability to speak convincingly about sexual violence in terms of security and persuade other state representatives to view the issue as an urgent one.

Advocates' use of the "weapon of war" frame and repeated assertions of the link between sexual violence, protracted conflict, and flawed peace processes appealed to states' more traditional security interests. Although PSVI's core goal of ending impunity for sexual violence addresses a wider scope of sexual violence and cites previously unrecognized victims and survivors, the international lobbying efforts tied to the initiative recall the frame that made previous Security Council resolutions and national efforts successful. Just as in the development of US policy toward sexual violence in the DRC, eradicating sexual violence in conflict-affected states looked promising to those British foreign policy officials who were concerned with curbing extremism and promoting stability abroad. To this end, representatives from the United Kingdom broached the subject of sexual violence in consultations with the governments of fragile states. Referring to PSVI's efforts in Somalia, one state that the United Kingdom has worked to stabilize, a British official remarked:

We very visibly want to help build [the state] up and help advance the aims of the government and yet we're pushing the president and his new government to take this issue more seriously and to be more actively engaged in this issue at a time when they want to do that but they want to do it slowly. We're rushing them. For me, if it was purely about, if our only interest was to build up the government of Somalia then we wouldn't need to focus on this right now. There are many other stabilization issues that we need to address. So by addressing sexual violence we are kind of contradicting that. Somalia is a friend of ours that we as the West are trying to build up and yet we're pushing the government on sexual violence. (a British official, in a discussion with the author, Washington, April 2013)

On the surface, highlighting sexual violence can appear to be (and often is) a shaming tactic, one that stands to hinder bilateral political relationships. In working simultaneously to improve a government's capacity and implement measures to reduce and prevent sexual violence, foreign policy officials must tread lightly; but the very fact that combating sexual violence would factor in to a state's foreign policy efforts is in itself a measure of progress. Through PSVI, the UK government stands to contribute to security and stabilization as well as to women's empowerment and humanitarian concerns. Foreign policy rooted in morality and humanitarian concerns need not be divorced from strategic priorities and interests—it can serve both.

Epigraph

This is a quotation from Hague (2013a).

Notes

1. For a report on the objectives, discussions, outcomes, and anticipated next steps, see Foreign and Commonwealth Office (2014c).

2. For a critical discussion of the proposed connection between efforts to end impunity and potential reduction in the use of sexual violence, see the research by Paul Kirby (2015).

3. See, e.g., HRW (2014) and International Campaign to Stop Rape & Gender Violence in Conflict (2014).

4. For illustrative examples, see Foreign and Commonwealth Office (2012a, 2013a) and Hague (2012a, 2012b, 2013b).

5. Insights based on information gathered from an interview with a British official, Washington, April 2013. For publicly available sources, see Kirby (2015, 460n17) and Wintour (2016).

6. For more discussion of the feasibility of deterrence through legal mechanisms, see Kirby (2015, 464–68). Also see Inal's (2013) research on the legal prohibition of sexual violence through international law and courts.

7. Hague, like Wilberforce, is a conservative politician who found himself at the helm of a liberal humanitarian cause; see Allan (2012). This alliance is not unlike that of US conservative politicians and advocates who championed a response to sexual violence both within US policy and at the UN Security Council.

8. See, e.g., Eriksson Baaz and Stern's (2013, 89) critique of Western "white savior" activists and celebrity advocacy in the DRC.

9. Rwanda held the Security Council presidency in April 2013 and chaired the open debate on sexual violence in armed conflict. No new resolutions were put forward at that time.

10. The resolution's cosponsors included Argentina, Australia, Austria, Belgium, Bosnia-Herzegovina, Bulgaria, Canada, Chile, Costa Rica, Croatia, Cyprus, the Czech Republic, Denmark, Estonia, Finland, France, Germany, Greece, Guatemala, Hungary, Iceland, Ireland, Israel, Italy, Japan, Latvia, Lebanon, Liberia, Lithuania, Luxembourg, Montenegro, the Netherlands, Norway, Poland, Portugal, Romania, Slovakia, Slovenia, South Korea, Spain, Sweden, Togo, Ukraine, the United Kingdom, the United States, and Uruguay (United Nations Security Council 2013c).

11. Remarks by Emma Wade, foreign policy counselor at the British Embassy in Washington, to the Missing Peace Symposium, Washington, February 14, 2013.

12. An important caveat is the summit agenda's exclusion of academic research and researchers. Amelia Hoover Green observed that the summit's agenda failed to include academic speakers or to recognize research on the complexity of sexual violence, despite the initiative's repeated efforts to acknowledge sexual violence in conflict as a complex phenomenon (Hoover Green 2014).

13. The sense of Hague's centrality to the initiative's success is frequently conveyed in coverage of PSVI. In the course of this research, Hague's role became clear through multiple sources, both public and anonymous (British official, in a discussion with the author, Washington, April 2013; remarks by Wade to the Missing Peace Symposium).

Chapter 5

The Legacy of the "Weapon of War" Frame
Implications for Research, Policy, and Practice

> No one is paying enough attention to sexual violence in Syria
> and Libya. Even human rights groups say it's not happening or,
> if it is, we can't talk about it.
> —*A legal expert, in a discussion with the author,*
> *New York, June 2012*

To return to the question I posed at the outset of the book: What impact has the "weapon of war" frame had on international political efforts to end conflict-related sexual violence? Specifically, how has this dominant frame helped or hindered efforts to implement an anti–sexual violence agenda? The previous three chapters offered case studies demonstrating how advocates' use of the "weapon of war" frame persuaded state leaders and members of the UN Security Council to view sexual violence as an instrument of warfare and strongly condemn it, and to make both short- and long-term commitments of resources in response. Each chapter also pointed to the ways in which the frame constrains both the conceptual understanding of conflict-related sexual violence and also—by extension—comprehensive efforts to address the full spectrum of abuses, victims/survivors, and perpetrators. Sexual violence used as a weapon *is* horrific, and efforts to condemn such tactics are absolutely warranted. The object of critique of the "weapon of war" frame is not to curtail attempts to mitigate instrumental sexual violence but rather to call attention to the many other situations and contexts in which individuals suffer from sexualized violence. Acknowledging the progress that has been made in the past two decades, this chapter views the "weapon of war" frame through a more critical lens in order to discuss what the frame obscures and what it offers advocates who use it to appeal to states and international organizations (IOs).

The chapter proceeds in two sections. The first explores the complexities that are left out of the simplified narrative on conflict-related sexual violence. I highlight the victims/survivors, perpetrators, and forms of sexual violence that are largely absent from discussions of conflict-related sexual violence, suggest that the focus on instrumental sexual violence leads to inconsistent recognition of conflicts involving sexual and gender-based violence, and highlight emerging research on the perversity of condemning wartime sexual violence. The second section observes that, despite having knowledge of the frame's limitations, advocates use the "weapon of war" narrative to engage states and IOs. I offer an assessment of why advocates employ the frame before concluding with a preliminary discussion of why advocates target security-focused entities to address sexual violence.

What the "Weapon of War" Frame Obscures

The success of the "weapon of war" frame comes at a cost. Although it appeals to states and situates sexual violence within the context of threats to peace and security—and therefore makes it a relevant concern for IOs like the United Nations—the frame places constraints on action and implementation of efforts to prevent and respond to sexual violence. The "weapon of war" frame, like any international issue's frame, must discount some aspects of the broader picture of sexual violence in order to achieve its appealing simplicity and conceptual coherence and to suit the relevant institutional and state interests, mandates, and constraints. This concern is at the heart of academic critiques of the securitization of sexual violence (Eriksson Baaz and Stern 2013; Davies and True 2015; Meger 2016), and the one most closely tied to the international community's ability to implement comprehensive efforts to eradicate conflict-related sexual violence. Individuals, forms of violence, and conflict cases are unintentionally left out of or deliberately excluded from recognition; the result is variation in the willingness and ability to implement the lofty goals set by the UN Security Council, by individual states in their foreign policies, and by the multilateral (and, indeed, global) forums on sexual violence.

Obscured Individuals and Forms of Violence

The image of sexual violence as a weapon of war brings to mind, and focuses policy on, a perpetrator–victim dynamic involving male-bodied combatants and female-bodied civilians. The advantage of this perception of sexual violence is that it focuses on a "short and clear causal chain (or story) about who bears responsibility" (Keck and Sikkink 1999, 98), and this concise story of a wartime atrocity makes political and legal condemnation and efforts to assist victims and punish perpetrators more feasible. Short and clear links between perpetrator and victim facilitated the "weapon of war" frame's diffusion through the international community, and the male-combatant-perpetrator/female-civilian-victim dichotomy has worked well in advocates' appeals for support from states and IOs. However, the actual identities of perpetrators, victims, and survivors of sexual violence in armed conflict and the postconflict transition period are far more complex than the "weapon of war" frame suggests, and international efforts to address wartime sexual violence overlook the complex range of survivors' and victims' identities. The dominant male perpetrator / female victim dichotomy that characterizes much of the rhetoric on sexual violence conceived as a weapon serves not only to limit the effectiveness of responses to sexual violence but also to reinforce the gender essentialisms or stereotypes that make sexual violence a powerful threat in the first place (Boesten 2015, 3). Accordingly, this section focuses on several groups of people who are vulnerable to wartime sexual violence but do not readily fit within the dominant frame: men, boys, and lesbian, gay, bisexual, transgender, and queer (LGBTQ) individuals—persons who do not easily fit within the dominant image of a cis female victim of male-perpetrated violence; civilians and combatants who experience opportunistic sexual violence, sexual exploitation, or intimate partner or family violence; civilians, especially women and girls, who share some aspect of a perpetrator group's identity (whether it is a political, ethnic, religious, national, or other identity relevant to the conflict); and children born of wartime rape. Individuals belonging to one or more of these groups experience neglect and nonrecognition despite the increase in commitments to improving survivor assistance and strengthening the capacity of investigation and prosecution mechanisms. Existing research addresses the difficulties faced by these groups of victims and survivors, and this section synthesizes these observations with my focus on the centrality of the "weapon of war" frame and its impact on the implementation of efforts to respond to wartime sexual violence.

The "weapon of war" frame for sexual violence draws on entrenched understandings of who constitutes a civilian; the practical understanding of "civilian" is inherently gendered and prioritizes the protection of women and children over military-aged men and older boys despite the fact that the latter are often just as or even more vulnerable in conflict situations and are also targeted for sexual violence. In her work on the civilian protection regime, Carpenter finds that "civilian" has become synonymous with "women and children" in international humanitarian relief efforts and policies; the result is a flawed picture of civilians that simultaneously includes "some combatants (female and child soldiers) and excludes some noncombatants (adult civilian men)," while emphasizing dangerous notions of women's vulnerability and ignoring the "gender-based vulnerabilities that draft-age civilian males face in armed conflict" (Carpenter 2005, 296). Helen Kinsella (2011, 88) similarly observes that the frequent repetition of the phrase "especially women and children" in speeches, policies, and resolutions on civilian protection reinforces, and thus reproduces, the gendered principle of civilian immunity. By focusing on sexual violence as a weapon used by combatants against the civilian population, the "weapon of war" frame taps into collective understandings of who is most vulnerable in war—and these understandings are flawed. Until very recently, political discourse and initiatives focused on sexual violence excluded male victims and survivors of sexual violence because these individuals are less likely to be viewed as innocent and vulnerable civilians. And even when men and boys have been included in efforts to address wartime sexual violence, their role has been limited to that of the "soldier-rapist" or the indirect victims of sexual violence who bear the emotional and psychological trauma of witnessing the rape of "their" women.

The conversation on wartime sexual violence has broadened somewhat in recent years to include males as direct victims of sexual violence, including in the forms of castration, mutilation, and rape.[1] Rhetoric and policies have begun to use gender-neutral language and to make specific references to male-bodied victims and survivors, but with much less frequency than discussions of female victims and survivors. Although UN Security Council Resolution 2106 recognizes that men and boys are affected by sexual violence and the 2015 secretary-general's report on conflict-related sexual violence acknowledges that LGBTQ individuals are targeted for "corrective violence" (United Nations Security Council 2015a, 7), recognition of victims and survivors who are beyond the ideal-typical "vulnerable woman and child" is only beginning to take shape. For instance, in her study of the systematic exclusion of men and boys from political discussions of sexual violence, Lewis (2014, 223) observes that the Security Council's debate on Resolution 2106 included 325 references to female victims and survivors but only 19 references to male victims and survivors. In addition, simply including references to men and boys still does little to improve recognition of those individuals who do not fit easily within binary conceptions of gender and heteronormative discourse. Thus, LGBTQ individuals have been almost completely absent from the international political discussion of sexual violence.

A September 2015 *New York Times* article exposed the gap in the recognition of survivors of sexual violence, citing reports that members of the US military services are instructed to "look the other way" when they encounter sexual abuse of boys by their Afghan allies. Colonel Brian Tribus, the spokesman for the US command in Afghanistan, told the *Times:* "Generally, allegations of child sexual abuse by Afghan military or police personnel would be a matter of domestic Afghan criminal law." He noted that the exception would be "when rape is being used as a weapon of war" (Goldstein 2015). Because boys are being victimized by the members of an allied military service in a way that does not resemble rape as genocide or the systematic attacks by armed groups that grab headlines, the "weapon of war" frame is difficult to apply. And the fact that Colonel Tribus noted the exception implies that the "weapon of war" frame is sufficiently compelling that states would condemn allies that engage in such tactics but that sexual abuse of boys did not clear this bar. Despite progress in recognizing the diversity of victims and survivors, the focus on international condemnation remains on women and girls because they still constitute the documented majority of victims and survivors and—most important here—fit within the "weapon of war" frame as states and IOs have accepted it.

Intimate partner violence, transactional or "survival" sex, and opportunistic sexual violence are problems in wartime as in peacetime but receive little attention from advocates, states, and IOs.[2] The response to crimes committed by UN peacekeepers notwithstanding, sexual violence, abuse, and exploitation occurring within the context of armed conflict and postconflict reconstruction but outside what is perceived to be an orchestrated tactic of war tend to be excluded from international political consideration.

Reliance on the "weapon of war" frame for sexual violence has led to the nearly complete nonrecognition of opportunistic sexual violence, the broader spectrum of conflict-related sexual and gender-based abuses, and the individuals affected by these acts. The types of sexual and gender-based violence excluded by the "weapon of war" frame include sexual exploitation by peacekeeping forces, humanitarian aid workers, and deployed state or international military forces; rape and other forms of sexual violence committed by combatants of their own volition and outside the context of military strategy; intimate partner violence during and in the aftermath of armed conflict; and the daily forms of sexual and gender-based violence experienced before, during, and after armed conflict as a result of gender inequality and structural violence. The forms of sexual and gender-based violence that exist in society before the outbreak of active armed conflict do not cease to exist—indeed, may worsen—during war and postconflict reconstruction.[3] Furthermore, systematic sexual violence as a wartime strategy inevitably has a basis in social and cultural understandings of gender and sexuality, and these understandings are often similarly expressed in other forms of sexual and gender-based violence that persist outside active armed conflict. With the exclusion of these forms of sexual violence and exploitation from the dominant frame, the victims and survivors of these abuses are similarly overlooked. The immediate consequences of this neglect by aid workers, international courts and transitional justice mechanisms, and national policies is that survivors' experiences are discounted and devalued and their access to medical, psychological, and social support services is limited or entirely absent.

Sexual violence in wartime is linked to gender-based violence and inequality in daily life before, during, and after active armed conflict. Beyond the direct consequences for survivors of these forms of sexual violence and exploitation, there is a theoretical implication, one that Boesten (2010, 2014) explores in her research: Women's—and men's—experiences of sexual violence and exploitation related to armed conflict shed light on gender dynamics within society and in the practice of war, but we cannot fully understand these complicated dynamics if experiences that do not fit within the "weapon of war" frame are silenced. As Special Representative Zainab Hawa Bangura remarked: "If women are seen as second-class citizens in peacetime, their rights will not be respected when there is unrest. If they are viewed as unimportant before war breaks out, they will be treated as expendable during conflict. Of course addressing conflict-related sexual violence ultimately must be about prevention" (remarks to the Missing Peace Symposium,

Washington, February 14, 2013). Too narrow a focus on sexual violence as a weapon creates a situation in which a great deal of work is devoted to one particular type of atrocity along the very broad and complex spectrum of sexual and gender-based violence.

Sexual exploitation by peacekeepers is a notable exception and a concern that the UN has reiterated and attempted to address through various institutional approaches.[4] The UN Conduct and Discipline Unit has tracked reports of sexual exploitation and abuse (SEA) by personnel deployed on peacekeeping operations since 2006, doing so initially as the Department of Peacekeeping Operations Conduct and Discipline Team, which was established in 2005.[5] The secretary-general has worked with the Department of Peacekeeping Operations and the Conduct and Discipline Unit to increase the UN's ability to prevent SEA and hold personnel accountable when abuses occur. In 2016 the secretary-general appointed a special coordinator on improving the United Nations' response to sexual exploitation and abuse, following the recent allegations of abuse of civilians (including children) by UN peacekeepers in the Central African Republic.[6] In March 2016, the Security Council adopted Resolution 2272, which further condemns exploitation and abuse by peacekeepers, endorsing the secretary-general's plan to repatriate units that tolerate such behavior by their members and hold troop-contributing countries accountable (including by replacing their contributed units with units from other member states) when they do not adequately investigate allegations of abuse (United Nations Security Council 2016). Under the current architecture of peacekeeping, the responsibility for enforcement ultimately rests with troop-contributing countries, but the commitments made by UN agencies signal a strong interest in eliminating the threat posed by its own peacekeepers, and the threat of repatriation presents states with a serious cost for noncompliance, given that troop-contributing countries have both material and reputational incentives to participate in the UN's peacekeeping functions.

Related to the issue of the neglect of victims and survivors of opportunistic sexual violence and the broader spectrum of violence and exploitation is the fact that the "weapon of war" frame excludes survivors and victims (whether they are combatants or noncombatants) who share characteristics of the perpetrators' identity. Even when the international community responds to a case of sexual violence as a weapon of war, it does not fully recognize the experiences of all individuals who are affected by sexual violence in that particular conflict. Discussing the retaliation against Serbian women in the Bosnian War, Askin (1997, 283–84) explains that the international community's failure to address sexual violence as vengeance committed against Serbian women stemmed from the fact that "they are the wives, sisters, and daughters of the aggressors. There is hardly a journalist who feels motivated to seek them out, to check up on what has happened to them and thus offer propaganda material to the Serbian side—that is, the 'bad' side, the side 'responsible for the war.'" Serbian women did not readily fit within the dominant narrative of systematic sexual violence in Bosnia-Herzegovina, so the sexual crimes perpetrated against them went unrecognized, even in the midst of the massive transnational mobilization around violence against women in the former Yugoslavia and the International Criminal Tribunal for the Former Yugoslavia's (ICTY's) mandate to address rape as a crime against humanity.

Doris Buss's analysis of the International Criminal Tribunal for Rwanda (ICTR) finds that a similar dynamic occurred in response to sexual violence in Rwanda; although Rwandan women were sexually violated before, during, and after the genocide for various political reasons, and in spite of complex social, familial, and marital ties that blurred the distinction between the Hutu and Tutsi ethnic identities, the narrative of rape in the Rwandan genocide focused on Hutu perpetrators and Tutsi victims and survivors and offered only a partial understanding of the scale and scope of sexual violence that occurred during the conflict. Buss (2009, 155) highlights the importance of simplicity, noting that "rape as a modality of violence is treated as relatively uniform in practice and experience. The emphasis is on shared patterns of violence (Tutsi women attacked by Hutu men) and continuity of impact (destruction of a community) rather than considering variances and exceptions." Much of the variation in experiences of sexual violence and exploitation in conflict results from the complexity of identity and the international community's tendency to simplify identities and groups to establish clear-cut images of perpetrators and victims. Weitsman (2015) contends that scholars must address the ways in which ethnic identity and gender roles interact in order to understand how war and genocide are planned and executed. Although the simplification of sexual violence to its use as a "weapon of war" helps to elicit stronger international responses to sexual violence during conflicts and in their aftermath, striving to analyze the complex relationship between identity (political, national, ethnic, or religious) and gender dynamics would enable the international community to establish more comprehensive mechanisms for responding to atrocities and providing aid that would encompass a broader range of victims and survivors.

Finally, the most vulnerable individuals affected by wartime sexual violence are those whose existence emanates from violence: children born of war rape, whether the crime was the result of an individual's opportunism or an armed group's systematic use of sexual violence. The "weapon of war" frame and the resulting international response to wartime sexual violence are squarely focused on ending impunity for perpetrators, helping survivors to heal both physically and psychologically, and—more broadly—facilitating reconstruction and reestablishing state and human security. The narrative of sexual violence as a weapon of war focuses on the perpetrator/combatant-victim/civilian dichotomy and ends with consideration of how sexual violence serves as a tool of violence and destruction. Efforts to address sexual violence have not sought to extend protection to the children born of forced impregnation, mass rape, or any of the other forms of strategic or opportunistic sexual violence; instead, these children fall through the proverbial cracks of local, national, and international humanitarian assistance and efforts to respond to wartime sexual violence. Carpenter (2007b) finds that little academic research or humanitarian work has been done to assess and respond to the needs of children born of war rape, despite the devotion of resources to initiatives focused on children in armed conflict and sexual violence against women, two categories to which "war babies" inherently belong. Forced impregnation and maternity are viewed as crimes against the rape survivor, the mother of the child; as Weitsman (2015) observes, the international community regards children born of rape as evidence of these crimes. These children, if carried to term, are frequently the victims of neglect; of exclusion from both the mother's and father's ethnic communities; and of infanticide, abuse, illegal adoption, and human trafficking. Although "war babies" suffer their own human rights violations as a result of the stigma attached to their births, the dominant frame for wartime sexual violence excludes these victims from consideration.

Evidence, Politics, and Neglected Conflict Cases

When exogenous advocates and decision makers perceive sexual violence to be opportunistic or when sexual violence is difficult to document convincingly as a widespread, systematic attack on civilians, the conflict fails to elicit a response from the international community. Perception of the systematic nature of sexual violence is also susceptible to political influence and to complications stemming from alliances, economic concerns, and power politics. If a state, a group of states, or an organization does respond to a conflict in which sexual violence does not resemble a weapon of war, that response is likely to be limited in scope and strength and may come months or years after initial reports of sexual violence. Highly publicized, salient conflicts—including those in the former Yugoslavia, Rwanda, and the Democratic Republic of the Congo (DRC)—brought more attention to the general issue of wartime sexual violence and provided the basis for the "weapon of war" frame, but these conflicts tended to eclipse other cases of wartime sexual violence, especially when those other conflicts involve sexual violence in different forms or on a smaller scale (whether this difference is the result of underreporting or difficulty of access to witnesses, merely perceived, or actual).

One illustrative example of the potential for variation in the international response is the nonresponse to sexual violence in Chechnya. Limited evidence of sexual violence in both the First Chechen War and Second Chechen War resembles strategic sexual violence, but the international community failed to respond to this case. Confirmation of sexual violence in the First Chechen War (1994–96) was difficult due to limited access to witnesses and civilians in Chechnya and also to those social and cultural stigmas linked to sexual violence that prevented survivors and victims' families from speaking openly about what had happened to them (Vandenberg and Askin 2001). The First Chechen War also coincided with the very early stages of transnational advocacy and international recognition of wartime sexual violence; the international community was grappling with thoroughly documented systematic sexual violence in the former Yugoslavia and Rwanda and the presence of a very vocal transnational network calling for a response to these two cases. The political discussion of sexual violence at the time—and in the years that followed—focused entirely on the atrocities committed during these two conflicts.

Despite the difficulty of documenting sexual violence during the First Chechen War, international human rights groups were able to compile accounts of sexual violence committed by Russian government forces during the Second Chechen War (August 1999–April 2009). Amnesty International reported on sexual violence throughout

2000—incidentally, its reporting coincided with the debates on UN Security Council Resolution 1325 on Women, Peace, and Security—and noted that there were indications that Russian government forces were using sex crimes as "instruments of torture, terror, and destruction" against men, women, and children (Vandenberg and Askin 2001, 142–43). States and IOs did not respond to sexual violence in Chechnya with any discernible strength.

The case of Chechnya demonstrates that several factors can influence variation in the international response to a given case of wartime sexual violence. First, lack of access to witness accounts (as in the First Chechen War) makes documenting sexual violence extremely difficult, and states and IOs will respond to a situation of wartime sexual violence only when the atrocities are credibly reported as systematic and were committed on a large scale. Second, highly publicized conflicts can overshadow other, concurrent or subsequent, cases of wartime sexual violence; this is especially true if the characteristics of the unrecognized conflict do not resemble those of the salient conflict.[7] Third, political influence is a factor that can shape the international community's perception of the nature of sexual violence. Russia was a party to the conflict in both Chechen wars and—just as important—its various government forces and agencies were the alleged perpetrators of sexual violence against Chechen men, women, and children. Russia's role in the conflict and its veto power at the UN Security Council certainly limited any possible action the UN might have taken. A frame is only as influential as the powerful actors that are willing to wield it. Thus the frame is more easily applied to the "other" state agencies or armed groups that commit sexual violence than to organizational comembers and world powers that do the same. In April 2000 a Chechen nurse was in the process of filing a case against Russian government forces with the European Court of Human Rights; at the same time, British prime minister Tony Blair was engaged in an unrelated diplomatic meeting with Russian president Vladimir Putin, suggesting that sexual violence in Chechnya either did not register on the international community's proverbial radar for sexual violence as a weapon of war or—if it did—strong states were unwilling to condemn another powerful state (Vandenberg and Askin 2001, 140).

Responses are still—more than a decade later—neither automatic nor guaranteed, and are contingent on a case's "fit" (or lack thereof) within the "weapon of war" frame and intervening political factors. More recently, the international community—including not only states and IOs but also, for a long time, nongovernmental organizations (NGOs)—has been similarly slow to respond to sexual violence in the wars in Libya and Syria. As chapter 4 discusses, the United Kingdom began to address sexual violence in Syria, and its involvement was investigative and heavily focused on providing concrete evidence of systematic sexual violence in order to assist with prosecution and postconflict justice mechanisms. Evidence and a clear causal chain are key. The landmark inclusion of sexual violence as a crime against humanity, and as an instrument of genocide in the statutes of the ICTY and ICTR, shaped not only the international legal responses to sexual violence but also the implementation of the anti–sexual violence agenda by states and IOs. For sexual violence to constitute a crime against humanity, the abuses must

> [be] committed as part of a widespread or a systematic attack against a civilian population. In general, to attribute responsibility to the state or political or military authorities, there would need to be proof that the crimes were ordered or condoned by the leaders, or that they were committed on such a largescale basis that the superior authorities knew or should have known of the crimes, and failed to take necessary and reasonable measures under the circumstances to prevent, halt, or punish the crimes. (Vandenberg and Askin 2001, 146)[8]

To consider sexual violence an act of genocide, there must first be proof that the conflict itself involves genocidal aims. Following from the international legal conception of crimes against humanity and genocide, international political efforts similarly seek evidence of a widespread, systematic attack against civilians. Absent documentation of systematic sexual violence deliberately used against civilians on a massive scale, states, IOs, and even NGOs are less likely to make material, institutional, or human commitments and may hesitate to condemn perpetrators and jeopardize political relationships until a conflict fits within the "weapon of war" frame.

The Unintended Consequences of the "Weapon of War" Frame

Despite the immense increase in rhetorical condemnation of wartime sexual violence, the commitment of funds and personnel to efforts addressing it, and the increased institutionalization of organizational and government efforts to respond to it, the impact of all these activities on the daily, lived experiences of victims and survivors is uncertain. States' and organizations' focus on ending impunity and calls for combatants to cease their attacks on civilians have not eradicated sexual violence.[9] Reports indicate that the prevalence of sexual violence in armed conflict is not decreasing. Highly publicized commitments by states and organizations send the message that sexual violence is a serious issue and that survivors must be given assistance and care; even if this does not have an immediate impact on potential perpetrators' decision-making processes, it shifts incentives for individuals and organizations. Although recognition is an unquestionable improvement over the historical silence and neglect surrounding survivors in the past, the perverse outcome is what some observers have deemed the "commodification" of sexual violence, such that it becomes a veritable industry. In addition to the incentive structures in both conflict and postconflict zones, there is little evidence of an internalized norm among states that they *must* prioritize sexual violence as an issue of peace and security.

With respect to the first point, there is an international consensus that sexual violence is an unacceptable tactic of war and that armed groups should exclude such attacks from their campaigns. The motivating logic holds that condemnation and improved mechanisms for monitoring, reporting, gathering evidence, and prosecuting perpetrators will decrease the incentives to commit sexual violence and increase the incentives to abstain from or proscribe it. However, as discussed in chapter 4, the short-term impact of politically condemning armed groups may be negligible. The unintended consequence of calls to end impunity, threats of prosecution after a war's end, UN Security Council resolutions expressing the urgency of the issue, and widespread media coverage of sexual violence may be that such attacks actually become more attractive to armed groups. We need only look to armed groups that widely publicize their use of sexual and gender-based violence in their operations to instill fear in the opposition or surrounding civilian populations. The prospect of enhanced notoriety is a net positive for some armed groups, and in such cases, the international political condemnation, institutional commitments, and legal mechanisms in place to prosecute perpetrators and end impunity are insufficient to raise the perceived costs of committing or tolerating sexual violence.[10] Furthermore, as discussed above, perpetrators of opportunistic violence and exploitation and those who commit intimate partner and family violence are largely excluded from the international political agenda.

Combating these injustices requires shifting norms and laws pertaining to gender equality and fully reversing the stigma away from survivors and onto perpetrators; such shifts require long-term investments in and commitment to changing societal structures (Hudson et al. 2012; Davies and True 2015).

At the other end of the spectrum, international condemnation of sexual violence creates financial incentives for humanitarian aid organizations to focus their efforts on programs related to sexual and gender-based violence and creates situations in crises and conflict zones where civilians face incentives to exaggerate the scope and severity of sexualized threats. Research on international aid programs, and specifically those operating in the DRC, has found that states' and donor organizations' public commitments to ending conflict-related sexual violence against women and girls translate into pressure for aid organizations to focus their efforts on specific forms of sexual violence and to reduce their focus on other forms of gender-based violence or violence more generally (Autesserre 2012; Eriksson Baaz and Stern 2013; Meger 2016). Because these aid organizations face pressure to increase their anti–sexual violence and survivor assistance programming, stories of victimization become valuable commodities for women in conflict and postconflict zones, an outcome of what Meger (2016) aptly dubs the "fetishization of sexual violence." This is not, of course, to say that civilian reports of rape and other forms of sexual violence should be discounted or ignored by aid organizations, the media, and states, but rather to highlight the fact that the increased focus on sexual violence as a security priority has changed the incentive structures in conflict zones and crisis situations in ways that states and organizations did not anticipate.

The second point begs a comparison with other security concerns that were previously tolerated by states but now represent so-called red lines: the use of chemical weapons and antipersonnel land mines. Sexual violence is a violation of international law—as established by the ICTY, the ICTR, the Rome Statute of the International Criminal Court (ICC), and the multilateral consensus that it constitutes a grave breach of the Geneva Conventions. The ICC and any future ad hoc tribunals created by the UN, regional organizations, and states have legal jurisdiction to prosecute perpetrators of sexual violence. However, no universal treaty unites signatory states in a shared responsibility to prevent or eradicate sexual violence. Still, UN member states are bound to follow through with any action items in Security Council resolutions on sexual violence and, more broadly, on the Women, Peace, and Security (WPS) agenda. States can pledge to make good on their commitments to WPS concerns through their respective national action plans and can voice their support or misgivings during the annual open debates on the WPS agenda and on the specific topic of conflict-related sexual violence. The Ottawa Treaty on antipersonnel land mines and the Chemical Weapons Convention both entered into force, in 1999 and 1997 respectively, as the world was grappling with systematic sexual violence in Europe and Africa.[11] The two treaties require signatories to alter their military tactics and tools because of the collective realization that indiscriminate weapons extend the devastation of war to civilians, often for many years after the end of active hostilities. The high-level political discussion of and commitments to address sexual violence as a weapon of war bear the same hallmarks as discussions of other weapons that defy the civilian immunity principle, but no such effort has been made to control its strategic use and opportunistic occurrence *directly*.[12] Even the strongest political and legal efforts discussed here carry repercussions for perpetrators only in the long term, if they are apprehended and if the investigative units have sufficient capacity. Although the international community has taken great strides to address sexual violence in war, especially in comparison with recognition and nonrecognition in the past, states and IOs have not yet reached the point where a normative taboo against sexual violence influences combatants' behavior or guarantees action by exogenous international actors.

Barriers to action increase when sexual violence does not clearly resemble a weapon of war, which is quite often. The centrality of the "weapon of war" frame leads to hesitation on the part of decision makers within states and IOs, who feel they may be justified in responding to a case of wartime sexual violence only once it is clear that this violence was used as a tactic of war in that conflict (an official of the US Agency for International Development, in a discussion with the author, Washington, September 2012; a legal expert, in a discussion with the author, New York, June 2012). Despite its simplicity, the "weapon of war" frame for sexual violence is difficult to apply to armed conflicts as they unfold, often with ambiguous or sparsely documented cases of sexual violence due to situational constraints and limited resources and capacity for monitoring and documentation. It is incredibly difficult to demonstrate a military strategy involving mass rape or strategic sexual violence in the course of active armed conflict, especially if humanitarian organizations or journalists have limited access to civilians, political prisoners, and other presumed victims. Aside from the implications for political action, the reliance on proof that sexual violence was used as a weapon creates a moral issue: a hierarchy of victims/survivors, which implies that some experiences are more traumatic, more threatening, and therefore more worthy of consideration than others. As chapter 1 noted, and as the epigraph at the start of this chapter indicates, international political efforts to respond to sexual violence in conflicts in Guinea, Colombia, Haiti, Mexico, Libya, Syria, and other states have been weak, slow to start, or altogether absent—especially when compared with the international political responses and material commitments to address and mitigate sexual violence in the former Yugoslavia, Rwanda, the DRC, and (to a lesser extent) Darfur (a British official, in a discussion with the author, Washington, April 2013). The difference stems from the highly publicized use of sexual violence as a weapon in the latter cases. The effect of the "weapon of war" frame on decision makers' ability or willingness to respond to cases of wartime sexual violence points to the two broad implications of the frame, which were discussed above: the prioritization of some groups and conflicts, and the exclusion of others.

Of course, states are generally loath to recognize sexual violence in conflicts to which they are parties, especially if the allegations are against state forces or suggest that the state has insufficient capacity to govern its population. As illustrated in chapters 2 through 4, states and IOs have worked to institutionalize mechanisms for responding to wartime sexual violence, findings that appear on the surface to run counter to interest-based expectations of state behavior. The international framework for monitoring and responding to wartime sexual violence—primarily embodied in Security Council Resolutions 1820, 1888, 1960, and 2106—institutionalizes the UN membership's response to sexual violence and creates a shaming mechanism that has the potential to clash with member states' interests. The debate during the 6,722nd meeting of the UN Security Council—in response to then–special representative to the secretary-general on sexual violence in armed conflict Margot Wallström's report on sexual violence in armed conflict, in compliance with Resolution 1960—demonstrates states' opposition to the report's naming and shaming of perpetrators (United Nations General Assembly 2012). Russia, Syria, Kenya, and Egypt, among other states, voiced opposition to what they considered the special representative's "overstepping" of her mandate through the inclusion of sexual violence in postconflict situations and situations of unrest; these states or their allies had been cited as perpetrators or sites of sexual violence in armed conflict (United Nations Security Council 2012b). It is through examples like this, as well as the discussion of strategic advocacy in the previous chapters, that the use of the "weapon of war" frame becomes more clearly linked to states' interests. The frame is successful because it does not overtly threaten most states' interests when condemnation and implementation of commitments stay within the frame's narrow scope.

Whether states will respond to sexual violence when doing so actively jeopardizes their national or foreign policy interests—as may be the case for the question of how the US military should respond to Afghan troops' sexual abuse of boys—remains a question; implementation of the response to sexual violence has dramatically improved in the past decade, but far from consistently and comprehensively. Still, efforts to institutionalize the anti–sexual violence agenda have created shaming mechanisms that are not universally popular, along with state policies and initiatives that have additional costs. Sexual violence in wartime is neither a red line nor a red herring. States condemn and respond to sexual violence outside the context of an adversarial relationship or the buildup to war. Although there is much room for improvement in the implementation of responses to and broader recognition of sexual violence, state and organizational responses have nonetheless been more than just bluster.

There are gaps and flaws in the discourse and commitments prompted and perpetuated by the "weapon of war" frame. The frame places political, institutional, and logistical constraints on both action and recognition. The critical take I present here and the observations made in the extant research, however, should not detract from the larger point: The "weapon of war" frame has provided advocates with a powerful tool that has enabled them to not only enter the arena of international security politics but also to expand the anti–sexual violence agenda over time to account for previously marginalized groups and conflicts. It is to this point that I now return.

What the "Weapon of War" Frame Offers Advocates

The "weapon of war" frame for sexual violence has been as influential as it has been because it streamlines the definition and scope of sexual violence for the purposes of generating (and maintaining) international political attention, condemnation, and action. Recall that advocates choose frames that will resonate with their intended audience. In 2007 and 2008, advocates' deliberate framing of sexual violence as a weapon in their efforts to convince UN Security Council members to prioritize the issue vividly illustrates why they choose specific frames for their appeals. For states and IOs to be able to respond to the broader spectrum of sexual violence in both wartime and postconflict situations, they would need to engage with broader issues of gender equality and human rights; some states are increasingly willing to do this, but many are not. Although NGOs and advocates routinely call for a more comprehensive international response to sexual violence, action in the high-level international political forums is currently limited to the one clearly defined area of wartime sexual violence—security issues—that resonates strongly with security-minded states and organizations as well as with international legal precedent.

Therefore, when advocates discuss sexual violence as a weapon, they situate it within the context of international security issues. As Letitia Anderson (2010, 247–48) argues, sexual violence is a threat to peace and security—and therefore a concern for organizations like the UN Security Council—when it "constitutes a *crime of international concern*, is *commanded/condoned, civilians are targeted*, a *climate of impunity* prevails, it has *cross-border implications* and/or it entails a *ceasefire violation*" (emphasis in the original). Each of these conditions is tied to armed conflict and the deliberate or widespread use of sexual attacks. The "weapon of war" frame does not completely close the door to future consideration of other forms of conflict-related sexual and gender-based violence; the frame provides a foundation from which advocates can work to broaden international awareness of conflict-related sexual violence in particular and gender-based violence in general by securing an audience with states and IOs that are concerned about the threats to security and stability posed by systematic sexual violence. Jody Williams—a Nobel Peace Prize winner (1997), cofounder of the Nobel Women's Initiative, and cochair of the International Campaign to Stop Rape & Gender Violence in Conflict—highlighted the importance of mobilizing action using the "weapon of war" frame, even when the goals are broader:

> [Addressing rape as a weapon] is an entry point into trying to address the larger continuum of violence against women. Since there is so much awareness because of the understanding of sexual violence

and rape as a tactic of war for destroying ethnic communities, feelings of manhood, etc., it would be illogical not to use that as an entry point. But I see it as a means to broaden the discussion: While the Campaign might use "rape as a weapon" as an entry point, we are working to end all rape and gender violence in conflict. The Campaign chose the word "conflict" specifically, rather than "war" or "armed conflict," because "conflict" encompasses situations much broader. (Jody Williams, in correspondence with the author, March 2013)

Activists are aware of the "weapon of war" frame's persuasive power and its capacity to facilitate relationships between advocates, states, and organizations. When persistent advocates, especially embedded advocates, wield the frame as a tool, the prospect of considering the broader spectrum of sexual violence remains a possibility.

In his speech launching the Preventing Sexual Violence Initiative (PSVI), British foreign secretary William Hague indicated such consideration by remarking on the link between the elimination of wartime sexual violence and women's broader political and economic empowerment: "[Tackling sexual violence] cannot be separated from wider issues of women's rights. We will not succeed in building sustainable peace in conflict areas unless we give the issue of sexual violence the centrality it deserves; alongside the economic and political empowerment of women and their vital role in peacebuilding" (Foreign and Commonwealth Office 2012a). Similarly, and in addition to its explicit recognition of LGBTQ individuals as targets of sexual violence, the UN secretary-general's 2015 report on conflict-related sexual violence observes that all situations cited in the report share one common issue: "that waves of conflict-related sexual violence take place against a backdrop of structural gender-based discrimination, including in formal and informal systems of law, and the exclusion of women from political life" (United Nations Security Council 2015a, 4). At the time of writing, the international response is, in practice, still firmly rooted in the "weapon of war" frame, but rhetorical recognition and discussion are expanding and, in some respects, are returning to their roots in the WPS agenda and the women's human rights movement.

Responding to sexual violence in the context of military tactics and/ or strategy, despite their conceptual limitations, gives states and IOs an identifiable atrocity to condemn without potentially implicating the exploitative, opportunistic behavior of civilians and of states' and IOs' own personnel in conflict, postconflict, and humanitarian operations. For advocates who simply want to keep conflict-related sexual violence on the agenda of strong states and organizations like the UN Security Council and to maintain pressure on these entities to make good on their commitments, this is a strategic advantage. Its narrow scope allows the frame to remain clear, conspicuous, and easily understandable—traits that have contributed to its diffusion among states and IOs.[13] Civil society advocates and NGOs often highlight the limitations of the dominant understanding of sexual violence while remaining optimistic about the possibility of a broader approach. In a discussion of the progress of implementation at the Security Council and among states, one advocate observed the following about recognition of different forms and perpetrators of sexual violence:

> In the last few years there has been a growing acceptance by Security Council and states that sexual violence is an issue that needs to be addressed and resources need to be dedicated to it. Sexual violence by peacekeepers hasn't had the support that sexual violence in conflict has; it's a politically fraught issue but we've seen instances of systematic abuse—for example, sexual abuse in the Central African Republic by French soldiers—and those instances have catapulted the issue to the forefront and forced the UN and member states to be more accountable. Up until now, there was acceptance that sexual violence by armed forces and nonstate actors needed to be tackled, and now there is more pressure to address sexual violence by peacekeepers. (the executive coordinator of the NGO Working Group on Women, Peace, and Security, in a discussion with the author, telephone, August 2015)

Advocates and NGOs recognize the limitations of the "weapon of war" frame, even as they also recognize its ability to compel state action. Using the frame to gain entrance into the conversation and put sexual violence on states' and organizations' agendas has allowed transnational civil society advocates to maintain pressure on these international actors over the long term to recognize other forms of sexual violence.

Advocates, States, and the UN Security Council

Before concluding, one question is worth revisiting: Why do advocates for human rights and gender issues target states and organizations like the UN Security Council in the first place? The uncomfortable alliance between feminist women's rights advocates and institutions dominated by state power politics is well documented in the literature.[14] The former work toward lasting peace and equality through broad social, structural, and normative change; the latter seek to alleviate security threats and secure peace through the means available to states (predominantly, though not exclusively, military means). The "weapon of war" frame for sexual violence works because it appeals to state-centric notions of threats (weapons) and instability (war) and sets aside the structural and normative nuances of gender inequality and factors related to identity that give rise to sexual violence in wartime and in peacetime. There is a legitimate concern, then, that the broader goals of women's human rights advocates—goals oriented toward gender equality, the empowerment of women and marginalized groups, and peace (not only in the sense of an absence of war but also in terms of daily, lived freedom from fear and want)—risk co-optation within international security organizations. Nevertheless, transnational advocates targeted the UN Security Council, the United States, and the United Kingdom (among other states and organizations), seeking to persuade these actors to put sexual violence on the international political (inter*state*) agenda as a security issue. The motivation for this engagement is the pursuit of an international political consensus on the gravity of conflict-related sexual violence and an effective normative taboo prohibiting its use.

As advocates quoted throughout this book have observed (especially as discussed in chapter 3), the mobilization in response to Bosnia and Rwanda placed sexual violence on the agenda of international courts and secured legal precedents for prosecution, and the next logical target was the UN and, specifically, the Security Council. Resolution 1325 (in 2000) addressed issues related to gender, gender-based violence, and peace and security broadly speaking, recognizing sexual violence as an element of war's impact on women and girls but focusing on women's empowerment and conflict prevention. In subsequent years, the secretary-general and advocacy groups spoke of sexual violence as a weapon or tactic; and as evidence from the DRC came to light, pressure on the Security Council increased, both from within council members' inner circles and from exogenous advocates. In essence, the effort to build and implement the anti–sexual violence agenda is one of consensus building across institutions. Advocates account for states' interests in their work, targeting specific states when opportunities for strategic alliances arise, knowing that they can maximize their influence through embedded advocates and sympathetic administrations. An example, described in chapter 3, is that women's rights groups appealed to Namibia to propose what became Resolution 1325 during the state's Security Council presidency, knowing that Namibia's leadership supported the cause of women's participation and gender mainstreaming in both peace and security matters. To recall what one of the advocates who described that process observed: "International lobbying is a give-and-take; it is not an all-or-nothing game" (the international coordinator of the Global Network of Women Peacebuilders, in a discussion with the author, Skype, February 2016). To influence the agenda, to build a consensus toward a norm, and to direct attention and resources to conflict-related sexual violence, advocates play the "game." In a world that is still governed by states, advocates need states and state-based institutions on their side.

Beyond the goal of building legitimacy and a consensus, state support for the anti–sexual violence agenda also stands to change the incentives within armed conflicts, given sufficient political will and institutional capacity. Once states internalize an anti–sexual violence norm—and have sufficient resources to follow through on their commitments—prevention and prosecution of sexualized violence committed by state security forces and nonstate armed groups will be done more effectively as the potential consequences shift from possible international condemnation to more concrete disincentives closer to home. As Security Council resolutions on the WPS agenda and the secretary-general's annual reports on conflict-related sexual violence routinely address the need for UN member states to engage more proactively with efforts to prevent and respond to sexual violence, an internalized norm is still a distant prospect. However, to make this prospect a reality that elicits the support of states is an important step, and the "weapon of war" frame has helped advocates with their efforts to achieve such a norm.

Notes

1. For a thorough consideration of how gender-based violence specifically affects men and boys, see Adam Jones (2010, 132).

2. For research on transactional sex in the Democratic Republic of the Congo (DRC), see Maclin et al. (2015). For a brief discussion of nonstate armed groups' motives for sexual violence in the DRC, see Kelly (2010). For further examination of opportunistic violence and the spectrum of sexual and

gender-based violence in wartime and peacetime, see Moon (1997), Goldstein (2001), Kronsell and Svedburg (2012), Hudson et al. (2012), and Boesten (2014).

3. For a public health approach to ascertaining the proportion of sexual violence committed by combatants relative to partners and family members, see Stark and Wessels (2012).

4. For research on sexual exploitation and peacekeeping operations, see Whitworth (2004), Allred (2006), and Higate (2007).

5. For access to statistics and more information on the Conduct and Discipline Unit's efforts to address SEA, see the Conduct and Discipline Unit's website, https://cdu.unlb.org/.

6. For more information on the February 2016 appointment of Jane Holl Lute as special coordinator, see UN News Centre (2016). It is important to note that SEA in the Central African Republic is not the first case of peacekeeper-perpetrated sexual exploitation; nor is it the first to emerge on the secretary-general's or Security Council's agenda. Personnel deployed on peace operations in Cambodia, the DRC, Bosnia-Herzegovina, Kosovo, and Timor Leste have also been implicated in SEA. WPS resolutions have referenced sexual abuse in peacekeeping operations directly and indirectly, calling for gender advisers and gender awareness training on missions. For further discussion of the UN's efforts to address the problem, see Crawford, Lebovic, and Macdonald (2015); and Karim and Beardsley (2016).

7. A similar situation arose concerning sexual violence in Kosovo; accounts of sexual violence in Kosovo frequently referenced the fact that perpetrators did not use rape camps, unlike the perpetrators of sexual violence in Bosnia-Herzegovina. At the time, the use of rape camps and forced impregnation signaled "systematic sexual violence," and demonstrating that other methods could be similarly systematic was a difficult endeavor; see Inal (2013, 182–83).

8. Also see Alona Hagay-Fey (2011, 97).

9. For an overview of a claim made by the *Human Security Report 2012* (Human Security Report Project 2012) that sexual violence is on the decline, see Nordås (2012).

10. On the unintended consequences of condemning sexual violence, see Autessere (2012); Crawford, Hoover Green, and Parkinson (2014); and Meger (2016). On the differences between strategic, ordered sexual violence, and sexual violence that commanders simply tolerate or condone, see Cohen, Hoover Green, and Wood (2013).

11. The Ottawa Treaty was signed on December 3, 1997, and became effective on March 1, 1999. The Chemical Weapons Convention was signed on January 13, 1993, and became effective on April 29, 1997.

12. Sexual violence is arguably a *discriminate* weapon when used against civilians, in the sense that its deliberate nature subverts the principle of distinction. When civilians are targeted, it is because of their legitimate expectation of a protected status; and it is this extreme violation of social norms and the laws of war that makes sexual violence an effective weapon when it is used as such. Unlike land mines and chemical weapons, which certainly pose grave threats to civilians, sexual violence is generally not used to attack an armed group physically. Rather, the direct target of sexual violence is the victim/survivor, whether the act is opportunistic or strategic. The impact on armed groups is symbolic and is linked to constructions of gender roles and responsibilities.

13. On the importance of conceptual clarity, see Kier and Mercer (1996).

14. See, especially, Tickner (1992), Otto (2009, 2010), Kronsell and Svedburg (2012), and Gizelis and Olsson (2015).

Conclusion

> To make a difference in the lives of women and girls and in international peace and security, this unprecedented momentum must be matched by drastically greater political and financial support from the most powerful decision makers, including all the countries that packed the Council's chamber yesterday.
>
> —*From the "Statement by UN Women on the Adoption of UN Security Council Resolution 2242"*

The international community cannot stand back and applaud its success in ending the problem of conflict-related sexual violence just yet, as there is much work that remains if the ultimate goal is to change the daily lives of real people—of all ages, genders, and identities—by assisting survivors and truly deterring would-be perpetrators. At the same time, we must also pause ever so briefly to reflect on the progress that advocates working both within and outside states and organizations have achieved in the last two decades. That sexual violence is a topic of academic discussion, that it receives press coverage, that humanitarian relief and human rights organizations work tirelessly to monitor abuses and treat survivors, and that heads of state recognize it as a problem are substantial achievements that represent a massive shift in recognition that has overturned a long history of silencing the problem. Accordingly, the "weapon of war" frame is a useful tool for advocates, even as its flaws, constraints, and gaps are apparent. As the preceding chapters detail, the "weapon of war" frame has led to state and multilateral efforts to emphasize the importance of and create and fund protection mechanisms for civilians—especially women and girls—in armed conflict. Paired with the concern for physical protection is the long-term goal, discussed in chapter 4, of ending impunity for perpetrators of sexual violence, and thus preventing its occurrence.

The central argument I have presented here is two-pronged: the "weapon of war" frame does, in fact, constrain efforts to implement the anti–sexual violence agenda by virtue of the situations, concepts, and people excluded from the dominant narrative; however, the frame allowed civil society and embedded advocates to gain unprecedented access to the agendas of states, the United Nations Security Council, and other international organizations, and this in turn has allowed advocates, over time, to incrementally expand the range of recognized individuals and forms of violence. Framing sexual violence as a weapon of war has enabled both advocates and policymakers to elicit meaningful political responses to a historically neglected problem in the relatively short span of two decades, and this is a phenomenon worthy of examination. As recognition of wartime sexual violence focused more exclusively and explicitly on sexual violence as a weapon of war, states and international organizations (IOs) began to commit financial resources, establish institutional mechanisms for monitoring and responding to wartime sexual violence in the long term, and devote human resources (rapporteurs, special representatives, gender advisers, and entire offices of staff) to addressing sexual violence in war. Still, as chapter 5 suggests, there are substantial gaps in the dominant narrative that have consequences for real human lives. And as the tables in each of the case study chapters illustrated, the international response to wartime sexual violence has not yet reached what I would consider "stage 5," or a level of reliable commitment that would signal the internalization of a normative taboo. Action from states, especially, but from IOs as well, still depends on the exertion of pressure from embedded and exogenous (civil society) advocates, many of whom in the latter category commonly cite a lack of political will to take the next steps in eradicating sexual violence by chipping away at the social norms and structural factors that contribute to gender inequality and make sexual and gender-based violence more prevalent. It is the central role of states—as both champions and impediments—in the international response to conflict-related sexual violence that makes the dynamics surrounding the "weapon of war" frame's use so compelling. Understanding why and when states initiate or support efforts to implement the anti–sexual violence agenda tells us more about the intersection of strategic interests and normative concerns and the role of individual decision makers who act as embedded advocates.

I present concluding thoughts in the following two sections. The first speaks to the point above: that the development and effectiveness of the "weapon of war" frame for sexual violence offers fruitful ground on which scholars from several camps within the academic discipline of international relations (IR) may engage with one another. The second section outlines unanswered questions and evolving issues.

The "Weapon of War" Frame and the Prospect of Dialogue

The "weapon of war" frame's impact speaks simultaneously to the strength of ideas and transnational advocacy in shaping states' behavior and to the influence of individuals within or linked to the state to serve, of their own volition and through their own moral imperatives, as interlocutors between civil society and the state. The frame's narrowness was not an accident but rather the result of strategic decisions concerning how best to present the issue to influential entities. Systematic sexual violence in Bosnia and Rwanda, shifting security priorities in the early 1990s and 2000s, and established international law regulating behavior in armed conflict made the "weapon of war" frame for sexual violence the ideal advocacy tool to foster states' support without compromising states' interests (or mandate, in the case of the UN Security Council as an institution). Speaking of sexual violence in terms of security was not a move to shift the discussion away from civil society advocates, although it did have the effect of distancing the anti–sexual violence agenda—in practice—from the broader Women, Peace, and Security (WPS) agenda and women's human rights agendas. Securitizing sexual violence has been a give-and-take process through which states have sought to focus on and commit resources to a limited set of deliberate wartime atrocities against specific populations, and civil society and embedded advocates have worked within those constraints and pushed to expand the range of persons and situations included in the anti–sexual violence agenda.

The "weapon of war" frame speaks to states' interests and (military) capabilities by focusing efforts on protection of civilians from harm. It works within the constraints of organizations like the Security Council, and the UN more broadly, which must reconcile new concerns with organizational mandates and the diverse and often conflicting views and priorities of member states. The "weapon of war" frame does not bear all the hallmarks of the feminist advocacy that brought about international legal condemnation of sexual violence and established the WPS agenda in the first place; but it does provide space in the agendas of states and organizations for such concerns to be voiced, given advocates' persistence and the presence of an allied embedded advocate. Over time, advocacy efforts have pushed states, organizations, and the public discourse on sexual violence toward something resembling a normative taboo, albeit with uneven impact on states' long-term political will and the daily realities of war and postconflict instability.

Taking this long-term normative negotiation process into account, implementation of the anti–sexual violence agenda has implications for the study of IR, particularly for international security studies scholars and constructivist scholars who focus on transnational advocacy networks and the development of new norms. Much (but certainly not all) of the IR research on sexual violence before, during, and after war to date speaks to or from feminist security studies in some degree, as explorations of the causes and implications of and responses to sexual and gender-based violence are natural questions for feminist scholars. By focusing on states, why transnational advocacy networks and individual advocates target states, when sexual and gender-based violence becomes a state and international security concern, and what effects this concern has on states' and organizations' agendas, I have endeavored to demonstrate that there are opportunities for rich and important dialogue across research areas.

When sexual violence is used as a weapon of war, or when states view it as such, then it is an issue that IR scholars must engage in order to gain a full understanding of how modern warfare is designed and fought, how civilians are victimized in war, the long-term security and peacebuilding implications of sexual violence, and the role of gender dynamics in war. As the previous chapters have discussed, sexual violence in war is not a new phenomenon. In one sense, it is perhaps the most conventional of weapons, with roots that can be traced back to the earliest documented battles. Yet, sexual violence has only gained recognition as a systematic, deliberate weapon or tactic of war and a matter of concern for states and international organizations during the past two decades. Only since the mid-2000s, especially with the adoption of UN Security Council Resolution 1820 in 2008, has sexual violence gained explicit recognition as a stand-alone security issue relevant to states and international politics. Feminist scholars have raised awareness of systematic sexual violence and its links to political economy, gender norms, and militarism since the mid-1990s, and more extensive recognition of and scrutiny using the concepts most at home within mainstream international security studies and constructivist IR, more broadly, would also yield important insights on the impact of wartime sexual violence on long-term security-building and reconstruction efforts as well as purely humanitarian and normative concerns. (See, especially, Enloe 1990, Whitworth 2004, Leatherman 2011, and Heineman 2011.)

Strategic sexual violence is far from incompatible with traditional understandings of security, violence, and warfare in IR. The prospect of its use as a weapon presents a threat to state security and the monopoly over the use of force; unfortunately, sexual violence is a cheap, relatively easily deployed, and highly destructive tactic that can be used within and across state borders to incite terror, mass displacement, and demoralization. As the nature of armed conflict has shifted, such that intrastate and asymmetric wars are the norm rather than the exception, establishing an understanding of the military tactics used against both combatants and civilians is vital for crafting sound scholarship and policy. K. R. Carter (2010, 346) notes that sexual violence "as a weapon of war may increasingly figure into postmodern warfare, as neither employs the clear frontlines or the clear combatant/civilian lines characteristic of traditional war." As states and the UN Security Council turn their focus to combating/countering violent extremism and international terrorism, extremist groups' use of sexual slavery, rape, and gender-based violence as tactics of intimidation has become a frequent point of emphasis, as embodied in Security Council Resolution 2242 and in studies and debates within the UN and state agencies (Couture 2014; United Nations Security Council 2015c; Crawford 2015). The issues of which forms of sexual and gender-based violence "count" as existential threats from the perspectives of states and international organizations, and when these issues become matters of security, are related questions of interest to scholars focused on securitization.

From the perspective of constructivist approaches to IR scholarship, studies of sexual violence can speak to questions of just war theory and "justice, shame, responsibility and reconciliation in, and after, war" (Carter 2010, 365). The question of when and why states and IOs condemn sexual violence, especially explorations of variation in condemnation and the caricature of perpetrators as barbaric states, is a fitting avenue for further research on shifting norms, taboos, and values in IR. Such questions include the nature and legacies of the states and IOs at the center of international efforts to condemn sexual violence, including those I have discussed here. Writing about the Preventing Sexual Violence Initiative, Boesten (2015, 3) makes the observation that observers ought to pause at the realization that the Global Summit was "spearheaded by countries that sustain massive military industrial complexes and who regularly engage in postcolonial wars," a point that resonates with Leatherman's (2011), Eriksson Baaz and Stern's (2013), and Meger's (2016) observations about the dynamics inherent in perpetrators' incentives to commit sexual violence and states' and aid organizations' modes of responding to sexual violence. To what extent do states' efforts to condemn and mitigate sexual violence reflect their economic and security concerns or their complicity in armed conflict, the international arms trade, or exploitative economies? As states and international organizations continue to commit themselves and their resources to mitigating conflict-related sexual violence, these relationships merit continued research.

For IR scholars to pursue questions related to conflict-related sexual violence fully, the field needs to permit further exploration of gender dynamics in both peacetime and wartime. To understand and explain the circumstances under which sexual violence gains the destructive power necessary to be useful as a weapon or through which perpetrators of opportunistic and intimate partner or family violence come to operate with impunity, scholars must acknowledge varying understandings and realities of gender and gendered disparities in social dynamics and agency. Scholars (as well as advocates and policymakers) need to pay more attention to gender in order to explain more fully and accurately *how* sexual violence—in all its forms—becomes so prevalent, lest we risk perpetuating dangerous perceptions of gender roles. In her discussion of genocide in Bosnia, and in speaking to the discourse on sexual violence as a weapon, Weitsman (2015) cautions against the blanket acceptance of the use of forced impregnation as a method of genocide, arguing that to accept the idea that children born of war rape inherit only the father's identity and bring shame to the mother and her ethnic community (the rationale for forced impregnation and maternity as a method of ethnic cleansing) is to accept and propagate the perpetrators' beliefs about identity and gender. We might instead discuss forced pregnancy as sexual violence, without reinforcing the genocidal component. Sexual violence in conflict and instability reflects societal "issues of power asymmetry, patriarchy, masculinity, and the devaluation of women that are pervasive even in settings not affected by armed conflict" (Stark and Wessells 2012, 677). Although sexual violence as a weapon of war resonates with traditional understandings of security and warfare in IR, research must also acknowledge the gender dynamics that underpin the decision to deploy sexual violence as a weapon, or to tolerate its opportunistic occurrence, in the first place.

Avenues for Further Research and Action

One of the most exciting yet bewildering aspects of studying a contemporary phenomenon is that it constantly changes over the course of researching and writing a book. The world does not pause for an author to write up her findings. As a result, I have come away with many unanswered questions, some that must be left for future reflection as policies and initiatives evolve, and some that speak to complementary areas of research and practice. By way of a conclusion, I now turn to these reflections.

The "weapon of war" frame's implications raise several questions that promise avenues for fruitful research in what is already a dynamic academic research agenda. Variation in the response to conflicts involving different methods and varying scales of sexual violence certainly merits further research. The international response to wartime sexual violence is still a relatively new political phenomenon, and the "weapon of war" frame focuses international attention on a specific subset of conflicts: those in which advocates and policymakers perceive that sexual violence has the characteristics of a systematic weapon or tactic of war. I have focused on the longitudinal implementation of the anti–sexual violence agenda over time, but an important question arises from this research: What is the threshold beyond which a case of wartime sexual violence generates an international response, whether this response is media coverage or political condemnation, commitment of states' or organizations' resources, or some form of humanitarian intervention? From this central question, others emerge. Must there be a minimum number of documented attacks or victims/survivors? Must states and IOs wait for evidence of sexual violence as an official military policy before they can respond? Is the use of sexual violence as a weapon against a very small but politically significant group considered as egregious as the widespread strategic rape of civilians?

Related to the study of variation in the response, future research on the international anti–sexual violence agenda may be able to ascertain whether an internalized norm condemning wartime sexual violence will someday exist or whether sexual violence is a unique security concern that will always require the persistent dedication of advocates. Additional study of the victims and survivors who are included in or excluded from the "weapon of war" frame also merits further study. Will the agenda continue to expand? If so, is this expansion principally the work of civil society advocates or embedded advocates, or partnerships between them? In addition, although scholarship has highlighted the groups that are commonly excluded from international efforts to address sexual violence, a better understanding of how and why humanitarian aid agencies, states, and international organizations prioritize certain groups of victims/survivors over others would have important implications for normative IR research, especially for an understanding of the civilian immunity principle and humanitarian intervention efforts.

The final set of remaining questions has both academic and policy relevance, especially as the international community works to strengthen its response to wartime sexual violence in certain conflicts and in general. What does the securitization of sexual violence, its discussion in the language of weapons, mean for those who are affected by it? How does international attention affect the capacity and capability of local law enforcement, judicial processes, and medical services to assist survivors and mitigate sexual violence? Research grounded in ethical and responsible dialogue with first responders, humanitarian relief workers, and other agents with firsthand knowledge of how international laws and policies translate to action and results (or a lack thereof) on the ground will shed light on these questions and point advocates, decision makers, and academics toward best practices. One such example is the policy-relevant research undertaken by a group of researchers affiliated with the Human Rights Center at the School of Law of the University of California, Berkeley, where Kim Thuy Seelinger, Julie Freccero, and their colleagues find that specialized units devoted to the investigation and prosecution of sexual and gender-based violence and international crimes promise greater national-level accountability in areas of conflict and political instability but that there is a need for improved resources to overcome daily structural and social challenges and for better coordination among such units (Seelinger and Freccero 2015). On the other side of the coin, what is the impact of international condemnation of wartime sexual violence on combatants' decisions to use it strategically? Despite improvements in international recognition of wartime sexual violence, rape and other sexual atrocities continue to be destructive weapons and common outgrowths of conflict-related instability. Sexual violence is an attractive weapon; it is cheap, easily mobilized, and highly destructive. If combatants seek notoriety, then growing international condemnation of sexual violence may paradoxically improve the weapon's appeal and increase the payoffs associated with its widespread use.

Ethically conducted research on the impact of international condemnation on perpetrators' motivations and rationale for using sexual violence against civilians will promote better understanding of the potential consequences of international criticism, policies, and actions. If states and international organizations are truly committed to understanding conflict-related sexual violence and how best to mitigate it, adequate funding for research must be a priority, in addition to service delivery.

The international community has come a long way from the historical silence surrounding sexual atrocities in war. The fact that the UN Security Council's members, government officials, and participants in public symposia and summits openly discuss and decry the use of sexual violence as a weapon against civilians demonstrates that the issue has gained significant traction in policy circles since its introduction as an international concern in the mid-1990s. But the fact that states and IOs commit funds, personnel, and institutional efforts to recognizing, mitigating, and preventing sexual violence in war is a far greater achievement. Nevertheless, much work remains, both to develop a more comprehensive and internalized international taboo surrounding conflict-related sexual violence and to pursue academic research on the issue, especially within the IR field. Scholars and practitioners alike have far more to do to right the wrongs done by sexual violence and its historical invisibility; but, given the advances in both spheres, there are reasons to be optimistic.

Epigraph

Quotation from the "Statement by UN Women on the Adoption of Security Council Resolution 2242 on Women, Peace and Security" (UN Women 2015).

References

Alison, Miranda. 2007. "Wartime Sexual Violence: Women's Human Rights and Questions of Masculinity." *Review of International Studies* 33, no. 1: 75–90.

Allan, Alice. 2012. "What Can William Hague Do to Prevent Sexual Violence in Conflict?" *The Guardian*, April 10. www.theguardian.com/global -development/poverty-matters/2013/apr/10/william-hague-sexual-violence -conflict.

Allred, Keith J. 2006. "Peacekeepers and Prostitutes: How Deployed Forces Fuel the Demand for Trafficked Women and New Hope for Stopping It." *Armed Forces and Society* 33, no. 5: 5–23.

Amnesty International. 2012. "DR Congo Must Investigate Assassination Attempt on Activist Dr. Denis Mukwege." October 26. www.amnesty.org /en/latest/news/2012/10/dr-congo/.

———. 2013. "G8 Commitment to Tackle Impunity for Rape in Conflict Welcomed by Human Rights Groups." April 12. Accessed April 20, 2016. www.amnesty.org.uk/press-releases/g8-commitment-tackle-impunity-rape -conflict-welcomed-human-rights-groups.

Amowitz, Lynn L., Chen Reis, Kristina Hare Lyons, Beth Vann, Binta Mansaray, Adyinka M. Akinsulure-Smith, Louise Taylor, and Vincent Iacopino. 2002. "Prevalance of War-Related Sexual Violence and Other Human Rights Abuses among Internally Displaced Persons in Sierra Leone." *Journal of the American Medical Association* 287, no. 4: 513–21.

Anderlini, Sanam. 2012. "Preventing Sexual Violence during War and Conflict: It's Time to 'Just Do It.'" *Global Gender Current*, November 20. http:// globalgendercurrent.com/2012/11/preventing-sexual-violence-during-war -and-conflict-its-time -to-just-do-it/.

Anderson, Letitia. 2010. "Politics by Other Means: When Does Sexual Violence Threaten International Peace and Security?" *International Peacekeeping* 17, no. 2: 244–60.

Arieff, Alexis. 2010a. "Sexual Violence in African Conflicts." Congressional Research Service, Washington, DC, June 10.

———. 2010b. "Sexual Violence in African Conflicts." Congressional Research Service, Washington, DC, November 30.

———. 2011. "Sexual Violence in African Conflicts." Congressional Research Service, Washington, DC, February 23.

———. 2014. "Democratic Republic of Congo: Background and US Policy." Congressional Research Service, Washington, DC, February 24.

Arieff, Alexis, and Thomas Coen. 2013. "Democratic Republic of Congo: Background and US Policy." Congressional Research Service, Washington, DC, July 29.

Askin, Kelly Dawn. 1997. *War Crimes against Women*. Cambridge, MA: Martinus Nijhoff.

Austin, J. L. 1962. *How to Do Things with Words*. Cambridge, MA: Harvard University Press.

Autesserre, Séverine. 2010. *The Trouble with the Congo: Local Violence and the Failure of International Peacebuilding*. New York: Cambridge University Press.

———. 2012. "Dangerous Tales: Dominant Narratives on the Congo and Their Unintended Consequences." *African Affairs* 111, no. 443: 202–22.

———. 2014. *Peaceland: Conflict Resolution and the Everyday Politics of International Intervention*. New York: Cambridge University Press.

Ayotte, Kevin J., and Mary E. Husain. 2005. "Securing Afghan Women: Neocolonialism, Epistemic Violence, and the Rhetoric of the Veil." *NWSA Journal* 17, no. 3: 112–33.

Balzacq, Thierry. 2005. "The Three Faces of Securitization: Political Agency, Audience and Context." *European Journal of International Relations* 11, no. 2: 171–201.

Barnett, Michael. 1999. "Culture, Strategy and Foreign Policy Change: Israel's Road to Oslo." *European Journal of International Relations* 5, no. 1: 5–36.

Bellamy, Alex J. 2009. *Responsibility to Protect*. Malden, MA: Polity Press.

Ben-Porath, Eran. 2007. "Rhetoric of Atrocities: The Place of Horrific Human Rights Abuses in Presidential Persuasion." *Presidential Studies Quarterly* 37, no. 2: 181–202.

Bob, Clifford. 2005. *The Marketing of Rebellion: Insurgents, Media, and International Activism*. New York: Cambridge University Press.

———, ed. 2009. *The International Struggle for New Human Rights*. Philadelphia: University of Pennsylvania Press.

Boesten, Jelke. 2010. "Analyzing Rape Regimes at the Interface of War and Peace in Peru." *International Journal of Transitional Justice* 4, no. 1: 110–29.

———. 2014. *Sexual Violence during War and Peace*. New York: Palgrave Macmillan.

———. 2015. *On Ending Sexual Violence, or Civilising War*. International Development Institute Working Paper 2015-2. London: King's International Development Institute.

Brownmiller, Susan. 1975. *Against Our Will*. New York: Simon & Schuster.

Buss, Doris E. 2009. "Rethinking 'Rape as a Weapon of War.'" *Feminist Legal Studies* 17: 145–63.

Buzan, Barry. 1983. *People, States & Fear: The National Security Problem in International Relations*. Chapel Hill: University of North Carolina Press.

Buzan, Barry, Ole Wæver, and Jaap de Wilde. 1998. *Security: A New Framework for Analysis*. Boulder, CO: Lynne Rienner.

Carpenter, R. Charli. 2005. "'Women, Children and Other Vulnerable Groups': Gender, Strategic Frames and Protection of Civilians as a Transnational Issue." *International Studies Quarterly* 49, no. 2: 295–334.

————. 2007a. "Setting the Advocacy Agenda: Theorizing Issue Emergence and Nonemergence in Transnational Advocacy Networks." *International Studies Quarterly* 51, no. 1: 99–120.

————, ed. 2007b. *Born of War: Sexual Violence, Children's Human Rights, and the Global Community.* Bloomfield, CT: Kumarian Press.

————. 2011. "Vetting the Advocacy Agenda: Network Centrality and the Paradox of Weapons Norms." *International Organization* 65, no. 1: 69–102.

Carter, K. R. 2010. "Should International Relations Consider Rape a Weapon of War?" *Politics & Gender* 6, no. 3: 343–71.

Cassimatis, Anthony. 2007. "International Humanitarian Law, International Human Rights Law, and Fragmentation of International Law." *International and Comparative Law Quarterly* 56, no. 3: 623–39.

Cohen, Dara Kay. 2013. "Explaining Rape during Civil War: Cross-National Evidence (1980–2009)." *American Political Science Review* 107, no. 3: 461–77.

Cohen, Dara Kay, Amelia Hoover Green, and Elisabeth Jean Wood. 2013. *Wartime Sexual Violence: Misconceptions, Implications, and Ways Forward.* Special Report, Washington, DC: US Insitute of Peace.

Cohen, Dara Kay, and Ragnhild Nordås. 2014. "Sexual Violence in Armed Conflict: Introducing the SVAC Dataset, 1989–2009." *Journal of Peace Research* 51, no. 3: 418–28.

————. 2015. "Do States Delegate Shameful Violence to Militias? Patterns of Sexual Violence in Recent Armed Conflicts." *Journal of Conflict Resolution* 59, no. 5: 877–98.

Cohen, Roberta. 2000. "'What's So Terrible about Rape?' and Other Attitudes at the United Nations." *SAIS Review* 20, no. 2: 73–77.

Cohn, Carol, Helen Kinsella, and Sheri Gibbings. 2004. "Women, Peace and Security Resolution 1325." *International Feminist Journal of Politics* 6, no. 1: 130–40.

Cook, Sam. 2009. "Security Council Resolution 1820: On Militarism, Flashlights, Raincoats, and Rooms with Doors—A Political Perspective on Where It Came From and What It Adds." *Emory International Law Review* 23: 125–39.

Copelon, Rhonda. 2011. "Toward Accountability for Violence against Women in War: Progress and Challenges." In *Sexual Violence in Conflict Zones: From the Ancient World to the Era of Human Rights*, edited by Elizabeth D. Heineman. Philadelphia: University of Pennsylvania Press.

Couture, Krista London. 2014. "A Gendered Approach to Countering Violent Extremism: Lessons Learned from Women in Peacebuilding and Conflict Prevention Applied Successful in Bangladesh and Morocco." Brookings Institution, Washington, DC, July.

Crawford, Kerry, ed. 2015. *Conflict and Extremist-Related Sexual Violence: An International Security Threat.* PeaceBrief 187. Washington, DC: US Institute of Peace Press.

Crawford, Kerry, Amelia Hoover Green, and Sarah Parkinson. 2014. Wartime Sexual Violence Is Not Just a "Weapon of War." *Washington Post* blog,

September 24. www.washingtonpost.com/blogs/monkey-cage/wp/2014 /09/24/wartime-sexual-violence-is-not-just-a-weapon-of-war/.

Crawford, Kerry, James Lebovic, and Julia Macdonald. 2015. "Explaining the Variation in Gender Composition of Personnel Contributions to UN Peacekeeping Operations." *Armed Forces & Society* 41, no. 2: 257–81.

Davies, Sara E., and Jacqui True. 2015. "Reframing Conflict-Related Sexual and Gender-Based Violence: Bringing Gender Analysis Back In." *Security Dialogue* 46, no. 6: 495–512.

Donnelly, Faye. 2013. *Securitization and the Iraq War: The Rules of Engagement in World Politics*. New York: Routledge.

Doswald-Beck, Louise, and Sylvain Vité. 1993. "International Humanitarian Law and Human Rights Law." *International Review of the Red Cross* 33, no. 293: 94–119.

Doty, Roxanne Lynn. 1997. *Imperial Encounters*. Minneapolis: University of Minnesota Press.

Ellis, Mark. 2007. "Breaking the Silence: Rape as an International Crime." *Case Western Reserve Journal of International Law* 38, no. 2: 225–47.

Enloe, Cynthia. 1990. *Bananas, Beaches, and Bases: Making Feminist Sense of International Politics*. Berkeley: University of California Press.

———. 2010. *Nimo's War, Emma's War*. Berkeley: University of California Press.

Eriksson Baaz, Maria, and Maria Stern. 2013. *Sexual Violence as a Weapon of War? Perceptions, Prescriptions, and Problems in the Congo and Beyond*. New York: Zed Books.

Farr, Kathryn. 2009. "Extreme War Rape in Today's Civil-War-Torn States: A Contextual and Comparative Analysis." *Gender Issues* 26, no. 1: 1–41.

Finnemore, Martha. 1996. *National Interests in International Society*. Ithaca, NY: Cornell University Press.

Finnemore, Martha, and Kathryn Sikkink. 1998. "International Norm Dynamics and Political Change." *International Organization* 52, no. 4: 887–917.

Foreign and Commonwealth Office, United Kingdom. 2012a. "Foreign Secretary Launches New Government Initiative to Prevent Sexual Violence in Conflict." May 29. www.gov.uk/government/speeches/foreign-secretary-launches-new -government-initiative-to-prevent-sexual-violence-in-conflict.

———. 2012b. "International Meeting on Support to the Syrian Opposition." November 16. www.gov.uk/government/news/international-meeting-on -support-to-the-syrian-opposition.

———. 2012c. "Wilton Park Conference on Preventing Sexual Violence in Conflict and Post-Conflict Situations." November 14. www.gov.uk /government/news/wilton-park-conference-on-preventing-sexual-violence -in-conflict-and-post-conflict-situations.

———. 2013a. "Declaration on Preventing Sexual Violence in Conflict." April 11. www.gov.uk/government/publications/g8-declaration-on-preventing -sexual-violence-in-conflict.

———. 2013b. "Foreign Secretary Marks First Anniversary of the Preventing Sexual Violence Initiative." May 29. http://blogs.fco.gov.uk/williamhague/2013/05/29/foreign-secretary-marks-first-anniversary-of-the-preventing-sexual-violence-initiative/.

———. 2013c. "G8 Declaration on Preventing Sexual Violence in Conflict." April 11. www.gov.uk/government/news/g8-declaration-on-preventing-sexual-violence-in-conflict.

———. 2013d. "Human Rights and Democracy: The 2012 Foreign and Commonwealth Office Report." April.

———. 2014a. "International Protocol on the Documentation and Investigation of Sexual Violence in Conflict: Basic Standards of Best Practice on the Documentation of Sexual Violence as a Crime under International Law." June.

———. 2014b. "London Ministerial on Security in Nigeria: Communiqué." June 12. www.gov.uk/government/publications/london-ministerial-on-security-in-nigeria-communique.

———. 2014c. "Summit Report: The Global Summit to End Sexual Violence in Conflict." www.gov.uk/government/publications/summit-report-the-global-summit-to-end-sexual-violence-in-conflict-june-2014.

———. 2014d. "UK National Action Plan on Women, Peace and Security 2014–2017: Country-Level Implementation Plan." December.

———. 2014e. "UK Response to Reports of Sexual Violence in the Syrian Conflict." April 10. www.gov.uk/government/case-studies/uk-response-to-reports-of-sexual-violence-in-the-syrian-conflict.

———. 2014f. "United Kingdom National Action Plan on Women, Peace & Security." June.

———. 2016. "Baroness Anelay Welcomes House of Lords Report on Sexual Violence in Conflict." April 12. www.gov.uk/government/news/baroness-anelay-welcomes-house-of-lords-report-on-sexual-violence-in-conflict.

Geneva Convention. 1949. "Geneva Convention (IV) Relative to the Protection of Civilian Persons in Time of War." August 12.

George, Alexander L., and Andrew Bennett. 2005. *Case Studies and Theory Development in the Social Sciences.* Cambridge, MA: Belfer Center for Science and International Affairs.

Gettleman, Jeffrey. 2007. "Rape Epidemic Raises Trauma of Congo War." *New York Times,* October 7.

———. 2009. "Symbol of Unhealed Congo: Male Rape Victims." *New York Times,* August 4.

Gizelis, Theodora-Ismene, and Louise Olsson, eds. 2015. *Gender, Peace and Security: Implementing UN Security Council Resolution 1325.* New York: Routledge.

Goetz, Anne-Marie, and Letitia Anderson. 2008. "Report on the Wilton Park Conference: Women Target or Affected by Armed Conflict—What Role for Military Peacekeepers?" S/2008/404. June.

Goldstein, Joseph. 2015. "US Soldiers Told to Ignore Sexual Abuse of Boys by Afghan Allies." *New York Times*, September 20.

Goldstein, Joshua. 2001. *War and Gender: How Gender Shapes the War System and Vice Versa*. New York: Cambridge University Press.

Hagay-Fey, Alona. 2011. *Sex and Gender Crimes in the New International Law: Past, Present, Future*. Boston: Martinus Nijhoff.

Hague, William. 2010. "Human Rights Are Key to Our Foreign Policy." *The Telegraph*, August 31.

————. 2012a. "Preventing Sexual Violence in Conflict." *Huffington Post UK*, May 30. www.huffingtonpost.co.uk/william-hague/preventing-sexual -violence-in-conflict-_b_1554928.html.

————. 2012b. "UK Announces Support for Victims of Sexual Violence in Conflict." UN Multimedia, September 25. /uk-announces-support-for-victims-of-sexual-violence-in-conflict/.

————. 2013a. "Historic G8 Agreement to Tackle Rape in War Zones." *Evening Standard*, April 11.

————. 2013b. "Sexual Violence in War Is Our Generation's Slave Trade." *Huffington Post*. January 28. www.huffingtonpost.com/william-hague/sexual -violence-in-war-is_b_2551284.html.

Hansen, Lene. 2000a. "Gender, Nation, Rape: Bosnia and the Construction of Security." *International Feminist Journal of Politics* 3, no. 1: 55–75.

————. 2000b. "The Little Mermaid's Silent Security Dilemma and the Absence of Gender in the Copenhagen School." *Millennium: Journal of International Studies* 29, no. 2: 285–306.

Harrington, Carol. 2010. *Politicization of Sexual Violence: From Abolitionism to Peacekeeping*. Burlington, VT: Ashgate.

Hartigan, Richard Shelly. 1967. "Noncombatant Immunity: Reflections on Its Origins and Present Status." *Review of Politics* 29, no. 2: 204–20.

Heck, Axel, and Gabi Schlag. 2012. "Securitizing Images: The Female Body and the War in Afghanistan." *European Journal of International Relations* 19, no. 4: 891–913.

Heineman, Elizabeth D. 2008. "The History of Sexual Violence in Conflict Zones." *Radical History Review* 101: 5–21.

————. ed. 2011. *Sexual Violence in Conflict Zones: From the Ancient World to the Era of Human Rights*. Philadelphia: University of Pennsylvania Press.

Henry, Nicola. 2011. *War and Rape: Law, Memory, and Justice*. New York: Routledge.

Higate, Paul. 2007. "Peacekeepers, Masculinities, and Sexual Exploitation." *Men and Masculinities* 10, no. 1: 99–119.

Hirsch, Michele Lent. 2012. "Women Under Siege: Bosnia." www.womenunder siegeproject.org/conflicts/profile/bosnia.

Hirschauer, Sabine. 2014. *The Securitization of Rape: Women, War and Sexual Violence*. New York: Palgave Macmillan.

Hirschkind, Charles, and Saba Mahmood. 2002. "Feminism, the Taliban, and Politics of Counter-Insurgency." *Anthropological Quarterly* 75, no. 2: 339–54.

Hoover Green, Amelia. 2011. "Repertoires of Violence against Non-Combatants: The Role of Armed Group Institutions and Ideologies." Doctoral dissertation, Yale University.

———. 2014. "Ignoring the Evidence at the End Sexual Violence in Conflict Summit." Women Under Siege Project, June 17. www.womenundersiege project.org/blog/entry/ignoring-the-evidence-at-the-global-summit-to-end -sexual-violence-in-confli.

HRW (Human Rights Watch). 1996. *Shattered Lives: Sexual Violence during the Rwandan Genocide and its Aftermath.* New York: HRW.

———. 2002. *The War within the War: Sexual Violence against Women and Girls in Eastern Congo.* New York: HRW.

———. 2008a. "Congolese Women Appeal to the UN Security Council to Help End Sexual Violence." June 12.

———. 2008b. "UN: Finally, a Step toward Confronting Rape in War." June 18.

———. 2009. *Soldiers Who Rape, Commanders Who Condone: Sexual Violence and Military Reform in the Democratic Republic of Congo.* New York: HRW.

———. 2014. "Democratic Republic of Congo: Ending Impunity for Sexual Violence." June 10. www.hrw.org/news/2014/06/10/democratic-republic -congo-ending-impunity-sexual-violence.

Hudson, Natalie Florea. 2010. *Gender, Human Security and the United Nations: Security Language as a Political Framework for Women.* New York: Routledge.

Hudson, Valerie M., Bonnie Ballif-Spanvill, Mary Caprioli, and Chad F. Emmett. 2012. *Sex and World Peace.* New York: Columbia University Press.

Hultman, Lisa. 2012. "UN Peace Operations and Protection of Civilians: Cheap Talk or Norm Implementation?" *Journal of Peace Research* 50, no. 1: 59–73.

Human Security Report Project. 2012. *Human Security Report 2012: Sexual Violence, Education, and War—Beyond the Mainstream Narrative.* Burnaby, BC: Simon Fraser University. http://hsrgroup.org/docs/Publications/HSR2012 /2012HumanSecurityReport-FullText-LowRes.pdf.

Hunt, Krista, and Kim Rygiel, eds. 2006. *(En)gendering the War on Terror: War Stories and Camouflaged Politics.* Burlington, VT: Ashgate.

Inal, Tuba. 2013. *Looting and Rape in Wartime: Law and Change in International Relations.* Philadephia: University of Pennsylvania Press.

International Campaign to Stop Rape & Gender Violence in Conflict. 2013. "113 Countries Commit to Stop Rape in Conflict With Historic Declaration at UN." September 25. www.stoprapeinconflict.org/113_countries_commit _to_stop_rape_in_conflict_with_historic_declaration_at_un.

———. 2014. "Minova Verdict: The DRC Must End Impunity for Sexual Violence in Conflict." May 8. www.stoprapeinconflict.org/the_campaign _calls_on_drc_to_end _impunity_for_sexual_violence_crimes.

Joachim, Jutta. 2007. *Agenda Setting, the UN, and NGOs: Gender Violence and Reproductive Rights.* Washington, DC: Georgetown University Press.

Jones, Adam. 2010. "Genocide and Mass Violence." In *Gender Matters in Global Politics,* edited by Laura J. Shepherd. New York: Routledge.

Kaldor, Mary. 2007. *Human Security.* Malden, MA: Polity Press.

Karim, Sabrina, and Kyle Beardsley. 2016. "Explaining Sexual Exploitation and Abuse in Peacekeeping Missions: The Role of Female Peacekeepers and Gender Equality in Contributing Countries." *Journal of Peace Research* 53, no. 1: 100–115.

Keck, Margaret, and Kathryn Sikkink. 1998. *Activists beyond Borders: Advocacy Networks in International Politics.* Ithaca, NY: Cornell University Press.

———. 1999. "Transnational Advocacy Networks in International and Regional Politics." *International Social Science Journal* 51, no. 159: 89–101.

Kelly, Jocelyn. 2010. *Rape in War: Motives of Militia in DRC.* Special Report. Washington, DC: US Institute of Peace Press.

Khong, Yuen Foong. 1992. *Analogies at War: Korea, Munich, Dien Bien Phu, and the Vietnam Decisions of 1995.* Princeton, NJ: Princeton University Press.

Kier, Elizabeth, and Jonathan Mercer. 1996. "Setting Precedents in Anarchy: Military Intervention and Weapons of Mass Destruction." *International Security* 20, no. 4: 77–106.

Kinsella, Helen. 2011. *The Image before the Weapon: A Critical History of the Distinction between Combatant and Civilian.* Ithaca, NY: Cornell University Press.

Kirby, Paul. 2012. "How Is Rape a Weapon of War? Feminist International Relations, Modes of Critical Explanation and the Study of Wartime Sexual Violence." *European Journal of International Relations* 19, no. 4: 797–821.

———. 2015. "Ending Sexual Violence in Conflict: The Preventing Sexual Violence Initiative and Its Critics." *International Affairs* 91, no. 3: 457–72.

Kristof, Nicholas. 2008. "The Weapon of Rape." *New York Times,* June 15.

Kronsell, Annica, and Erika Svedburg, eds. 2012. *Making Gender, Making War: Violence, Military, and Peacekeeping Practices.* New York: Routledge.

Leatherman, Janie L. 2011. *Sexual Violence and Armed Conflict.* Cambridge: Polity Press.

Lebovic, James H., and Erik Voeten. 2006. "The Politics of Shame: The Condemnation of Country Human Rights Abuses at the UNCHR." *International Studies Quarterly* 50, no. 4: 861–88.

Leiby, Michele L. 2009. "Wartime Sexual Violence in Guatemala and Peru." *International Studies Quarterly* 53, no. 2: 445–68.

Lewis, Chloé. 2014. "Systematic Silencing: Addressing Sexual Violence against Men and Boys in Armed Conflict and Its Aftermath." In *Rethinking Peacekeeping, Gender Equality and Collective Security,* edited by Gina Heathcote and Dianne Otto. New York: Palgrave Macmillan.

Lieber, Francis. 1863. "Instructions for the Government of Armies of the United States in the Field, General Order No. 100." April 24. www.icrc.org/ihl.nsf/FULL/110?OpenDocument.

MacFarlane, S. Neil, and Yuen Foong Khong. 2006. *Human Security and the UN: A Critical History.* Bloomington: Indiana University Press.

MacKenzie, Megan. 2010. "Securitizing Sex." *International Feminist Journal of Politics* 12, no. 2: 202–21.

Maclin, Beth, Jocelyn Kelly, Justin Kabanga, and Michael VanRooyen. 2015. "'They Have Embraced a Different Behaviour': Transactional Sex and Family Dynamics in Eastern Congo's Conflict." *Culture, Health & Sexuality* 17, no. 1: 119–31.

McSweeney, Bill. 1996. "Identity and Security: Buzan and the Copenhagen School." *Review of International Studies* 22, no. 1: 81–93.

Meger, Sara. 2010. "Rape of the Congo: Understanding Sexual Violence in the Conflict in the Democratic Republic of the Congo." *Journal of Contemporary African Studies* 28, no. 2: 119–35.

———. 2016. "The Fetishization of Sexual Violence in International Security." *International Studies Quarterly* 60(1):149–59.

Mendelson, Sarah E. 2005. *Barracks and Brothels: Peacekeepers and Human Trafficking in the Balkans.* Washington, DC: Center for Strategic and International Studies.

Meron, Theodor. 1993. "Rape as a Crime under International Humanitarian Law." *American Journal of International Law* 87, no. 3: 424–28.

Mertus, Julie. 2008. *Bait and Switch: Human Rights and US Foreign Policy.* New York: Routledge.

Moon, Katharine H. S. 1997. *Sex among Allies: Military Prostitution in US–Korea Relations.* New York: Columbia University Press.

Nalaeva, Galina. 2010. "The Impact of Transnational Advocacy Networks on the Prosecution of Wartime Rape and Sexual Violence: The Case of the ICTR." *International Social Science Review* 85, nos. 1–2: 3–27.

Niarchos, Catherine N. 1995. "Women, War, and Rape: Challenges Facing the International Tribunal for the Former Yugoslavia." *Human Rights Quarterly* 17, no. 4: 649–90.

Nordås, Ragnhild. 2012. *Sexual Violence on the Decline? Recent Debates and Evidence Suggest "Unlikely."* CSCW Policy Brief. Oslo: Centre for the Study of Civil War.

Öberg, Marko Divac. 2005. "The Legal Effects of Resolutions of the UN Security Council and General Assembly in the Jurisprudence of the ICJ." *European Journal of International Law* 16, no. 5: 879–906.

Ogata, Sadako. 2001. "State Security—Human Security." Fridtjof Nansen Memorial Lecture. http://archive.unu.edu/hq/public-lectures/ogata.pdf.

O'Reilly, Ciaran. 2008. "Primetime Patriotism: News Media and the Securitization of Iraq." *Journal of Politics and Law* 1, no. 3: 66–72.

Otto, Dianne. 2009. "The Exile of Inclusion: Reflections on Gender Issues in International Law Over the Last Decade." *Melbourne Journal of International Law* 10: 11–26.

———. 2010. "Power and Danger: Feminist Engagement with International Law through the UN Security Council." *Australian Feminist Law Journal* 32: 97–121.

Pankhurst, Donna, ed. 2008. *Gendered Peace: Women's Struggles for Post-War Justice and Reconciliation*. New York: Routledge.

Pankhurst, Donna. 2010. "Sexual Violence in War." In *Gender Matters in Global Politics: A Feminist Introduction to International Relations*, edited by Laura J. Shepherd.

Peace, Security, and Cooperation Framework for the Democratic Republic of the Congo and the Region. 2013. Addis Ababa, February 24. http://responsibility to protect.org/SESG%20Great%20Lakes%20Framework%20of%20Hope .pdf.

Peterman, Amber, Tia Palermo, and Caryn Bredenkamp. 2011. "Estimates and Determinants of Sexual Violence against Women in the Democratic Republic of Congo." *American Journal of Public Health* 101, no. 6: 1060–67.

Prendergast, John, and Sasha Lezhnev. 2015. "Suffocating Congo's War." *Foreign Policy*, February 7.

Price, Richard. 1995. "A Genealogy of the Chemical Weapons Taboo." *International Organization* 49, no. 1: 73–103.

———. 1998. "Reversing the Gun Sights: Transnational Civil Society Targets Land Mines." *International Organization* 52, no. 3: 613–44.

Puechguirbal, Nadine. 2010. "Discourses on Gender, Patriarchy and Resolution 1325: A Textual Analysis of UN Documents." *International Peacekeeping* 17, no. 2: 172–87.

Rees, Madeleine, and Christine Chinkin. 2015. "Why We Support the PSVI." Women's International League for Peace & Freedom, June 17.

Rutherford, Kenneth R. 2000. "The Evolving Arms Control Agenda: Implications of the Role of NGOs in Banning Antipersonnel Landmines." *World Politics* 53, no. 1: 74–114.

Rythoven, Eric Van. 2015. "The Perils of Realist Advocacy and the Promise of Securitization Theory: Revisiting the Tragedy of the Iraq War Debate." *European Journal of International Relations* Online, 1–25. http://ejt.sagepub .com/content/early/2015/09/02/1354066115598635.abstract.

Sartori, Anne E. 2002. "The Might of the Pen: A Reputational Theory of Communication in International Disputes." *International Organization* 56, no. 1: 121–49.

Security Council Report. 2016. "UN Security Council Working Methods: Penholders and Chairs. January 29." www.securitycouncilreport.org /un-security-council-working-methods/pen-holders-and-chairs.php.

Seelinger, Kim Thuy. 2014. "Domestic Accountability for Sexual Violence: The Potential of Specialized Units in Kenya, Liberia, Sierra Leone and Uganda." *International Review of the Red Cross* 96, no. 894: 539–64.

Seelinger, Kim Thuy, and Julie Freccero. 2015. *The Long Road: Accountability for Sexual Violence in Conflict and Post-Conflict Settings*. Berkeley: Human Rights Center of the School of Law of the University of California, Berkeley.

Sellers, Patricia Viseur. 2009. "Gender Strategy Is Not Luxury for International Courts Symposium: Prosecuting Sexual and Gender-Based Crimes Before

International/ized Criminal Courts." *American University Journal of Gender, Social Policy & the Law* 17, no. 2: 301–25.

Shepherd, Laura J. 2008. "Power and Authority in the Production of United Nations Security Council Resolution 1325." *International Studies Quarterly* 52, no. 2: 383–404.

———. 2011. "Sex, Security and Superhero(in)es: From 1325 to 1820 and Beyond." *International Feminist Journal of Politics* 13, no. 4: 504–21.

Skjelsbæk, Inger. 2010. *The Elephant in the Room: An Overview of How Sexual Violence Came to Be Seen as a Weapon of War.* Oslo: Peace Research Institute Oslo.

Smith, Alastair. 1998. "International Crises and Domestic Politics." *American Political Science Review* 92, no. 3: 623–38.

Stark, Lindsay, and Mike Wessells. 2012. "Sexual Violence as a Weapon of War." *JAMA* 308, no. 7: 677–78.

Steinberg, Donald. 2011. "An Agenda for Action." In *Women and War: Power and Protection in the 21st Century*, edited by Kathleen Kuehnast, Chantal de Jonge Oudraat, and Helga Hernes. Washington, DC: US Institute of Peace Press.

Tadjbakhsh, Shahrbanou, and Anuradha M. Chenoy. 2007. *Human Security: Concepts and Implications.* New York: Routledge.

Tarrow, Sidney. 1998. *Power in Movement: Social Movements and Contentious Politics.* New York: Cambridge University Press.

Taureck, Rita. 2006. "Securitization Theory and Securitization Studies." *Journal of International Relations and Development* 9: 53–61.

Tickner, J. Ann. 1992. *Gender in International Relations: Feminist Perspectives on Achieving Global Security.* New York: Columbia University Press.

Townsend, Mark. 2015. "William Hague's Summit against Warzone Rape Seen as 'Costly Failure.'" *The Guardian*, June 13.

True, Jacqui. 2003. "Mainstreaming Gender in Global Public Policy." *International Feminist Journal of Politics* 5, no. 3: 368–96.

UK House of Lords. 2016. "Sexual Violence in Conflict: A War Crime." HL Paper 123. London.

United Nations Development Program. 1994. *Human Development Report 1994: New Dimensions of Human Security.* New York: Oxford University Press.

United Nations General Assembly. 1993. "Vienna Declaration and Programme of Action."

———. 1998. "Rome Statute of the International Criminal Court (last amended 2010)." July 17.

———. 2012. "Conflict-Related Sexual Violence: Report of the Secretary-General." A/66/657-S/2012/33. January 13.

———. 2013. "A Declaration of Commitment to End Sexual Violence in Conflict." September 24.

United Nations Secretary-General, Office of the. 2000. "UN Secretary-General on the War in the Congo: Statement to the United Nations Security Council." December 6.

———. 2001. "UN Secretary-General on the War in the Congo: Statement to the United Nations Security Council." New York, February 21.

United Nations Security Council. 1999a. "Letter Dated 23 July 1999 from the Permanent Representative of Zambia to the United Nations Addressed to the President of the Security Council." S/1999/815. July 23.

———. 1999b. "Resolution 1279." S/Res/1279. November 30.

———. 2000. "Resolution 1325 (2000)." S/Res/1325. October 31. http://www .refworld.org/docid/3600f4672e.html.

———. 2008a. "5,916th Meeting." S/PV.5916. New York, June 19.

———. 2008b. "Resolution 1820." S/Res/1820. June 19.

———. 2008c. S/2008/403. June 19.

———. 2009. "6,195th Meeting." S/PV.6195. September 30.

———. 2010. "Resolution 1925." S/Res/1925. May 28.

———. 2012a. "Resolution 2053." S/Re/2053. June 27.

———. 2012b. "Security Council Presidential Statement Condemns Sexual Violence in Conflict, Post-Conflict Situations, Urges Complete, Immediate Cessation of Such Acts." SC/10555. February 23.

———. 2013a. "Letter Dated 7 June 2013 from the Permanent Representative of the United Kingdom of Great Britain and Northern Ireland to the United Nations Address to the Secretary-General." S/2013/335. June 7.

———. 2013b. "Resolution 2106." S/Res/2106. June 24.

———. 2013c. "6,984th Meeting." S/PV.6984. June 24.

———. 2014a. "Note by the President of the Security Council." S/2014/268. April 14.

———. 2014b. "Report of the Secretary-General on the Implementation of the Peace, Security and Cooperation Framework for the Democratic Republic of the Congo and the Region." S/2014/4697. September 24.

———. 2015a. "Conflict-Related Sexual Violence: Report of the Secretary-General." S/2015/203. March 23.

———. 2015b. "Report of the Secretary-General on the Implementation of the Peace, Security and Cooperation Framework for the Democratic Republic of the Congo and the Region." S/2015/173. March 13.

———. 2015c. "Resolution 2242 (2015)." S/Res/2242. October 13.

———. 2015d. "7,533rd Meeting." S/PV.7533. October 13.

———. 2016. "Resolution 2272." S/Res/2272. March 11.

UN News Centre. 2016. "Seasoned Official Appointed to Coordinate UN Efforts to Curb Sexual Abuse by Peacekeepers." February 8. www.un.org/apps/news /story.asp?NewsID=53185#.VyEFa0Zy5Q4.

UN News Service. 2010. "Tackling Sexual Violence Must Include Prevention, Ending Impunity–UN Official." April 27.

UN Women. 2013. "UN Women Welcomes the Unanimous Adoption of Security Council Resolution 2106." June 27. www.unwomen.org/en/news /stories/2013/6/un-women-welcomes-the-unanimous-adoption-of-security -council-resolution-2106.

———. 2015. "Statement by UN Women on the Adoption of Security Council Resolution 2242 on Women, Peace and Security." October 14. www.un women.org/en/news/stories/2015/10/ed-statement-unsc-resolution-1325.

US Department of State. 1994. "Zaire Human Rights Practices, 1993." Washington, DC.

———. 1996. "State Department on Refugee Crisis in Central Africa." In *Historic Documents of 1996*. Washington, DC: Congressional Quarterly.

———. 2000. "Remarks to the National Summit on Africa." February 17.

———. 2003. "Implementation of Security Council Resolution 1325 on Women, Peace and Security." October 29.

———. 2004a. "Conflict in DRC." December 20.

———. 2004b. *Democratic Republic of the Congo, Report on Human Rights Practices, 2003*. Washington, DC: US Department of State.

———. 2009a. "Remarks on the Adoption of a United Nations Security Council Resolution to Combat Sexual Violence in Armed Conflict." September 30.

———. 2009b. "Roundtable with NGOs and Activists on Sexual and Gender-Based Violence Issues." Goma, Democratic Republic of the Congo, August 11.

———. 2009c. "Testimony before the US Senate Subcommittees on African Affairs, and Human Rights, Democracy, and Global Women's Issues." May 13.

———. 2010a. "Quadrennial Diplomacy and Development Review." Washington, DC.

———. 2010b. "Remarks on the 15th Anniversary of the International Conference on Population and Development." January 8.

———. 2011. "Election Outcome and Governance in the DRC." December 15.

———. 2012. "US Department of State Policy Guidance: Promoting Gender Equality to Achieve Our National Security and Foreign Policy Objectives." March.

———. 2015. *US Relations with Democratic Republic of the Congo*. June 15. www.state.gov/r/pa/ei/bgn/2823.htm.

US House of Representatives. 2003a. "Conflict Diamonds Resolution." 2003 H. Con. Res. 239.

———. 2003b. "Foreign Operations, Export Financing, and Related Programs Appropriations Act, 2005." 2003 H.R. 4818.

———. 2005. "UN Organization Mission in the DRC: A Case for Peacekeeping Reform." March 1.

———. 2009. "International Violence against Women: Stories and Solutions." Report 111-64, October 21. www.gpo.gov/fdsys/pkg/CHRG-111hhrg52986 /html/CHRG-111hhrg52986.htm.

———. 2011. "The Democratic Republic of the Congo: Securing Peace in the Midst of Tragedy." March 8.

US Senate. 1997. "The Challenge in the Congo." Report 9851. June 3.

———. 2005. "Democratic Republic of the Congo Relief, Security, and Democracy Promotion Act of 2005." S. 2125.

———. 2007. "Exploring the US Role in Consolidating Peace and Democracy in the Great Lakes Region." October 24.

———. 2008. "Rape as a Weapon of War: Accountability for Sexual Violence in Conflict." April 1.

———. 2009. "Confronting Rape and Other Forms of Violence against Women in Conflict Zones, Spotlight: DRC and Sudan." S. HRG. 111-161. May 13.

———. 2013. "Examining Ongoing Conflict in Eastern Congo." S. HRG. 113-136. April 16.

Vandenberg, Martina, and Kelly Dawn Askin. 2001. "Chechnya: Another Battleground for the Perpetration of Gender Based Crimes." *Human Rights Review* 2, no. 3: 140–49.

Vincent, Saffiene. 2012. "Conference Report: Preventing Sexual Violence in Conflict and Post-Conflict Situations." WP1199. November.

Voeten, Erik. 2009. *Think Again: The UN Human Rights Council.* November 4. http://themonkeycage.org/2009/11/think_again_the_un_human_right/.

Wæver, Ole. 1995. "Securitization and Desecuritization." In *On Security*, edited by Ronnie D. Lipschutz. New York: Columbia University Press.

Weitsman, Patricia A. 2008. "The Politics of Identity and Sexual Violence: A Review of Bosnia and Rwanda." *Human Rights Quarterly* 30, no. 3: 561–78.

———. 2015. "Constructions of Identity and Sexual Violence in Wartime: The Case of Bosnia." In *Genocide and Gender in the Twentieth Century: A Comparative Survey*, edited by Amy E. Randall. London: Bloomsbury.

Whitworth, Sandra. 2004. *Men, Militarism & UN Peacekeeping: A Gendered Analysis.* Boulder, CO: Lynne Rienner.

Wilton, Paul-André. 2015. "The End Sexual Violence in Conflict Summit Was Worth It, but It Was Only Ever the Beginning." Care International, June 22.

Wintour, Patrick. 2016. "Plan to Tackle Sexual Violence during Wars 'At Risk without William Hague.'" *The Guardian*, April 12.

Wolfe, Lauren. 2012. "What the UK Can Do to Stop Sexualized Violence in Syria." Women Under Siege Project, November 15. www.womenundersiegeproject .org/blog/entry/what-the-uk-can-do-to-stop-sexualized-violence-in-syria.

———. 2014. "Unarmed and Dangerous." *Foreign Policy*, March 7.

———. 2015. "How Dodd-Frank Is Failing Congo." *Foreign Policy*, February 2.

Women's International League for Peace and Freedom. 2008. "Security Council Debate on Sexual Violence in Conflict, June 2008 (SCR 1820)." New York, June 19.

Wood, Elisabeth Jean. 2009. "Armed Groups and Sexual Violence: When Is Wartime Rape Rare?" *Politics & Society* 37, no. 1: 131–61.

———. 2012. "Rape during War Is Not Inevitable: Variation in Wartime Sexual Violence." In *Understanding and Proving International Sex Crimes*, edited by Morten Bergsmo, Alf Butenschorn Skre, and Elisabeth J. Wood. Beijing: Torkel Opsahl Academic EPublisher.

Index

Tables are indicated by t *following the page number.*

About the Author

Kerry F. Crawford is an assistant professor of political science at James Madison University in Harrisonburg, Virginia. She received her BA in Political Science from St. Mary's College of Maryland (2007) and her PhD in Political Science from the George Washington University (2014). She was the 2015–2016 recipient of the International Studies Association's James N. Rosenau Postdoctoral Fellowship.

CPSIA information can be obtained
at www.ICGtesting.com
Printed in the USA
LVOW11*1555170418

573805LV00007B/140/P